CW01656376

Suzanne Brøgger

Deliver Us From Love

TRANSLATED FROM THE DANISH BY THOMAS TEAL

QUARTET BOOKS LONDON

Published by Quartet Books Limited 1977
A member of the Namara Group
27 Goodge Street, London W1P 1FD

First English edition published in the United States 1976
by Delacorte Press/Seymour Lawrence, New York

ISBN 0 7043 2132 7

Excerpts from "Daguerrotypes" and "A Fire Speech" by Karen Blixen in Chapter 6 are reprinted from *Essays* by Karen Blixen by permission of the University of Chicago Press and the Rungstedlund Foundation.

Printed in Great Britain by litho at The Anchor Press Ltd
and bound by Wm Brendon & Son Ltd
both of Tiptree, Essex

dedicated to
Diane and Philippe Baude

CONTENTS

FOREWORD

Many people feel that it has become superfluous to write fiction when society itself is pure fiction and fabrication. It does seem preposterous to try to force your material into some specific GENRE when there is no clearcut totality to reflect. That kind of literary process could occur only at the expense of immediacy, and at the moment, immediacy seems more important than elegance.

The following mixed bag of reporting, essays, interviews, and fiction—or whatever it ought to be called—represents conscious, intentional, undigested subjectivity, and expresses nothing but what was happening while I wrote the book.

Nevertheless, some of it unavoidably points back in time. That is because the book is about the necessity and the difficulty of throwing psychophysical baggage overboard. For that reason I have had to rewrite myself and reality whenever they got in the way. I have done whatever I had to do to become whomever I needed to be.

The people who appear in this book—and who may feel themselves exposed—have nothing to do with real life.

Therefore I will wail and howl,
I will go stripped and naked:
I will make a wailing like the dragons,
and mourning as the owls.

—MICAH 1:8

Deliver Us From Love

1 The Very Last Tango

Love's death dance

The tango is playing to full houses all over the world, even though it is the last tango in Paris. It is almost impossible to dance it anymore, although even a death dance has its rules. "It is a ceremony," says Marlon Brando. The dancers know the steps but never see each other's faces. It is a mechanical ritual, which, like individual romantic love, excludes other people. "We have ritualized security," says Marianne to Johan in one of Bergman's *Scenes from a Marriage*. "Our mistake was that we didn't break away from the beginning and create something on our own terms."

What became of Marianne and Johan? Well, we know what became of An American Family. Or, if we don't yet have all the details, television will undoubtedly give them to us in due time. This year we're getting not one but two versions of the selfsame Nora slamming the door to the selfsame doll's house. Wouldn't one be enough? No, not in these times. For there is something in the times that doesn't quite fit, and even if it does, that is not to say that we do. Ibsen clearly implies that the problem is not a new one—but neither is it an eternal human problem. The problem of marriage dates from the moment that love began to crowd its way into the family, which was not designed to accommodate it. Hence the misery . . .

There have been several different rebellions against the family as a "repressive institution"—by the French Surrealists, by Ibsen, by Freud, by Wilhelm Reich, and so forth. But they all changed their minds, thanks to the First World War, and then thanks to the Second World War, and then thanks to the Cold War. It is possible that it would now take an atomic war to bring desperate characters to their senses and to get rid of the irrepressible questions surrounding the nucleus and fundament of society. Some people would rather see mankind eliminated than the family. Not because they are sadists, but on purely emotional grounds. In defiance of the anthropologists, they make mankind synonymous with the family, which they see as the last cell of security in a world whose mentality is being, as they put it, "collectivized." Some people maintain that the whole thing is a private problem and no one else's business, while others feel that privacy has become a convention, a camouflage for galloping anonymity and life's staggering lack of authenticity—not to mention its lack of love.

"There is no love in marriage," says Mrs. Jacoby to Marianne in one of Bergman's *Scenes from a Marriage.* We know that Marianne knows very well what Mrs. Jacoby means. Our own Pastor Krarup does not. For him it's enough that there *ought* to be—if only people were different and if only they didn't make their lives frivolous and empty. Søren Krarup has not expressed his opinion of Mrs. Jacoby's marriage, but a few months ago he did write about a great many others in an article called "On Marriage," where he said that wedlock had become a lot of damned nonsense when people could separate without pain and then get together again over a cup of coffee and have a nice chat about the old days—which is the way magazines depict "modern broad-mindedness." "The love of two people cannot be turned into this kind of an empty parenthesis without making everything else meaningless at the same time," he writes. And then—as a contrast to the decadence of the times—he mentions a case (also reported in the papers) in which a young man from a provincial town in Jutland murdered his wife out of jealousy. "It appeared," Krarup writes, "that he would rather kill the woman he loved than see her in the arms of another man. . . . For him, these things were not nonsense. For him, they had meaning and form." For him, love was . . . death.

Now it is not especially logical for a priest to chastise people for their foundering marriages, which they are trying desperately to patch up or gloss over or sweep under the carpet so that they can somehow go on living. If our pastor were logical, he would chastise them for impiety instead. Because, after all, it is not that people have suddenly lost their senses, but that marriage itself became senseless the moment it ceased to be constituted on God's terms. When the king is no longer God's representative on earth, he no longer has any significance. And the same is true of marriage. As soon as it becomes a private matter, a matter of personal taste and pleasure, it no longer has any meaning, and "fidelity" is nothing but duty and nonsense. At this point in history, both monarchy and marriage are dead institutions, even if they do still have an archaic hold on people. Marriage as an institution was meant to make up for the "infinite qualitative difference between God and man," and as such, to symbolize the otherwise impossible union with God. Otherwise it is a lot of damned nonsense. Furthermore, marriage was intended to last for a lifetime (through thick and thin), but according to divorce statistics, it does not do so, so in this way too it is meaningless. And once an institution has become meaningless, then people might just as well try to invent other lifestyles, which, for that matter, they seem to be busily doing, even though their attempts look mostly like bursts of rebellion. But it does no good for the pastor to insist that there is love in marriage, for people themselves are the best judges of that. The pastor would do better to point out that there are many *other* things in marriage that are more important than love—marriage as an end in itself, for example. . . . But the man has no business dangling love in front of us.

If we no longer live together two by two because it is "right" to do so, but simply in order to have a good time, this means that, historically speaking, cohabitation has taken on a new significance. Whether the new morality is good or bad is not something I'm going to pronounce upon. I don't know whether it expresses some diabolical hedonism or whether it is essential to the success of this new phenomenon called "love." But it has nothing to do with the meaning of marriage.

As everyone knows, marriage is not built on love. Love forced its way into the family at a moment when the family was in a state of disintegration. Marrying for love goes back a hundred years at most, and only in this century did it become widespread in all social classes. No one can know for certain if marriage is a deathtrap for love. Marrying for love is too recent for that. If placing so much importance on love is the work of the devil, then people must be absolutely possessed, now that they've had a taste of it. . . . It might have been wiser to have left love as the private preserve of princes, cunning courtiers, and novelists, but the damage has been done, Herr Pastor.

Last Tango in Paris is only one of thousands of signs of this desperation. Bertolucci doesn't hold out any hope for intimacy—not within marriage, which has become "pop," nor outside it, in the romantic, individual passion of a detached eros. Perhaps the bankruptcy of this passion is due to its being nontranscendental, for it holds "fucking God" outside, along with everything else. It is love not in order to know, but in order to forget. It is a death wish. It is an EC-STA-SY, occurring beyond permanence where time no longer exists—"Verweile doch du bist so schön" and all that shit. It is death, and only in death have European lovers ever been able to unite in any satisfactory manner. I don't know if it is immoral to flee from other people. But I do know it is death. With their external antennae lopped off, the lovers run mechanically through the traditional sadomasochistic humiliation ritual, loving each other at different times so that they never meet (partly because there is not now and never has been any reciprocity between the sexes) and ending, as usual, in death. This is truly the damnation of the flesh! Nor is marriage much more life-affirming:

"How do you see marriage?" asks the heroine's husband-to-be.

"Everywhere, always," she says. "On walls, on housefronts, on billboards." Marriage is POP, a little enterprise consisting of two smoothly operating functionaries. If it goes to pieces, you simply fix it.

Her fiancé films her from morning to night, and he means to continue despite her protests. "It's a love story," he confides to her. Married life is a fiction and a convention. He can see her only through a lens and is constantly at work on his optical illusions, trying to find new perspectives on unreality.

It is the Yankee who gives the heroine a real going-over—from the bottom up—on the subject of the "fucking family." "I'll tell you about the family, the holy family that tames the savage, the church of good citizens, where children are taught to tell their first lie, where the will is broken by repression, where freedom is crushed by selfishness, the fucking family, oh, God, Jesus," he weeps.

Her future husband tells her they are mature adults.

But what do mature adults do?

"We have to invent new ways of being, new words," she says. And that's certainly a good idea, because otherwise things look fairly bleak for all of them.

When the American finally wants to know her better and tells her he loves her, then he too must die. And we might have known, for love without pain and death is to Europeans what yin without yang would be to many other peoples. The association love/death is as certain in our culture as the Amen is in church—as certain as the authenticity of European history, where we can pinpoint with great accuracy the origin of romantic passion—passion, of course, in the sense of torment.

The language and mechanics of Western love appear to have arisen in early twelfth-century Provence, as one element in the political, heretical struggle of the Cathar "guerrilla movement" against Europe's largest political party, the Roman Catholic Church, which had thrust its way across Europe and forced its marriage doctrine down the throats of the people. It is said that mysticism is sublimated eroticism. But in this case it was the other way around. The Cathars, the "pure," disguised their belief in the "Church of Love" as love for a human being, specifically, as love for a noble Lady (married and unattainable). And the heretical tidings were spread by the guerrilla activity of the troubadours, who carried their ballads from castle to castle in such a way that the Roman Church would not get wind of the fact that it was dealing with a rebellion against the Establishment. It was in this way that passionate love invaded the consciousness of the European elite, which had only recently been converted to Christianity and which suffered under the new doctrine of marriage.

Writing of the Catharist church, the "Church of Love," Denis de Rougemont says in his classic work, *L'Amour et L'Occident:*

> The Church of Love gave birth to innumerable more or less secret, more or less revolutionary sects whose features bear witness to a common origin, a consistently maintained tradition. All of these sects are characterized by their opposition to the dogma of the trinity (at least in its orthodox form); by their ecstatic spiritualism; by their doctrine of 'radiant joy'; by their denial of the sacrament and of marriage; by their absolute condemnation of every form of participation in war; by their anti-clericalism; by their predilection for poverty and asceticism (vegetarianism); and, finally, by their spirit of equality, which in some cases went as far as total communism.

Subsequently, the Cathars were completely exterminated in a Catholic crusade. But the "doctrine" of passionate love survived. And still survives. And therefore it is important to point out that its origins are nonmatrimonial, that it is a Western and, in its widespread popularity, a relatively recent phenomenon. The current view of love as a universal, eternal, unchanging human emotion, a riddle that we must either live with or give up on, according to whether or not we have a talent for it, is a complete misunderstanding. Love is only a riddle to the extent that we have made it a riddle for political purposes. When people become hurt and angry and dismiss any discussion of love as a pure waste of time, because you cannot express the inexpressible, or because "it is pointless to open the throat of the nightingale to reveal the secret of its song," or because, as Kierkegaard said, "Any attempt by the intellect to explain or to imagine love becomes ridiculous, which is to say that the intellect becomes ridiculous," their attitude is pure conditioned reflex, in keeping with the European mystical tradition.

One could no doubt maintain that feelings such as sorrow, joy, and love are the same the world over. But the importance attached to these feelings varies greatly from culture to culture. "Very few people would fall in love if they had never heard of romance," writes La Rochefoucauld, and many people outside of Europe would not allow the Western version of romance into the family. What has existed everywhere, and all through time, and what people have pursued outside of Europe, is various forms of eros. Plato would have found our passionate love tragicomic, and the ancient Chinese would have regarded it as unbecoming. Of course it has happened that non-Europeans have fallen in love, but when this kind of lunacy forces its way into the tribe or the family, the moonstruck lovers are condemned, not *celebrated,* as in the European tradition. De Rougemont writes, "I do not hesitate to define the European Romantic as a man for whom pain—and the pain of love in particular—is the best possible path to wisdom." The attitude of the European who spends his life asking, "Am I really in love, or am I only in love with love, or am I only in love with myself?" would be considered a symptom of insanity by a Chinese psychiatrist. We worship suffering and take insanity seriously—the publication of *The Sorrows of Young Werther* was all it took for an avalanche of suicides to roll across Europe. We note that "love is blind" with the same conviction as that "two and two are four," and ascribe qualities to the beloved object which no other mortal can perceive. When, subsequently, the infatuation is "over," we note that the whole thing was a mistake. But that does not explain it. Nature and instinct are not in the habit of making mistakes of that kind. So if there is a mistake, it must originate in the intellect, in an obsession.

Europeans are traditionally more in love with this obsession than they are with people. The secret of European passion is the desire to be struck down, flattened out, by the triumph of love—death at first sight! Our love mythology includes an alibi for insanity, that is, the magic potion or the poisoned cup, which will free us from responsibility and excuse our error. We can't help it. Love is stronger than we are. "C'est plus fort que nous," runs the refrain in one love story, *A Man and a Woman.* The magic potion is one of the chief ingredients of the Tristan and Isolde legend, which originated at the same time as the ballads of the troubadours and contains the basic elements of all European love literature. What would the novel be without love, that is, without the eternal triangle? We can see some version of the Tristan myth in every story of a middle-class triangle. Isolde is the lonely, frustrated, suburban housewife who reads *True Romance*; King Marc is the cuckold; and Tristan the young lover. The crucial part of all these stories is that the lovers' passion would not last as much as an hour if it weren't for the third party, the deceived husband, who keeps their passions at the boiling point. Similarly, it is absolutely essential for the plot of a satisfactory love story to be built around hopelessness and lack of fulfillment—in the form of separation, scandal, misfortune, or suicide. For we say that "happy love has no story," thereby indicating, perhaps, that in the field of love we are merely beginners—illiterates.

The middle class was never any threat to romanticism—in fact the two of them were formally betrothed. "Happy endings" are merely an expression of the desire to make use of the myth without paying too terrible a price for it—the romantic need for everything to run as smoothly as possible. The nice thing about happy endings is that they seem to blind the middle class to its intimate contradictions.

The last eight hundred years of European intimate history consists of the clash between love and marriage and implies that half of all the misery in Europe can be summed up under the heading Infidelity. But even if love has obsessed the imagination for all those years, that is not to say that it has been especially widespread in the social sense. Only slowly did love force its way into upper-class families, where people read novels, but even there it was always accompanied by drama and conflict, because love was not the purpose of family life. The purpose of the family was to raise children, and the purpose of the doctrine of marriage was God's purpose. When functions are lost, institutions die. Now that all the traditional criteria for mating have lapsed: rank, position, blood, land, property, dowry, an entirely new phenomenon—love—has arisen as a criterion for the social behavior of all social classes. But it is still the negation of marriage, and possibly of companionship in general. Love is too new for us to say very much about it.

We have freed pornography in order to be free from it. Sensuality has been excluded from everyday life and has only economic importance, as a commodity. Love has always been an anarchistic force, and in order to control it, we have made use of the divide-and-conquer principle and separated human beings into spirit and flesh, soul and body, intellect and sexuality. The modern tendency to reduce mankind to sex alone is the traditional defense of the heathen against the myth of unhappy love. Perhaps we are waiting for other myths. In any case, we now see a desire to unite our genius with our genitalia—they originally went together—and a desire, equally strong, to unite ourselves with others.

The intimate crises to be shown on film and TV screens in the years to come will deal with what hurts most of all—an upheaval in European history that I think is more important than the advent of the Common Market—the bankruptcy of individualistic love.

"Loneliness is total, companionship has to be invented," said Johan, or was it Marianne, or someone else?

2 From the Nuclear Family to Nuclear War

Familles, je vous hais.
—André Gide

For one whole year I flew down to the Loire valley about once a month to talk to Guy about marriage and the family and what they're supposed to be good for. The nuclear family was putting me into a cold sweat, and I did a great deal of reading trying to find theoretical support for my aversion. But it was Guy more than anyone else who helped me give a form to my anger and find a system in the madness.

All the Utopians agree that the institutionalized two-person relationship—the nuclear family—will not exist in Utopia. Yet the subject rarely comes up in everyday life, and the nuclear family is seldom the object of any criticism beyond what can be found in old Socialist tracts. This lack of criticism is due to the fact that

1. most Utopians today are either married or living with someone, and their wives/husbands would be annoyed if they started criticizing the family publicly.

2. Utopians who have been divorced and then criticize the family as an institution don't count, because they have had only bad experience.

3. Utopians who have never been married at all don't count either, because either they're so stupid and ugly that no one wanted them—and their grapes are sour—or else they are distinguished by an utter lack of "human" feelings.

I myself belong to this third category. But also to the second—the one with the bad experience—since after all I did grow up in a nuclear family. And yet I find it astonishing that people should look on the subjective and personal point of view with such suspicion. By those standards, we can suspect Freud of having invented this business about neurosis "merely" because he himself was neurotic, or nuclear physicists of wanting to split the atom "merely" because they were curious.

My own despair about the nuclear family is based "merely" on the fact that

1. I spent my childhood in an unhappy family.
2. Both of my parents came from unhappy families.
3. The families of my parents' friends were unhappy.
4. Most of my own friends' families are unhappy.

"Life is no bed of roses," someone will say, and that's all there is to it. But that's not enough for me. I have never set my foot inside the door of a nuclear family home and thought, This is how I would really like to live. I have always thought, This simply can't be true.

Guy helped me clarify some of my thoughts and find documentation for my skeptical attitude toward the justifications offered for the existence of the nuclear family in the latter half of the twentieth century—for which I love him. For a whole year we took long walks in President Pompidou's private hunting preserve with its "No Trespassing" signs and examined the nuclear family from every angle, told each other about what we had been reading since my last visit, and continued our discussions by the fireplace long into the wee hours.

One of the things that struck us was the disparity between the way people think and the way they live—between our ideas and our actual behavior. Now the fact is that people often find a certain satisfaction in acting against their own best interests, because it shows that they are "only" human. Being human has always been a good excuse. Everyone is familiar with the way married people start running down marriage the moment they get drunk. As a source of humor, marriage is an ancient theme, though of course that hasn't made it disappear. But what is new is that ordinary people are beginning to have "rebellious" ideas with regard to marriage, ideas they have never entertained before, ideas that are going to make marriage more meaningful and more up-to-date, as they put it.

We have heard a number of different attitudes expressed.

To begin with, people have begun to say that marriage is not a necessity at all! People can actually live without being married, and can make the decision for themselves. Secondly, it has become more and more common to look at marriage and divorce as two sides of the same coin. There are very few people any more who marry for eternity. Divorce has begun, in a manner of speaking, to be a part of marriage.

Nor do people think of marriage anymore as an absolute bastion of fidelity. They have come to the conclusion that both men and women ought to have a certain freedom (?)—without exactly going into details. But the one-to-one relationship is not to limit each partner's chance for personal development. On the contrary, the combination of resources is to make both of them stronger, freer, and "richer"—each independently. People are buying the idea that both the woman and the man should have the same obligations, rights, and privileges within the marriage. The woman shall not be the only one to take care of the baby and the dishes, and the man shall not be the sole provider. Tasks shall be divided equally between the partners without regard to sex, because that is only natural. The same thing applies to the woman's financial independence—she is to have her own bank account.

A readiness to sacrifice for one another and to smooth each other's rough edges, as it was always so nicely put at the wedding supper ("diamonds" was the favorite example), is no longer such good form. On the contrary, the idea today is for the partners to fulfill themselves. And both of them are to hold on to their old friends. "You have yours and I'll have mine. There's nothing to keep us from cultivating old friendships—or even new ones, for that matter. Marriage isn't going to keep me from going to the soccer games with Hans, I can tell you that. And you go on doing the things you want to do, too. Marriage isn't going to spoil anything. Everything's going to be just the way it was—only better."

People are generally ready to admit that in the long run marriage involves a certain sexual monotony, that a person may get a little bored over the years, but that it doesn't have to matter. It's natural. We have a whole (glossy) literature to document the fact that very few people are unprepared for marital boredom. All you have to do is put "life" back into the marriage. "Renewal" is a constant theme in talking about two-person relationships. In certain circles there is a compulsive tendency, say, to switch partners every Saturday, but the most common solution is still to rearrange the furniture or buy some new clothes.

The new view of marriage includes a more or less explicit suggestion of sexual freedom: we're not going to own each other, NO MATTER WHAT. People who want to own each other must be weak in the head. And that we're not. As for jealousy, who's jealous? Jealousy is a negative and deadly emotion. COMMUNICATION is the order of the day. A one-to-one relationship isn't supposed to be some sort of cubbyhole, an isolated enterprise. No, external communication will enrich the relationship internally. So for heaven's sake, the more communication the better! Within reason, of course.

> The idea of sexually exclusive monogamy and possession of another breeds deep-rooted dependencies, infantile and childish emotions, and insecurities. The more insecure you are, the more you will be jealous. . . . And jealousy, like a destructive cancer, breeds more jealousy.
> (*Open Marriage*, New York: Avon, 1973)

So write social anthropologists Nena and George O'Neill in their best seller, *Open Marriage*. They insist that people must have the will to find new ways of turning marriage into a creative, growing union rather than a static, or even stagnating form of thralldom.

Another attitude beginning to gain ground is a certain skepticism toward status symbols and conspicuous consumption. The old saw about material possessions not being everything is beginning to circulate afresh. It's silly to get caught up in a wave of wasteful and trivial consumption; people don't want to buy more than they really need. They take pollution seriously, for they've developed environmental consciousness. They don't want to help destroy any more than is absolutely necessary.

Money—we won't even mention. We have passed that stage. The children? They'll be free, of course—within certain limits. In any case they won't be dependent on their parents all the time. They'll be around other children and have a chance to develop on their own terms.

In short, a humane and libertarian ideology is gaining

the upper hand, in regard to marriage and in a broader sense as well. HUMANITY as a program:

People are to do as they please, or perhaps, as Rabelais would have it, they *must* do as they please. Anyone who doesn't do what he wants to do is a poor, frustrated idiot. Anyone who keeps him from doing what he wants to do is a frustrated busybody and authoritarian. If a man wants to commit suicide, then he ought to be allowed. It is inhumane to prevent him. Integration into THE SYSTEM is the most ridiculous and feebleminded goal a person can aspire to. "Frustrated" and "authoritarian" have become virtual expletives.

This libertarian ideology is hardly elitist. It is gaining a certain foothold in every home where people still talk to one another and is, I think, a fairly good expression of their attitudes.

But how, then, does life compare to these ideas?

The answer is easy enough, or rather, it is very hard, for life is just the reverse. Life within the institutionalized nuclear family turns out to be the exact opposite of what everyone had imagined. Looking this fact right in the eye is called losing your illusions, growing up. The fact that the number of people who try to kill themselves is so astonishingly small, and that the majority of the populace does survive, at least in purely physical terms (although the number of disability pensions for people in their forties is rising sharply) can be explained by pointing out that resignation is commonly supposed to be the same thing as maturity.

For how does it all work out in real life?

Let us begin with the apartment or "single-family" house that couples move into, as the purely geographical background to their future isolation. The "homes" being offered today are designed like military fortresses, in that all of the outside relationships that each of the partners had before will now necessarily become common property. The friends of the one will also be the friends of the other. If you go to visit someone who has started living in a one-to-one relationship, when you ring the bell you are necessarily visiting both of them—unless you have "arranged" it otherwise in advance. If one of the partners doesn't care for the interloper, there are two possibilities. Either the one-to-one relationship breaks up—which is not the purpose of such relationships—or else there is a break with the person from outside. This is what usually happens, and clearly it changes the tone of the relationship, for pretty soon one of the partners begins to say, "It's your fault I never see my friends anymore." But even as the atmosphere deteriorates, the relationship itself is strengthened by these small self-sacrifices, which eventually become the very meaning of life. The couple is forced to break with the outside world—except for professional and purely social purposes—in order to assure the continued existence of their marriage. The sociologists tell us that by the time we reach our forties here in Denmark we have an average of one and a half friends apiece who are worthy of the name. Some people have to make do with half a friend, and others have none at all. This is partially a spatial problem, since dwellings are all ingeniously arranged to prevent people who live together from developing independently.

But the couple's isolation is hardly due to architecture alone. The wonderful fellowship they envision would scarcely come about even if the architect provided every apartment with two front doors and two doorbells. Another factor is that when the couple goes out and meets other people, they both know that no matter what happens they will go home together, the same two people, unchanged. The best that can happen when they meet people they like is that they will go home afterward and talk about them. "Goodness, what nice people! Let's have them over." He knows perfectly well, and she knows perfectly well, in advance, that they will never get to know any of these people any better, that is, beyond the purely social level, unless they're prepared to get involved in lies and deceit, secrecy and dissimulation. All in all, people aren't prepared to endanger their one-to-one relationship, even though this relationship is always endangered merely by going out the door. But then what about indoors? Let us hasten to admit—married people are not unhappy ALL the time. There really are bright moments, times when they are actually happy. Of course, these happy times tend to be moments of resignation. For it is not becoming—except for a masochist—to declare, I've got a shitty job and a shitty car and a shitty house and a shitty wife. No, I've got a good job, a nice car, a lovely house, and a gorgeous wife. And this is the start of the happiness race. It takes two forms. The happiness declaration for external consumption (because we need witnesses): "We don't give a damn how life is treating you, but WE are happy." This declaration somehow confirms the notion that one-to-one relationships are possible. And then there is the happiness declaration for internal consumption, which invokes permanence and the future in its oath: "How happy we are!" What difference does it make that the other person is bored half senseless, the important thing is to get him committed to happiness and stability for the long haul. What's more, happiness is not always a lie. There ARE times when things are good, and since we know they are rare, we have a need to emphasize them. As they say in the women's magazines: "Oh, we buy a nice piece of beef and a bottle of good wine and we can sit there for hours and talk and enjoy ourselves—that's happiness."

I doubt that any other period in history has seen as

much publicity for marital happiness as we see today. All the marriages we read about in the magazines are luminously happy, right up to the moment they fall apart. I believe that these desperate advertisements for happiness are rooted in a terrible need to assert that marriage is possible, at least for other people. What difference does it make what sort of a marriage we have ourselves—the important thing is to preserve the faith.

One of the reasons we know so little about how married couples get along together is that all of their intimacy is reserved for each other. This is one of the functions of the relationship. Because if I can't say what I think to my own husband, then to hell with it. But hell can rest easy, for in fact people do talk mostly to their spouses—anything else would be disloyal. Moreover, it is a sign of weakness to feel anything inappropriate, or at least to let anyone else find out. We must never give ourselves away. But intimacy in a relationship is complicated, because what I say to my husband, I say with an eye to how I know he will react. In this way, we develop a code, as opposed to a language. But that doesn't matter. As long as the marriage can give me protection, I am perfectly prepared to think and feel in code. I can tell the rest of it to my psychiatrist. One of the reasons that a one-to-one relationship becomes isolated and dies is that the partners are exclusive and reserve all of their problems, in deformed versions, for each other. Antipsychiatrist David Cooper writes:

> One of the worst fates of a two-person relationship, and this is above all true of many marital relationships during most of their history, is that the two people enter into a symbiotic relationship with each other, so that each becomes the other's parasite, each becomes hidden in the inside of the other's mind. . . . This is really

"happy marriage," the price being simply a disappearance of one's human being.

(*The Death of the Family*, Random House, Vintage, 1971)

Isolation also shows itself in other ways. The couple is having a quarrel. The doorbell rings and another married couple arrives for a visit. The first couple begins embracing happily. This is not necessarily because they've forgotten everything that was happening five minutes before, but because it suddenly loses its significance. All at once they like each other again. And it's not altogether a lie. For one of the causes of their quarrel was that they were alone. And all it took to get them smiling again was to stop being alone.

Even if marriages don't work out according to people's original philosophical projections, and even if it is the woman who has to take most of the responsibility for the housework, and even if neither partner becomes independent and "free," and even if they lose their old friends, and even if the sexual monotony becomes deadly, and even if all the prescriptions for "renewal" fail, still most people stick with the marriage stoically FOR THE SAKE OF THE CHILDREN. But the pathetic fact is that nuclear families in general are unfit to care for children. According to several studies made by the National Institute of Mental Health in the United States, most married couples should not have children. Divorces occur most frequently where there are children. Childless marriages are the happiest, and every additional child represents an added danger to marital well-being. This does not mean that ALL parents are unhappily married. Some of them ARE happy and ought to have children, but these comprised only about 13 to 17 percent of the couples in the sample.

It appears to be virtually impossible to realize or fulfill our original ideas about marriage—but it's neither the police nor the Pentagon that keeps us from doing so. No, it is first and foremost the historical legacy that marriage represents. I think it is difficult to comprehend the misery of the times without having a clear picture of the disparity between our ideas and our behavior. And this gap is neither universal nor general but limited historically and geographically to the wage-earning era in prosperous societies. It's all very well to suggest that we simply throw out our ideas and live comfortably in the ruins, but we have fashioned these ideas for a purpose. They express certain of our needs in the specific situation we live in, and as everyone knows, it is traumatic to throw away any part of yourself, even though many people do their very best.

Of course "harmonious" marriages do exist. They are the ones where the traditional sex roles are applied to the letter. And as far as I can see, that is the only way to be married. We may have all sorts of progressive ideas about how we will use marriage and give it a new meaning. But marriage is a historical legacy and is accompanied by all of its spiritual baggage, including monogamy, fidelity, patriarchy, and mutual self-sacrifice.

Marriage is based on St. Matthew's assurance that $1 + 1 = 1$. This is a curious sum in terms of the arithmetic we learn in school, but of course his point was that the man and the woman would become one through marriage. And history shows us that there were many who did—men and women of thoroughly different sexes who "complemented" one another. It worked very well indeed, as long as the woman was 0. Because $0 + 1 = 1$. But today people are trying to revise this equation and insist that $1 + 1 = 2$. This is a great misfortune . . . for marriage. Because marriage is based on the notion that a woman will be a woman (0) so that a man can be a man (1).

Marriage worked as long as the partners had fairly definite functions about which there could be no mistake—functions based on sex. Each of them knew exactly when he or she had sinned against the regulations. People had something to abide by. But there is almost no one who wants that kind of marriage anymore. We've thrown away the regulations and the sex roles, since we're counting on being able to alter marital standards from within. But we don't really know how to go about it—beyond the fact that we ought to be "human," which is difficult since no one knows what being "human" means. But never has it been pointed out as forcefully and as often as it is today that we are HUMAN BEINGS.

But supposing someone, like myself, wants to speak out in favor of abolishing the family, marriage, and one-to-one relationships altogether? He or she will be called either a Utopian or a radical. As for the former, Utopianism is always the most practical alternative, providing you confine yourself to the laws of the universe, where the practical is also the ideal. (What, for example, would we do with eight arms?) As for the latter, the real radicals are the great majority who consider it possible to give marriage a "human" face and thus preserve it. And yet every attempt to reform marriage serves only to reveal its unsuitability and absurdity. Which is not to say that marriage will fall apart if one attempts to liberalize it from within. On the contrary—as we see before us every day—it is the marriage partners who will fall apart.

It is not uncommon for both the husband and the wife to have outside jobs. It *is* common for the woman to feel a greater responsibility for the home and not to insist that her husband give her adequate help with the housework. But marriage is simply not ready for a situation where *anyone* has to go outside to work and then come home and keep house. Marriage was never intended to accommodate the problems brought about by modern-day changes in sexual roles and the conditions of labor in an industrial society. The nuclear family household as it operates today is so inefficient and out-of-date that, instead of wearing each other down with mutual accusations of not doing enough to keep the household going, the partners ought rather to ask: Why keep it going at all? This is only one of the questions that the nuclear family never asks.

It can be shown that the nuclear family as we know it today was not known in any other age, since it is now completely defined and determined by the conditions of life in a highly industrialized, wage-earning society. And so it is strange to see so many people torturing themselves and one another in the belief that the failure of the arrangement is their own fault. Suppose for a moment that it simply cannot be made to succeed—except by people who are hopelessly benighted. How shocking, then, to realize that in the latter half of the twentieth century, a majority of people have reached the point where their chief mission in life is to make marriage work. There must be something way out of proportion somewhere.

And yet it is a fact that marriage has never played so important a role and had such enormous significance for the individual as it does today. The old social conventions are crumbling, and neighborhood solidarity has disappeared. The last refuge from the workaday world is a private relationship, the nuclear family. Those who think the nuclear family is dying are absolutely wrong. Never before have people taken it so seriously. The spectrum of affection used to be much broader, involving many more people than it does today. Today, people demand and expect EVERYTHING from the family: fellowship, passion, and communication. And that's not all. It is often the case that one of the partners must also meet the other's childish need for a father or a mother, and with the lack of metaphysical footing that most people unconsciously suffer from today, they often demand that this substitute parent be a virtual Our Father or a Madonna. As things now stand, most people regard their LIVES as successful if their marriages are successful. "Love is looking over on the divan and discovering that he's still lying there after sixteen years."

David Cooper writes: "The bourgeois nuclear family unit . . . has become, in this century, the ultimately perfected form of nonmeeting, and therefore the ultimate denial of mourning, death, birth and the experiential realm that precedes birth and conception." (*The Death of the Family*) And social psychologist Erich Fromm has said that while we really ought to have completed birth before we die, yet it is the tragic fate of most people to die before they are born.

But even if the one-to-one relationship is an organized form of nonliving, not everyone suffers. There are even those who blossom. In order to understand the mechanics of this process, we must have a look at their partners. Almost without fail they are shadows. It may be that there is an ineluctable law of nature to the effect that we blossom at each other's expense, but I find it indecent to legitimize and perpetuate this state of affairs through the institution of marriage.

The fact that love has been mixed into the economic arrangement marriage once was has not helped to free woman's potential. On the contrary, it has made her position even more vulnerable.

There is only one thing in a marriage worse than an oppressed woman. And that is a woman who no longer wants to be. A woman who, when there are guests, gives her husband a cutting glance and orders him to put the kid on the potty. A woman who screws around on principle. But the "oppression" cliché is an inadequate description of a married woman's situation. A woman who plays the traditional woman's role with all it implies and who fulfills all the expectations placed on her is not, to my way of thinking, "oppressed." She is merely a giant lizard or some other exotic creature from a bygone age. She has no real viability in a social or biological sense, because she helps to preserve an outworn picture of the world. In a way she is a little sinister, for she raises her brood to believe that it is quite all right to be a lizard, whereupon they all grow up with their brains in their tails. It doesn't become apparent until too late that the climate has altered despite the best wishes of the lizard mother, and that the environmental conditions for the survival of giant lizards are no longer present. The conformist woman is not oppressed, she is merely a traitor to the cause of human survival.

It is the really oppressed women that I worry most about. They were not born yesterday. Many of those who are still alive are forty to fifty or sixty to seventy years old. They are the women who dropped out years ago, the ones who couldn't make it anymore. They sensed that life was not what it pretended to be. But they couldn't prove it, partially because they had never learned how. And since they couldn't explain how the whole thing worked, and since they weren't qualified to change anything very significant—like society—they made do with a very simple reaction to the symptoms of falseness and injustice. They stopped cleaning. They refused to play the role expected of them—any other role, but not that one. Very slowly, but systematically, they killed their husbands by pulling the props out from under them and then retiring to the tavern where they refused to be held accountable. After that no one would dare count on them as women. And so gradually their husbands died and they themselves lived on, roleless and mythless, as pill freaks and alcoholics. They lived on any way they could. They spent the rest of their lives trying to forget the bad consciences that were eating them up. I know of no one who has succeeded in NOT playing the role expected of her.

This is the oppressed woman in marriage. She is ugly and touching. Those who stick to the regulations, on the other hand, present no danger. They will soon die out. It's too bad, in a way, because right at the moment the lizard ladies are the sweetest and the warmest ones around.

The fact that so many people believe they can alter marriage to suit their pleasure has to do with our having made marriage a private concern. We do not look on marriage and the one-to-one relationship as a cultural nucleus in a larger social context, but as something completely personal. And this is why people are misled into believing that "Our marriage will be different," or "We won't be like our parents or our unhappy friends." But of course they will. They will develop the same failing radiance as their parents and their unhappy friends, and they will come to give off the same dismal vibrations. For marriage is a social convention and only to some small extent a private matter. For example, even if you have never been jealous in your life, you will be in a marriage. Because in marriage people own one another, whether they want to or not. In one-to-one relationships, the desire to do what you want is a real danger to harmony, and therefore it is wrong to dismiss the broad anxieties of married people as imaginary or paranoid. Their anxiety has a real basis. For when people enter into one-to-one relationships, they marry not only other human beings, but a whole ready-made set of psychophysical reactions. The emotions that people come to feel are not necessarily their own—in most cases they are a historical inheritance. In twentieth-century marriage, people ARE anxious (unless they are utterly benighted), and they have good reason to be.

Tolstoy's observation that all happy families resemble

one another while each unhappy family is unhappy in its own way simply doesn't hold water. It is all the unhappy families that resemble one another. Marriage is a social behavior pattern and the participants share the same basic conflicts; it is only their manner of dealing with them that differs. The problem is the same for all of them—how to survive the clash between marital and societal structure. Because it is not the husband and wife who form the marriage but much more the marriage that programs the individuals—just as the atmosphere in a prison depends very little on the personalities of the prisoners.

But in order to get a clear picture of this programming, we have to take a look at the role played by the mini-family in the economic life of society.

Let us begin with the two people who have decided to move into their own fortress, both of whom earn money. Up to this point they have managed financially with separate apartments and separate households. Now anyone would suppose that it would be more economical to join forces, and that the two of them together will be better off with only one apartment, one household, and two incomes—congratulations! But the moment they become a couple, particularly a "young couple," something very remarkable occurs—they get into financial difficulties. The immediate explanation is that the "isolated" nuclear family is, by definition, a consumer unit, and as such it is more vulnerable to a consumer society than either the extended family or the individual, who, by virtue of being single, has relationships to many people. Even if we maintain that the nuclear family is free to set its own level of consumption in keeping with its own welfare and free to close its eyes to the blandishments of the consumer society, nevertheless it will appear that this freedom exists only in principle. Consumer industries concentrate exclusively on the nuclear family as a target group, and in practice it turns out that the nuclear family runs its household and lives its life in accordance with the demands made upon it by the consumer society.

There are several reasons why the nuclear family is incapable of controlling its own consumption.

One of them is the nuclear family's craving to pretend it is a large family from the olden days. It has retained the form of the extended family but thrown out its content—people. The little family upholds the traditions of the large family every time it sets the table for dinner, and sometimes for lunch and breakfast too. The minifamily maintains a kitchen with supplies and food reserves, machinery, tools, and appliances intended for a much larger group of people. There is thus a remarkable disparity between the traditions of the nuclear family and its actual function.

The interesting thing is that the nuclear family retains the traditions handed down from the age of farms and large families not only out of lethargy, but also because it has an apparent *need* for the rules, rituals, and ceremonies that symbolize community. If the nuclear family did not have the facade of fellowship, it would have nothing at all. But to retain the rituals and services of a large fellowship in order to sustain the lives of two to four people must be regarded as a senseless aberration. If the behavior of the minifamily were to agree with its function, it would either abandon the ceremonies and buy prepared food in aluminum foil, or else it would invite an additional twenty people for dinner.

The psychological explanation of the nuclear family's exaggerated and convulsive consumption, and of the remarkable fact that two people with sound economies separately need only move in together to create financial problems, can undoubtedly be found in this need to behave like a larger family. Nor, apparently, is there any doubt but what manufacturers have noticed this need—in themselves if nowhere else. In any case, we do produce an abundance of just those things the nuclear family needs in order to convince itself that it is a *family.* As soon as two people join forces, they suddenly need a lot of expensive equipment and paraphernalia. When we are single we don't buy dishwashers, but as soon as there are two of us, we do. It wouldn't cost any more to do dishes for ten. The various household appliances—the blender, the meat slicer, and so forth—are not really indispensable, but we do have a sudden need for them, as symbols of our having become a family. Moreover, we have a need to confirm our new happiness, which these acquisitions serve to do.

The arrival of a new object in the home—an enormously interesting phenomenon to observe—produces a noticeable JOY, which lasts for a day or two. I don't think this joy is imaginary. I think people's lives really are made better—which is of course a reification of joy. Naturally "canned happiness" is a myth, but insofar as they function, myths are not lies, and the acquisition of new things does give the relationship a sense of renewal. When the young couple buys a freezer, they kiss each other, and maybe that night they make love. In fact they are certain to, for the wife is happy and the husband is happy at having made his wife happy. That they experience this happiness as real is shown by the figures on industrial growth. Industry IS capable of selling canned happiness. The whole consumer goods industry is aimed at the nuclear family, which is thus sucked into a system that makes married people the object of a competitive struggle to lure from them their incomes and the fruits of their labor. The impoverishment is not only moral, it can be reckoned in dollars and cents, as people hurry to spend more money than they earn in order to achieve happiness and become the indebted slaves of the consumer society. But the nuclear family is an isolated consumer unit, and as such it is too vulnerable to be able to revolt against a system designed entirely with it in mind.

It is probably an exaggeration to say that society creates artificial needs. For that matter, how are we to distinguish between artificial needs and real ones? Is everything we make use of above and beyond the food in our mouths, the roofs over our heads, and the clothes on our backs an artificial need? I don't think there is any cause to be puritanical. The invention of the water bed, for example, was brilliant. It is an expression of a certain era's concept of comfort and well-being, and in ten years someone will come along and tell us we should all be sleeping on hard planks, and so we'll all sleep on hard planks and say, "Oh, how marvelous!" Life would be awfully dull without such small caprices. Nevertheless, criteria do exist for distinguishing between artificial and real needs. In any given society, economists figure on a certain level of demand. But this level is always dependent on the ideas and attitudes that the nuclear family attaches to its needs. The fundamental question ought to be: Shall we buy as much as possible, or as little as possible? To what extent is our consumption an enrichment and to what extent an impoverishment? Is an immediate, maximal use of our income preferable to a minimal consumption geared to more farsighted and differentiated goals?

These are only a few of the questions that the nuclear family does not ask itself—and which, in its isolation, it is perhaps incapable of asking—but which could lead to an unprecedented freedom for the little middle-class family. It is only the rich who travel around the world and have adventures and indulge in the study of interesting subjects. But it *could* be everyone.

The fellow who works at the post office, for example. He knows perfectly well that he is not at the top of the social ladder. He also knows that if his father had been rich, and if this, and if that . . . then maybe he'd be sitting in the postmaster general's chair instead of riding around on a yellow bicycle. But if he reduced his consumption enough to have a little money left over, he could acquire some freedom of choice. He could get some additional education to help him advance within his field, or an education of an entirely different kind. It's a perfectly obvious idea, a question of shaping your own life instead of living it from hand to mouth as the victim of the consumer society. The rich are not victims. The rich don't live from hand to mouth. Only the poor do that, and not only because their incomes are smaller, but also because everything is calculated to get them to spend everything they earn—and more—as quickly as they can.

I don't want to moralize and say that it's wrong to buy a pair of red patent-leather shoes. Whether or not a purchase is appropriate has to depend on how much thought has gone into it. But we have reached a point today where the interval between conceiving a desire to buy something and actually buying it involves neither discussion, reflection, nor analysis. Consumption has been automated.

The objection might be made that discussion of new material acquisitions is exactly what is most typical of the nuclear family's intellectual life. But the discussion is more likely to center on whether it's to be in plush or plastic. The process of deliberation is not related to real needs but has become an expression of human relationships. People buy a thing because the neighbors have one, or because they've been unfaithful and want to make amends. People buy things out of boredom, and they buy things as substitutes for what they can't express or never got around to saying. Say it with flowers. Say it with an orange kitchen ventilator or a hair dryer. People HAVE to buy things, because that is the way to find happiness. Buying something gives people a prompt and intense satisfaction, like a lesser orgasm. And they can use those orgasms. The people in minifamilies aren't exactly spoiled in that department.

The minifamily doesn't ask if it is necessary to eat meat several times a day. The more money you have, the more meat you eat. The more money you have, the more expensive things you buy. You don't ask yourself if you have too many rooms already. If you have money, you buy a bigger house. Automatically. If you get a raise, you choose a more expensive vacation. Regardless. Under all circumstances, you choose the most expensive alternative your means allow. But the nuclear family is in no position to criticize the system that justifies its existence. The minifamily is too confined and too weak to exert pressure. The consumer society's traps are set for the nuclear family, and so it unavoidably falls into them.

A larger group, an extended family or a collective, say, is necessarily more critical, because a larger fellowship contains more centers of power. In a larger group there is always someone who says, "I'll be damned if I will." All the more so since the economy of a collective—as opposed to the economy of a nuclear family—rests on the personal contribution of each separate member. Thus a large purchase always means that the members will have to pay more, and there will always be one or more who oppose it. A larger group automatically provides a more critical atmosphere and a natural base for resistance to the consumer society, because consumption will always be subject to discussion.

The nuclear family would probably not be so spineless a consumer unit if it were also a production unit. But all production occurs outside the family. The family has lost the productive function that originally justified its existence—and as if that weren't enough, it has crippled itself by making its lack of productivity a virtue, and by elevating its inactivity to alarming proportions. For even if the nuclear family does not produce much, there are still daily tasks that have to be performed. But even here the nuclear family has become absolutely and utterly nonfunctional and cannot take care of itself. We live in apartments or small houses full of devices and equipment that require a certain maintenance, which, however, the nuclear family is in no position to provide. We live within a framework of certain simple technical conveniences such as electric light, gas, radio, TV, washing machines, water pipes, windows, locks, walls that have to be painted or papered from time to time, and so forth. But in the face of these small chores, the nuclear family is usually helpless. Production outside the home is so organized that everyone is a specialist. So as soon as we come home and face a problem that doesn't lie within our area of specialization, we have no idea what to do—beyond calling for another specialist from outside. And that's what we do. We immediately call for the electrician, the glazier, the plumber, or the TV man to fix things we could just as well fix for ourselves—except that we give up before we start.

The nuclear family has pushed this waste of individual resources to such fantastic extremes of nonproductivity and nonactivity that pretty soon we will not be able to do anything for ourselves at all. This comprehensive helplessness underlines once again the nuclear family's dependent relationship to outside production. We don't even toast our own bread anymore, but buy an electric bread toaster that goes pop and eventually has to be repaired or thrown away. We are constantly buying helpful appliances and gadgets that are going to make life easier and that require maintenance we can't provide and so have to pay for. This is the nuclear family's vicious circle of moral and material impoverishment. Life is divided in two—outside the home we have highly specialized production, and inside the home pure nonproduction. Intellectuals are especially interesting in this regard, for they are not only more worthless than other people in practical terms, they are also prouder of it.

Of course the ineffectuality of the minifamily has broad socioeconomic repercussions. Not only does it spend more money than it has on the maintenance of its various iron lungs and life prostheses, but at the same time it helps to preserve and increase specialization outside the home. The growing helplessness of the nuclear family creates a growing need for thousands of people to spend their lives providing trivial services that, in principle, people could just as well provide for themselves. With the nuclear family in its present enfeebled state, there have to be people who spend their lives going from bathroom to bathroom tightening some screw. And thousands of people who spend their lives replacing thousands of small tubes in thousands of small television sets. The people in minifamilies are struck with horror at the idea of replacing their own tube or turning their own screw—the television set is a sacred object, which only specialists may touch.

Specialization makes work boring and private life trivial.

And what sort of children is it the nuclear family breeds? Well the apple doesn't fall far from the tree, though we have to admit that in many cases the children are a bit more capable than their parents. This is particularly true of children who live in groups and bands outside the home. For in larger groups, a person can always learn something. It is here in their rough-and-tumble years that they pick up a feeling for various practical skills that they will lose the chance to learn about later on. Once they've grown up and gone to work and closed themselves into their own nuclear families, that's the end of figuring things out. Preserving the nuclear family "for the sake of the children" is gallows humor at its best.

Collectives and extended families clearly have a much greater capacity for self-preservation. Evil tongues will insist that instead of three people who don't know anything, a collective has fifteen. But it isn't true. A collective has fifteen people with at least one skill each. A larger collection of people is a larger accumulation of knowledge. And in a larger group, people help one another and learn from one another, because they own their own resources. In the nuclear family, people tear each other down in a climate of general impotence. The couple starts quarreling as soon as a faucet doesn't work. "Well don't come and tell me about it, call the plumber!" If the nuclear family can be said to produce anything at all, it is a lot of dependent, ineffectual people who can be readily manipulated without ever catching on. It is perfectly amazing that the richest people in the world are willing to accept a life of such moral and material poverty.

But since the nuclear family's productive functions have disappeared, and since people are no longer born at home or learn anything at home or even die at home (except figuratively), then how do we explain the fact that the nuclear family appears to be surviving?

For one thing, the nuclear family still has an emotional and sexual monopoly, although this is gradually becoming a little frayed around the edges, what with the pill, and women who go out into the working world and meet other men. Still, the nuclear family is the only place where a person can reach out for his or her partner in the darkness without getting no for an answer. It is still a little easier to find immediate sexual satisfaction within the nuclear family, because the partners know they're SUPPOSED TO, and feel guilty if they don't. Sexuality is a part of marriage, and if people lose their desire, they feel they are betraying a higher purpose. Out in the working world, eroticism is more complicated—and different, too, because to a *slightly* greater degree it is based on mutual attraction.

Politiken, January 22, 1973
A deeply shocked, 46-year-old woman in Northern Sjælland discovered yesterday morning that the man she had just been in bed with was not her husband. She became aware of the mistake when she saw her husband asleep by her side in their double bed, while the false husband was scrambling to get away.

Police are now searching for the "false husband." He forced his way into the family's house through a pantry window. Before reaching the couple's bedroom he wandered through the whole house. Two of the couple's three grown children caught glimpses of him and simply supposed him to be a member of the family.

The woman thought it was her husband when, still half asleep, she felt herself being embraced. It was only the family dog who was suspicious. He growled to draw attention to the uninvited guest, but no one took any notice. It was not until the stranger had completed intercourse that the error was discovered.

Probably most people swear by the nuclear family for lack of anything better. They know their present misery, but have no idea what another kind of misery might be like. They have learned that nothing is perfect. Moreover, the nuclear family is the only place in society where there appears to be any sort of communism. It is pseudo-communism, of course, since no real communism is possible within the framework of a capitalist economy. Nevertheless, the nuclear family does practice the rule of "From each according to his abilities, to each according to his needs." Even if the wife doesn't earn anything, no one demands that she should therefore eat less or sleep on a poorer mattress than her husband. The children earn nothing either, but are permitted to eat as much as they like. In principle, everything in the nuclear family is held *in common*, as opposed to the situation prevailing in the working world, where each wage earner is paid individually for his personal contribution and is not theoretically entitled to use other people's belongings or spend other people's money. A person can do both in the nuclear family.

In reality, the minifamily lives on the myth of the original family communism, where everyone worked together on the soil and enjoyed the fruits of their labor in fellowship. Even the children worked. But in the nuclear family, neither the children nor the housewife works. The feminists can ascribe all the social value they like to the housewife's labor, but in fact it only serves to maintain the nuclear family and the ideology that are the background to her oppression—or, if not her own oppression, then that of other women.

The pseudo-Communist shared economy of the nuclear family stands in glaring contrast to the economic laws that obtain outside the home. Let's take the case of a bachelor—we'll call him Mr. Eckersberg—with an income that nicely supplies his needs. The moment he marries he is expected, as a matter of course, to share this income with one to three additional people. By the economic standards of our society, this is a wholly abnormal phenomenon, and if you tried to explain it to a businessman, he would either tear his hair or die laughing—unless of course he understood that it was a matter of women and children. For when it involves a nuclear family, society views this economic aberration as normal. If Mr. Eckersberg shared his salary with a friend, it would be considered terribly eccentric, and he risks a terrible row with his wife if he decides to send $30 a month to his aged mother. When a man is young, he does a lot of stupid things and throws away his money right and left—that's only natural. But when he grows older and responsible, he presents his salary to women and children. How are we to explain this uneconomic tendency on the husband's part? But perhaps it isn't so uneconomic after all. The explanation must be that women are consumer goods, and luxury articles at that. From his bachelor days, he already knows what it takes to have a good time—beer, pussy, and a little brass band. Or wine, women, and song, if you prefer. When, later in life, a man makes this irrational investment in a woman over a longer period of time, it is because it is associated with all of our social myths and notions about happiness. By giving his money away to women and children, he becomes a small-scale Lord and Father and acquires the power to exert influence, to mold the woman and make her dependent. Now we may well wonder if the man was really endowed with this much cunning by Mother Nature—and why he is interested in being a Lord and Father. But the fact is, Mr. Eckersberg himself may be wondering why he goes on working. And this is where the nuclear family comes to his aid, by providing him with the justification for an often dreary and trivial job. Promotion and wage increases would not be any satisfaction in themselves if the nuclear family didn't offer him a domain where he can exercise the power he is prevented from exercising at his place of work.

But the primary explanation of the fact that men accept this form of life is that they don't have any other options. It's family life or no life at all. The disparity between the individualized economics of production and the pseudo-communistic economics of the nuclear family has traumatic implications for both sexes. Naturally the man never feels that he gets enough for his hard-earned money. But it is far harder for the woman, who must constantly justify to herself the fact that she doesn't earn a thing. Deep down, she feels like an incompetent, because she lives in a society that defines the individual in accordance with the role he or she plays in the working world. We are familiar with those letters to the editor signed, masochistically, "A very average housewife," or, aggressively, "A very UNAVERAGE housewife." The housewife is the first one to realize that she has no social identity. She seeks to compensate for her nonproductive role by identifying with her husband's productivity and she thrusts him forward and upward. She is called the inspiration for his success. It is characteristic of this *inspiritress*, this secondary producer, to make a persistent effort to use up the better part of her husband's income. The explanation is to be found in her economic dependency, and in the fact that she earns nothing herself. Her only opportunity to intervene in economics . . . is to buy. The nonproducing woman, like the nonproducing family, is by definition a consumer. I know a woman who managed to buy two vacuum cleaners in the same day in order to have her revenge on fate.

The collective and the extended family are, at the moment, the only family forms that operate according to the financial principles of the business world. In the collective too there is a personal economic relationship between the individual and the group—unless we're talking about pure communism, and we can ignore that possibility. The idea is give-and-take, *quid pro quo*—just as in society. In a collective, it would be outrageous for the women not to work, because then the men would have to pay double. In the collective, Mr. Gyldenkrone pays $150 to the group, which roughly corresponds to what Mr. Gyldenkrone receives. They have figured it out. Give-and-take. The relationships in a collective are cynical and clear, just as they are in the business world. I don't claim that this is the best of all possible worlds, but it is the world we live in at the moment, and it is repressive tolerance to want to protect women from it.

The nuclear family appears to be a haven from the selfishness that has gradually come to be the distinguishing feature of capitalist society. In the family, the worth of the individual is not reckoned up in dollars and cents, and for that very reason many people are skeptical of any effort to dissolve it. They are quite right to ask if it is really necessary to let capitalist individualism and egotism force their way into the family, which still seems to be untouched by them. And they are quite right to wonder if it is really necessary to "alienate" the housewives who up to now have been cut off from a social identity and thus from the dehumanization that a social role implies: "I, a typewriter," "I, a button," "I, a pivot . . ."

One can imagine a more advanced society in which neither men nor women would have to take part in the world of production in order to have social worth. But we haven't reached it yet. The individual freedom that the middle class called for so loudly in its day is still a goal that everyone agrees on: the greatest possible individual freedom within the greatest possible sense of community. The middle class has indeed won many victories in the battle for individual freedom, and we cannot call that freedom idiotic merely because the middle class demanded it. It was a step forward for men to become wage earners rather than to remain financially dependent until their fathers died. The next step, which cannot be skipped over, however, is the financial independence of women and their participation in the world of production. But the middle class cannot make that leap, and so all further demands for individual freedom must necessarily occur at the expense of the middle class. The progressive role of the bourgeoisie was played out long ago. Confronted with further demands for freedom, the middle class has had to put on the brakes, first of all in order to keep women from taking an active part in production, and secondly, in order to preserve the nuclear family so as to secure the dependence of the individual upon the economic system.

Unfortunately, today, every effort to describe the formal role of the middle class suffers from a certain communicative drawback, namely, that no one identifies with it. Very few people nod in recognition of the monstrous oppressor role and say, "Yes, that's me to a T. I am a bourgeois, patriarchal capitalist." For that reason I will break all the rules and abolish the bourgeoisie as a distinct class, and call it instead an *aspiration*, shared by a cross section of the populace running all the way from the dying aristocracy to the proletariat. The middle class is all the wage earners, all the people who want to send their children to college, and all the Socialists who go off and establish nuclear families. It is all those women who say yes to the housewife role, thereby preventing the concept of sexual equality from becoming real. For in the eyes of the law, there is nothing in middle-class society to keep a woman from sitting down on her ass and studying stars and becoming world champion cosmologist or head astronomer. And therefore it is probably most practical to say that most people choose their own oppression. Many out of ignorance, and a few against their own better judgment. Of course it is THE SYSTEM that *makes* us what we are, but it is still most *practical* to say that we choose oppression, that we are "bearers" of the system the way mosquitoes bear malaria, that the system—is us.

One can always choose again, as long as there are any possibilities to be seen or any inspiration to be had. But we cannot exactly say that society encourages us to question the nuclear family, nor can we expect it to, since the result would be a new society. It has always been characteristic of societies to maintain themselves as long as they could. We have family guidance, social counseling, teachers, institutions, and commissions. But they are all working to "modernize" and patch up the family and to make marriage more "timely" and durable. The family is attacked only in very narrow circles and by people who are frustrated. (!) There is no antifamily movement worth mentioning, nor, for that matter, is there any course in school to give society's small citizens an honest orientation into what kind of an institution it is that they will spend the rest of their lives in—if all goes "well." If only there was an antifamily movement that could put marriage on the danger list and weaken the nuclear family, then we'd really see some fun. I am convinced that an active, radical struggle against the nuclear family is THE ONE THING that our otherwise tolerant-repressive society—where all the rebels are put on TV and wrapped in spun sugar as ornaments to democracy—would not tolerate. That the general public is not shocked by the occasional attacks on the family that do find expression, and that antifamiliasts are not persecuted, is simply because it isn't necessary. There is no reason to defend the status quo, for the family LIVES. And if it is not in the best of health, it is still full of life in the sense that most people still use it to live in. Not necessarily because it is the best way to live, but because it is the best-known, that is, the lesser of the only two evils people can imagine.

The statistics show that more and more people are marrying younger and younger. They all get married so as not to be alone—at the one moment in their lives when they are not. From the moment a child starts talking, it says, "I want to get married so I can have a big car." For marriage is the sole maturity model that society offers—or that we offer one another. But, Christ, it astounds me that there are married feminists! And it is a riddle to me why so many Socialists spend their everyday lives—when they're not at some meeting—in a one-to-one relationship of one kind or another. We are faced with the curious fact that the desire to alter society in a Socialist-Communist direction and the desire to marry are equally dominant and do not seem to strike the so-called revolutionaries as contradictory, in spite of the fact that the nuclear family simply will not exist in the society they are striving to achieve. All of the Communist theoreticians are in complete agreement on that point. The nuclear family is the fundamental social cell that determines the child's behavioral and emotional role. The nuclear family preserves and propagates our cultural values, and contains in miniature all of the antagonisms and psychological power factors that are developed and enlarged out in society. Social anthropologists perceive sexual differences not only as individual characteristics, but also as culturally inherited behavior patterns. And so it is intriguing and puzzling that so many Socialists, who want to change society's norms, choose to live their own lives in the cell that best preserves them. It is not granted to everyone to abolish capitalism. But everyone has the right and the opportunity to abolish the nuclear family.

Many of the political causes of the young have had social consequences—new attitudes toward narcotics addicts and psychiatric "patients," women's liberation, penal reform, and so forth. Why don't young people propagandize for the dissolution of the family? Why don't they boycott one-to-one relationships? Why don't the left-wing parties and the feminists put the elimination of the family at the top of their programs? It is no excuse to say we are victims of the system and the products of capitalism. Society isn't going to be transformed by "products," but by the people who cease to be products. Nor is the weak position of women an excuse for not taking radical steps. The liberation of women is not a prerequisite for abolishing the family, but one of its consequences.

If the people who call themselves revolutionaries would dissolve their own one-to-one commitments and take up the motto, "Don't Marry, Divorce!" and if they would help to bring out thousands of people to overrun the divorce courts, there would be definite political and economic consequences. In the first place, there would be confusion, wild confusion. Society would be traumatized, forced to ask some new and essential questions. Of course no one can predict in detail what situations would arise. The important thing is to shake the foundations, disrupt the way women and children and men relate to one another. Questions would be raised, and for the moment, that is enough.

But the fact that one-to-one relationships are not considered a serious political topic is probably because most "revolutionaries" regard them as secondary. "Down with the government! Down with capitalism! Down with private property!" And as for the rest of it, it will all take care of itself. But NOTHING takes care of itself—history's revolutionary experiments clearly show that absolutely nothing takes care of itself. All of the problems associated with the family and one-to-one relationships in general would be exactly the same as they are today even if the revolution were to come tomorrow, as they say (imagining, apparently, that it will come flying through the air like some giant beefsteak). Conversely, it is possible, and obvious, to accelerate cultural evolution within the framework of the present economic system and without the interference of the army or the police.

But left-wing politicians are afraid of scaring people away (as if they had any significant popular support). They are delighted to stick to wage issues—which has to be called dishonest when they know perfectly well that all wages and wage increases will be sucked out of people's pockets in any case, as long as the nuclear family is preserved. But the Socialists are afraid of publicizing a burning question to which they have no answer. Economic questions are very simple—the state has only to do this and the workers that. But when the question is rather more fundamental—how men and women are to propagate the race in a more appropriate and joyous manner than they do at present—they can't come up with an answer.

But do we have to have the answer just because we ask the question? It is only demagogues who ask and answer in the same breath. The forces that tear down have never been the same that built up, except in dictatorships. For the time being, then, we need only say, with concrete documentation, that the nuclear family is evil and we won't have it in the house. Because it is killing us. If someone still insists on an answer—if only to draw us out onto thin ice—then we will say that we want to replace family with community. And that takes care of that.

Ever since the Renaissance, when the patriarchal family finally won its foothold, the question has always been the dynamic HOW? in preference to the metaphysical WHY?

And since then, the family has acquired an independent value in itself.

Capitalism, growth, have acquired independent value.

Empirical science, an independent value.

The family has monopolized our emotional life.

Capitalism has monopolized our labor.

Empirical science has monopolized research and accumulated data.

But for what?

From the nuclear family to nuclear weapons . . . That is in brief the history of patriarchal culture.

* * *

One evening I asked Guy if he thought I would ever live in a nuclear family.

"If you do it'll probably be with me," he said.

"Oh, no, you don't," I said.

"Do you think the prospect pleases *me?*"

I would have liked to hide myself in his armpit for a hundred years, for then, perhaps, there will come a day when people can once again live two by two without endangering their lives.

January 12, 1973

I think the grocer's wife has left him. Anyway she hasn't been in the store for several months. His sister came to help at Christmas. Three weeks ago I walked in and clapped my hands. "Umm," I said, "what a wonderful smell of Christmas!"

Then I realized that there had been a fire. There had been a short circuit and all the bottles had exploded, he explained. Half of the store was a huge smoking hole.

I was at the grocer's again today. I hardly recognized him, his face was black and blue and he looked as if he'd been beaten up. Maybe he'd been in a traffic accident? I don't know, because I couldn't very well ask. But he was trembling convulsively and had trouble picking things up. His hands were like paws. He couldn't remember the prices and could only just barely talk. His eyes didn't focus, and he just stood there behind the counter very oddly, quivering like an animal that has given up hope and is going to let itself be eaten.

"You don't look well . . ." I said cautiously.

"Some kind of flu," I was able to read from the movements of his mouth.

But it couldn't have been influenza. Maybe he was just very drunk. But I've never seen anyone drunk like that.

"You ought to go to bed," I said. "You should close the store!"

"But I can't do that."

"Yes, but don't you know anyone who can help you?"

He didn't answer, just stared off into space.

"You can't just ruin your health." I was suddenly angry. "The money simply doesn't matter. You mustn't let it matter!"

"But it does matter," he said, and he looked at me as a tear ran down one cheek. He was wearing a green smock, and across the chest it said, "Your Independent Grocer."

3 Let Us Abolish Private Life

I once wrote an article called "Let Us Abolish Private Life"—and I still think it's a good idea, even though I never dreamed that one of the daily papers would run right over and abolish mine.

More and more people are wondering if we dare entrust our private lives to the distortions of the press, and the answer, of course, is that we do not. For the commercial press makes life more private than it really is. This is not because sensational journalists are especially morbid, nor because they suffer from glandular disturbances, as the actor Bendt Rothe insists. It is because the separation of the private and the public—or the private and the universal—is not only an artificial but a fatal distinction, and one that the press, as a result of its financial interests and thus of its conspicuous lack of feeling for our common human condition, helps to emphasize.

When the press, in its craving for scandal, meddles with our emotions and makes them sensational, our lives suddenly become private and lonely. I dislike having files kept on me without my knowledge, just as I dislike having my personal life distorted in the interests of privacy, and that is why I am so eager to see private life abolished.

But what is it exactly—private life? We all agree that every person has the right to have one. The alternative is unthinkable. But what we are to do with this privacy—aside from avoiding invasions of it—is a lot less clear.

We think of private life as a natural thing to have, but in fact the concept is probably most closely associated with societies such as ours—capitalistic and highly industrialized. The more anonymous we become, the higher we grow our protective hedges; the less authenticity our lives have, the more private we make them; the more conventional and empty they grow, the greater becomes the need to keep them secret. In short, the worse life is, the more imperative it becomes that other people stay out of it.

On the face of it, we all know perfectly well what privacy is—something about the right to lock your door. But the privacy that is quite natural in one context may seem to be asocial and secretive in others. For example, it would not look good for The Private Bank to keep its accounts a secret. What is more public than population statistics, and yet what is more private than our own kids at home? Those are two different things, but all the same it is dangerous to deny the connection.

In Amsterdam, I've noticed, it is not customary to put up curtains, so as you walk along the canals you can see right into people's living rooms. It's an old merchant tradition to show off the polished furniture. But if you stand in front of someone's window in Copenhagen, you run the risk of being pilloried as a Peeping Tom. In countries where whole families sleep in the same room, acts are performed that in our latitudes we consider private—and, in the presence of children, downright unsavory. But we in the West are always eager to protect our children from the realities of life. During the so-called "quilt lifting" debate, the editor in chief of one of the slick weeklies was attacked for having printed the statement of a Danish girl characterizing the English comedian Marty Feldman as a good lover. The motivation for the attack was that the remark would cause suffering to Feldman's six-year-old daughter. I can only say that it requires a very subtle—not to say perverted—mind to spot a source of pain in the fact that a girl has a good lover for a father. And having his name in the paper will hardly make him any worse.

But where does it come from, this privacy of ours? How was the idea invented?

The concept of privacy appears to have arisen in conjunction with the middle-class revolution in Northern Europe in the sixteenth and seventeenth centuries. It was here that cities began to grow large, and that the rich began to live in a different place from where they worked—namely, "at home." There was nothing by that name before; only now did "house" became "home." Up to that time, people had lived in large houses, fellowships, academies, or colleges, where they slept, lived, and were trained in all kinds of services and trades. The house was a miniature society, with its own agriculture and small industry, and included not only husband, wife, children, and relatives, but also servants, craftsmen, laborers, plowmen, shepherds, dairymen, and milkmaids. All the rooms in the house were connected with one another quite openly, so it is hard to imagine a private life of the kind we demand today.

According to the French social historian Philippe Ariès, the origins of privacy are closely linked to the breakup of large households. Gradually, the group that composed the household became a "nuclear family" consisting of parents and children who lived together in privacy and in growing isolation from the rest of society, of which they had previously been a part. Servants now comprised a separate, subordinate class who worked in the house for the pleasure of those who lived there and no longer produced anything for their own consumption or for other markets. "House" was becoming "home," as it cut itself off from the world of work and became a fortress for family life and leisure time.

Of course it's a mistake to underestimate the value of being able to lock your door and indulge in a little leisure. And yet the fact is that this new life-style was not well-established until the 1700s and is closely linked to industrialization and the economic system we call capitalism. The notion of privacy is intimately connected with the capitalist ideology. In fact privacy is an idea without which capitalism simply could not function, since capitalism is partly based on commercial secrecy. Commercial secrecy and privacy—our emotional commercial secrecy—are two sides of the same coin.

Alienation between people is partly the result of the disappearance of those broad bonds of solidarity that marked medieval and most other precapitalistic societies. Society today consists of small particles—nuclear families—which are alien to one another but which are held together by selfish interest and the necessity of mutual exploitation.

We are also social beings, with a need to feel that we are members of a group. And yet today we have become strangers to our own social concern. It is expressed in various public spheres: The Ministry of Social Welfare, narcotics centers, psychiatric wards, alcohol outpatient clinics—all of them far removed from private life. But what is more private than being an alcoholic? All of our social institutions are public, but at the same time they express the quality of our private lives. As Erich Fromm puts it:

> Separated from our private life as individuals is the realm of our social life as "citizens." In this realm the state is the embodiment of our social existence; as citizens we are supposed to, and in fact usually do, exhibit a sense of social obligation and duty. . . . What clearer example could there be of the separation between private and public existence than the fact that the same man who would not think of spending one hundred dollars to relieve the need of a stranger does not hesitate to risk his life to save this same stranger when in war they both happen to be soldiers in uniform?
>
> (*The Sane Society*, New York: Fawcett, 1973)

When a man kills for a cause, he doesn't feel he is committing the act himself, because our social and private selves have become alien to each other. But this separation between public and private is inextricably bound up with the way we have organized and structured our society—which more and more people are attacking on the grounds that in this society we have, as they put it, "lost contact with one another."

There is also some question as to how much, how wholeheartedly, we really like our privacy. There is still nothing wrong with sweeping our own doormats and locking our own doors, but what are we locking ourselves into, and what are we locking out? For even as we cling to our right to a private life, which we insist is sacrosanct, we may be simultaneously undermining it. Is it possible that we are sabotaging our own privacy because it bores us? And that this privacy, bound up as it is with the flowering of capitalism, is decaying at its foundations, because it has led us too far from each other and from ourselves, and because the specialized labor we do gives us no private satisfaction? Is it possible that we really don't care very much about our private lives?

After all, even in capitalist societies we have reached the point where private beaches and private forests are regarded as suspect. We have succeeded in asking some basic questions about the very idea of private property, to the point that in certain circles a thing as beneficial as private initiative is seen as the root of all evil. We are pretty much in agreement that secrecy and mystification provide the setting for authoritarian rule, political manipulation, and the abuse of power. We have therefore passed laws against administrative secrecy. Cheating on taxes is not considered a private matter. Nor is it a private matter for a member of parliament to traffic in liquor or supply arms to the Greek resistance. No, it is our emotional life—the sphere of activity that is supposed to bind us together—that is considered private. Family life is private. We consider it our natural, God-given right to have a private wife, a private husband, and private children. It is when we close the door to our single-family house that privacy—that is, our emotional commercial secrecy—comes into play. And it is not simply that we become self-sufficient and have no need for other people. It is worse than that. For other people become a threat, they become enemies, and we come to fear what we call snooping and interference from outside. Thus we have made commercial secrecy a way of life and turned privacy into a virtue *per se*, regardless of its nature. The emotional and the universal sphere, the area in which we ought to do things in common and come closer to each other—that part of our lives is no one's business. It is a private matter, and we are afraid of its becoming public or being publicized. But why?

I have made a note of some of the terms that are constantly cropping up in the current press-and-privacy debate—such as garbage journalism, smut, vileness, and filth. This kind of terminology in reference to stories about our private lives leads inevitably to the question of whether it is not our private lives themselves that are vile and filthy. If it's good enough indoors, why does it become so depraved as soon as it is publicized? And since these invasions of privacy are gobbled up by the wage-earning populace, does that mean we're all sick, that there *is* something wrong with our private lives, or is it only a glandular disturbance on the part of a dozen Danish journalists?

We have to work on the assumption that it is the "ruling class"—that is, the wage-earning middle class—that implicitly defines what is to be regarded as private and what public. The most egregious cases of smut in journalism are considered to be those associated with the revelation of infidelity and divorce. The middle class finds it morally reprehensible to publicize the fact that men and women leave *home* and move in with other men and women. To understand this point of view one must see it, of course, in the context of a threatened nuclear family. People are afraid that something will leak out—even though it may be humanly impossible to make a success of the family in its present form and within the framework of the existing society.

So the middle class is on its guard lest anyone defile its private life by describing it the way it is. But when, as happened recently, a young man is fined $20 in accordance with police regulations, par. 5, for having "manipulated his erect member," as they called it, in a public rest room, it is no longer looked upon as a private matter, even though we can assume that it was his own private penis that he "manipulated."

Privacy and concern for its invasion are to a great extent bound up with norms and taboos—especially of a sexual nature.

If the papers in Cairo, Damascus, or some other Arab

city were to reveal that Mrs. Avari had eaten pork, it would probably be the death of her, since she would be guilty of violating a taboo. But if Copenhagen is treated to the information that Mrs. Hansen eats pork, and if the newspaper prints a picture of her with the caption, "Mrs. Hansen in her ultramodern kitchen, preparing a delicious meal of roast pork," she would undoubtedly be very pleased and proud of the publicity. On the other hand, she would not be so happy to have the press publicize the name of her lover, no matter how much she loved him or how beautiful his name might be, because when all is said and done, it is not good form to have a lover—even though a lover is by no means an unusual thing to have.

I heard a radio program recently on which a woman complained about a particular housing project because there was so much gossip. When her girl friend came to visit her and her husband, all the other people in the entryway went around saying that they were having group sex. "And it's simply not TRUE," said the woman, beside herself with despair. "And when I go to the supermarket, I can see on people's faces that they think we have group sex, but we just DON'T, so the only thing we can do is move away." As far as I can see, her indignation at this malicious gossip is not so much due to the fact that her neighbors are especially wicked, but that she herself considers group sex worse than lice and vermin.

By the same token, we might suspect that people who are afraid of having their private lives made public have private lives of which they are not particularly proud. Here again, the question is whether we are well served by our privacy. For it is not inconceivable that the privacy mystique creates more distance between us than we care to live with, that it inhibits us and cramps our style more than it frees us and protects our integrity. It is possible that privacy has become an idea without content, an idea that is simply no longer in our own best interests. For after all we are no longer capitalists with the black mark of commercial secrecy on our foreheads. Most of us are wage earners, even if we do still cherish a dogmatic belief in the sublimity and inviolability of private life, despite the fact that it may have become downright impractical. For as things now stand, we have hardly anything in common but our tax problems—plus the mystique of privacy and family life that tells us not to mind each other's business.

It is perfectly natural, however, to want to attach prestige to private family life, as vulnerable as it has become in many cases. Hence the mystification. For as De Gaulle said, "Prestige is worthless without mystery. One honors only slightly what one knows too well."

But what do we mean by the vulnerability of family life? Well, as we said before, studies done in the United States show that children are by and large a threat to marital happiness. But if the nuclear family is not suited for raising children and perpetuating the race, then what is it suited for? For another thing, the family's vulnerability is reflected in the divorce rate. Something must be causing these hundreds of thousands of divorces, something not particularly pleasant.

But what? What goes on in our families? We know disastrously little about it, thanks to the privacy mystique. We all know that feeling of ringing someone's doorbell—our best friends', maybe—and sensing immediately that they were just on the verge of murdering each other. Some call it "vicious rage," others let it go as "a perfectly natural minor disagreement," as they say in the women's magazines. Anyway, this remarkable thing happens: as soon as an outsider appears on the scene, the atmosphere changes completely.

"How are things?"

"Just fine, thanks."

It is not right to involve other people. According to the terminology of private life, it is "disloyal" to tell anyone outside the nuclear family how things really are. Private life is a tacit reciprocal agreement whereby I won't meddle in your affairs if you won't meddle in mine.

For that matter, the immediate reconciliation of the fighting partners as soon as some third person knocks on the door is not entirely false. In the first place, they aren't alone anymore. In the second place, they, like the rest of us, have arranged their lives in small cells cut off from the activities of society at large, and this is a life-style that more or less requires spectators. We set up our homes like showrooms, and we communicate more by showing off things and children, by telling about our raises and vacation plans, than by revealing how we get along together privately.

In fact there can be no privacy without spectators. We need witnesses to our happiness. We need witnesses to the very fact that we exist. But there is no escaping the fact that the relationship of object to spectator is not the warmest one in the world, nor the most liberating, however reciprocal it may be.

I believe that privacy can be downright injurious to the health. We all need to know where we stand emotionally, but to do that we need frames of reference. The privacy mystique makes these frames of reference difficult to find.

It is almost impossible to learn anything about other people's private lives and their relationships to one another. Elizabeth Janeway writes:

> We are dependent on what husbands and wives tell us about themselves, on our estimates of their behavior (which is naturally related to our own experience), and on our judgment (which may be good or bad) of whether they are speaking and acting what they really

feel. When they say they are "happy" or "sad" or "bored" or "desperate" we have no way of knowing how they assess these words in their own minds, or how to compare the intensity and tone of their emotions with those of other happy, sad, bored, or desperate couples. (*Man's World, Woman's Place,* New York: William Morrow, 1972)

It is difficult under any circumstances to know anything about the way a family functions—and the privacy mystique doesn't make it any easier. And those who suffer most are the very ones who insist most firmly on their privacy. Why is it, for example, that one of the most common therapeutic techniques being used in psychiatric clinics is to let the patients talk to each other in groups? And what is it they are told to talk about? About their private lives, of course.

Private life is also the most interesting life we live, because it is universal, an expression of the human condition. But the press does not take privacy seriously. It makes it seem even more private than it really is. It is said that a country has the press it deserves, and no doubt it is our own attitude of mystification toward our crumbling privacy that permits bedroom journalism to flourish the way it does. For when we shroud our own private lives in mystery, it follows automatically that we will feel a certain malicious enthusiasm on seeing other people's private lives exposed. It is this more or less malicious delight on the part of its readers that the commercial press lives and thrives upon.

The press has been accused of destroying people by publishing the intimate details of their private lives. But if this is the case, then it is our own taboos that make it so. There cannot be many people who would object to a photograph that showed them playing parcheesi with their kids or baking liver pâté or spending an evening with good friends. It is almost exclusively sexual relationships that we feel are too private to be publicized, even though they are universal. But since we think of them as private, we gobble up details of other people's sexuality, especially famous people's, and in so doing we make bedroom journalism possible.

The fact that the commercial press can be dangerous, can even ruin people's lives, is due to its tendency to support and strengthen our taboos, and also, of course, to its conspicuous lack of taste and proportion. It speaks to our lowest emotions, and prospers by arousing our indignation and reaffirming our prejudices.

In my opinion, our private lives are so important that they must and ought to be made public, for no one who has not fallen into total human darkness can be indifferent to the way other people live. But precisely because private life is so important, it is essential that it not be distorted. And so it is not only a question of whether private life should be publicized, it is also a question of the character and quality of the press. There is nothing worthless, per se, in taking pictures of Jacqueline Onassis naked (if she is willing), but it is despicable and vulgar to present her nakedness as a sensation, as if her nakedness were more interesting than everyone else's. It represents a malicious, Peeping Tom mentality, trying to drag her down by the discovery of a roll of fat or a wart on her ass. Journalistic morality and taste are absolutely crucial, for to my way of thinking there is nothing about human beings that cannot be said or shown. It depends entirely on *how* it is said, and in what context.

The moment we make life private, we give the press free rein to prosper by peddling the universal as sensational. It is really we ourselves who have distorted life by making it private. When we wallow in the love lives of famous people and leap under the covers with prime ministers and film stars, it is not *their* actions that are interesting and intriguing and suspect, it is our own.

And therefore we will not have fewer invasions of privacy in the future, but more—and not only of actors and ministers of state. Our "filthy," "vile," "smutty" sex lives must be demystified by means of publicity, but by a press that does not merely mystify them further, as at present. For there are greater mysteries in the universe than sex. There are other, more urgent challenges to be met. Sexual liberation ought properly to mean liberation *from* sex, from sex as fixation, as trauma.

Erich Fromm writes:

> The division between the community and the political state has led to the projection of all social feelings into the state, which thus becomes an idol, a power standing over and above man. Man submits to the state as to the embodiment of his own social feelings, which he worships as powers alienated from himself.
>
> (*The Sane Society*)

As wage earners, we grow more and more powerless. It becomes harder and harder to influence social institutions, which seem to grow more and more impersonal. So it is important that we do not become impersonal ourselves. Our impotence and anonymity are not private matters, and so we need to know as much as we can about each other. We have a need for the most intimate kinds of information—on a voluntary basis, of course, out of a desire to know each other better, and not by means of hidden microphones and secret files. Therefore we must reach some agreement among ourselves. Do we mean to take our private lives seriously, or are we going to continue to make them mysterious? In my opinion, privacy has become an empty idea, and has little to do with respect for individual integrity. And I am seriously afraid that if we do not abolish privacy ourselves, out of a craving for fellowship, that it will be abolished for us, by machines, computer data banks, wiretapping, and outside force. This is not even a vision of the future. It is happening already, which may be why privacy has become the subject of debate.

And so the question of how far we dare entrust our private lives to the press depends on which private life and which press we are talking about. The lives we live today, and the press that makes them private, can go fly a kite for all I care. For once private life has lost its universality, private life is no longer worth living.

4 The Bargain

She stands there crying in the gray hall of the *pension*. Beside the telephone. She picks up the receiver and dials a number so she can cry some more. She calls every day to get some of the beating she clearly feels is coming to her.

Naturally it's hard for her to admit that she has spent at least half of her life in something close to an unconscious state. Literally. I don't know what these states are called. She simply couldn't walk through the house without something to hold on to, furniture or people. She has never wanted to admit it. But now that she has no house, much less anything to hold on to, she has—in an instant of self-knowledge, perhaps—thrown away all her high-heeled shoes. She has bought a pair of more or less foot-shaped shoes, with soles that reach out beyond her feet as if to make sure of their grip. She has grown smaller these last two years, a head and a half, I'd say, a bent figure with a pointed nose, waddling along so as not to fall down. To see her wearing those shoes, in which she is very certain not to fall, anyone might smile. Except for the fact that she radiates misery and wretchedness.

She calls to say she has now definitely stopped taking pills, and she calls to be punished. "Is it my fault he's in the closed ward? Ever since he was two, I could tell. . . . Ever since he was born. . . . Can I help it I was married to an insane alcoholic, who bought everything on installments so I had to go to work?"

She calls to say how popular she is at the tavern, and how she will probably move in with some man pretty soon. "I can pick and choose. . . . The minute I come in they say, 'Come and sit down over here, Ilse!' They all start shouting at the same time so they can sit with me. And the compliments! The man I was married to never said I was beautiful. Not once in twenty years."

She calls at 12:30 at night just to see how everything's going. . . . "I haven't been drinking," she always establishes first. Via stuttered consonants it appears that she has a man in her bed, and that is why she's calling. She has climbed out of bed and left her room, come barefoot into the hall to pick up the receiver and call and tell someone.

She calls the next day to say he was terribly cultivated, with a huge vocabulary.

But she wants more punishment. She searches out a superior force and embraces it as if she were seeking the hand of righteousness. Then she discovers she no longer has any say in the matter. It is somehow revealed to her, little by little, that she can no longer embellish reality with her insanity, that she is alone. It is a liberation, but one she has a hard time getting used to.

She has never been very familiar with freedom, but has worshiped whatever was handy instead. She was not accustomed to reaching out, and so whatever was handy came gradually closer and closer until in the end it was only within her. And she was entirely self-enclosed.

In all probability she has loved only two men in her life.

One of them was Hitler, who was adored in the nostalgic German schools around the Baltic (she herself was much praised in Racial Science class for her Aryan profile), and the other was her father, a Jewish businessman. But at home no one mentioned being Jewish, until the day she accidentally found herself with a report card on which there was a Jewish name. "Oh, ugh, how disgusting!" she said, and flung it down.

Her jovial father, who generally spent more time in the pursuit of business and pussy than he did on his children—although he loved them, of course—put her down on his lap and told her he was a Jew.

"But it's not something we consider very important in this house. Now run along and play," he added, with a loving pat on the cheek.

From that day on, naturally, she was terrified that he might come down and pick her up after school, although that wasn't very likely. Or that someone, anyone, would see him. Her beloved father.

But then he went to Sweden, and she got married. To the man who was handiest, the man who adored her most. During the war, moreover, marrying a non-Jew was the obvious thing to do, and for safety's sake she had her hair bleached too, and looked like a regular Valkyrie.

Ove played the piano, was always the center of attention, sang "Ain't Misbehavin'," and made people want to dance, so it was a natural match. They found an apartment on Ryesgade, where she lay in bed most of the day in pink Charmeuse and read Goethe and Graham Greene and smelled nice. Ove called her his silk doll. Housework and children bored her beyond description. She could cook only one dish—sausage—in spite of the fact that her father, at great expense, had sent her to the Maria School for several years. Nevertheless she did have children—two little girls, who quickly learned not to disturb her when she was lying in bed. She was so sweet and soft that no one had the heart to burden her. She began taking some pills that had just come out in order to calm her nerves. Occasionally she would climb out of bed and play Denmark's Melody Book for them in the semidarkness. They learned the songs by heart and sang them while she slept. But it didn't bother her.

She was by no means weak—neither physically nor psychologically. She walked from Ryesgade to Frederiksberg to have her little dog put to sleep. It ate like a vacuum cleaner. And she sang at the top of her lungs, "Is there anyone who'd want a little pree-tie girl like me, shooba dooba," or sometimes she whistled. No one else ever did that, so people stared at her as she bounced along on her long white thighs.

The fact that she nevertheless lay in bed all the time represented a kind of weakness which, for want of a better word we might call "cultural."

Out of boredom, but also because Ove spent all the money he earned on tailor-made suits and hand-sewn shoes—she took an evening job as a secretary. Even though it was beneath Ove's dignity. At work she found a lover, who soon came to the apartment in broad daylight and beat Ove repeatedly at chess. Dear Lord how she enjoyed it! Ove finally moved out, and Ole moved in, with his fingernail scissors and his statistics textbooks. But it made no difference that he had so few worldly goods, for this was love. She loved Ole more than Ove, partially because Ole was at the university headed for a Ph.D. Ove had merely been in business—at her insistence—even though he had been a musician to begin with. Ole was a whiz at figures, naturally, and helped the girls with their arithmetic. "There's nothing to it," he would say, and that's the way he was in everything. He used to hang his towel on his prick when he went to the bathroom in the morning.

When Ole was away from home, she began to lie in bed and call for Ove.

She would lie there and weep convulsively in the sour-sweet room where the drapes were always drawn. "He was so good to me, I want him back. Tell me he's coming back. . . ."

The girls were frightened, for of course their father had gone and was married to someone else, and there was nothing they could do to change that.

When things got very bad, her father arrived and presented her with an expensive suit from Fonnesbech's and told her to take a bath and get her hair done. The girls cheered up and cleaned her room. Sometimes, too, he would invite her for a weekend on Jutland, and then he would always get them a lovely double room with a balcony.

For several days afterward she would be up. She would lie and read fully clothed. She was so lovely as she lay there, her cheeks and hands and lips so soft. Everyone vied for permission to do her some favor. At happy times like these it was usually Ole who won. But when she nibbled a little at the food the children had prepared for her, they took it as a declaration of love. For she was so thin that they were afraid she might die. And then when everything was breathing harmony, she might suddenly conceive a desire for a piece of marzipan, after the store was closed. So Ole would drive off into the night in the unpaid-for Volkswagen to some entirely different part of town, and if in the meantime she changed her mind and wanted soft nougat, but ate the marzipan anyway, without bitterness, then everything was peaceful. And Ole and the children would sit around her as she reclined on her pillows and take turns rubbing her legs, for she liked that very much, as long as it did not interfere with her reading of course.

Ole called her his pearl.

Sometimes when he came home from work and leaned over the sofa to give her a kiss—they kissed a great deal during these ambulatory periods—she would draw back a little and say, "Phew, you smell. . . ."

"My little pearl," he whispered.

If someone suggested that this was only human, since he had been working all day, she would answer that she wasn't interested in what was human.

"It would never occur to me to sweat," she would declare, as if that were obvious, and the fact is that she never did. She had the fabulous capacity to alter reality in this way. Even when she lay in bed for days and the room smelled sour-sweet, it was never she herself who smelled. It was either the medicine or the blood that the girls wiped from between her thighs when they came home from school. Or perhaps some old cheese sandwich.

Strangers never came to the house, because they had now moved out to the suburbs and had a mortgage. "Why don't you invite people over?" the children often asked. But that simply wouldn't have worked.

Now and then she would take a secretarial job at a hospital. Partly because there were installments to be paid on everything, but mostly because it cheered her up to be surrounded by doctors. Especially surgeons, and most especially chief surgeons. The way they decided other people's fates in seconds. That appealed to her. She simply *adored* dynamic men. Psychiatrists were distinctly lightweights.

Then she got pregnant and suddenly had three children instead of two. But it made no real difference, for she paid with a knife to get Ove to buy her pills. But he preferred playing soccer, and anyway he figured that with all her crazy talk she must be feebleminded.

Be that as it may, she went back to work again, and Nils was put in a foster home during the week—for which, as a matter of fact, she despised him. His foster father tended the wash kettles in a laundry, and his foster mother stuffed him full of pastry and wiped off his mouth with a dishcloth. He grew chubby and pale, and for this his mother despised him all the more and called him "proletarian." Because she couldn't imagine having flabby children. *Her* children weren't just anybody! When he would cry on the weekends (if he fell down, for example—he was only two) she would hit him and tell him to stop his howling. It was more than a person could stand. The way he cried. The girls felt it was a little unjust, but they knew they would be called "disloyal" if they let on. And so they couldn't decently give their little brother much attention. It is never a good thing to set a child against his parent, and they didn't want to risk having their brother like them better than his mother. To think that people wanted to take her children from her.

For a short time she was in a mental hospital. In the closed ward. But that was a misunderstanding, for she didn't belong there at all, a fact of which she finally managed to convince the apes. There was nothing wrong with her but money worries and depression. And overwork. It wasn't easy to have three children and hold a job besides. But when it looked as though they meant to keep her for a little while anyway—just to be sure—she felt bullied and made herself pregnant in order to get an automatic release. She knew there was a paragraph in the law to that effect.

The obstetrician, meanwhile, advised her to have an

abortion, on the grounds that her health was i
But when she explained how much she loved
how they were the only thing in life that me
thing to her, they decided that sounded like
kind of talk—natural for a woman to feel that w
concluded that she ought to complete the pregn
psychological reasons. She weighed only about ei
pounds at the time, and the fetus never looke
bigger than a tennis ball beneath her black silk je
often wore evening gowns, as though she had so
to celebrate. She let the blonde grow out of her h
it turned out to be black. She was like an animal
from its cage, changing its coloration so as neve
recaptured. All during her pregnancy she was not
a black streak, fluttering about without rest, but
blissful curl to her lips and a demonic, victorious g
her black eyes, which seemed blacker than they
fore. She had beaten them, and what lay in her
belly was indeed a prize—though no larger than a
Her children always popped out of her like almond
their skins. In late summer she gave birth to a tiny
Leo child, who was put in an incubator. The two
barely survived.

Then came a turning point in her life. Of a sort.
work in Mombasa and later in Laos. Everyone agre
her life would be easier, now that she was going t
servants. And she did rally from her confinement an
a lot of books about those countries.

In Mombasa she had hallucinations. The childr
lieved in her visions, naturally. To counteract the
Austrian doctor gave her approximately enough me
to cover a tea table. And still she continued to ma
—and this with the clearest black eyes—that her
had come to Mombasa in command of a ship in

for a time. One of them was bridge, the other was Sung pottery—particularly Southern Sung.

She became the mascot of the Royal Laotian Bridge Club and played at the most expensive table. It was terribly important to her, and she dreamed of an opportunity of playing with her father, who had been bridge champion of Tallinn—just one rubber before he died. True, he had always ridiculed women who tried to play cards, but so much the better—he was right. She was invited home by the Laotian nobility, which does not generally mix with whites. But she was different and had overleaped some boundary. She was feeling very adventurous and traveled around to bridge tournaments all over Southeast Asia, bought a jade-green cheungsam with long slits in Hong Kong and a Sung frog in the Philippines. She lived mostly on pep pills during the day.

There was a Japanese who taught her to feel beauty. Taught her that it wasn't only sight. It was possible to date a vase with your eyes closed, by touch alone—its bottom, texture, shape, glaze. Her hands, which had always been long and slim and pale, grew even more so. When they were not playing expensive cards, they rested on white glazes. "Let us open our eyes to beauty," she quoted with a twinkle, pushing back the silken cover of a silken box with a cautious caress, removing the little silken cushion with two fingers to reveal a fog-white, hexagonal, ceramic powder case. When her eyes were tired, she replaced the cushion. Or the characters on the silken box might say: "Spring-rain-sky-blue-vessel-for-incense." Nails with flamingo-pink lacquer caressed the characters as she explained.

This was all insanely expensive, naturally, and there was not always food in the house. But she said that beauty was more important, and illustrated her assertion with an example from the year 1000—a Chinese potter who threw himself into his kiln and burned to a cinder in order to give his glaze the trace of extra oxygen it needed for perfection.

Yet money was always a problem. She claimed that Ole drank it up. At one point she tried to convince her older daughter, who was now past puberty, to prostitute herself to a rich Chinese merchant who had made the girl a lucrative offer just for lifting her skirt—no kissing. She didn't pressure the girl, it was just that she had her practical moments and thought it was petty to refuse a cultivated offer.

Aside from the financial problems, there was another snag in her new life of pottery and cards, and this was the fact that she had begun to find Ole less and less intelligent. He had learned a little Chinese, of course, in order to keep up with her, and he had also become quite a decent bridge player. But the higher esthetics cannot be learned, and she played cards at a level which mere practice cannot achieve. He grew stupider and stupider and drank whiskey in the afternoons. She checked the bottles. When he mixed up Tang and Sung, she refused to eat and went to bed with her pills for a week, and the whole house tiptoed and whispered so as not to fan the flames. Or when he played the wrong card or made a stupid bid, she would sit with an evil scowl on her face for days, and screw up her drugged eyes like black pottery—black Tang is my guess—and declare that it was impossible to live with an alcoholic barbarian.

And then he began to beat her now and then. But when she wept, it was mostly out of a sense of victory. Only he who dealt the blows had anything to lose. The servants circled around him in a great arc and approached only when it was time to get their pay.

One evening she drove off into the tropical darkness in

her nightgown. The next morning, the newspaper said that the body of a woman had been found in Pathet Lao country, shot by the Communists. But it was only a rumor. A death that dramatic would probably have suited her, if only the Communists had been strong enough. But she lived on as ever, on her own conditions, on her own terms. . . .

Things began to go wrong when they moved to the Arab countries. She despised Arabs because they lacked Chinese culture. She stopped eating when Ole began playing golf, and she stayed in bed for at least a year. She lay there and screamed about his disloyalty. No one had ever been as cruel to her as he.

"My little pearl," he would whisper.

She was moved from one hospital to another in many countries for several years, and she always brought along a little jade cat, to the point that it was with her when she would wake up in an oxygen tent. But the hospitals could do nothing for her, because there was nothing wrong with her. At the most, she was somewhat depressed and exhausted.

And so she would be carried home to bed, where she lay babbling about how her life was over—unlived. When Ole was sick of listening to her, and close to losing his job because he could no longer cope, and when he was tired of carrying her to the toilet because she simply refused to use her feet, he sent her home to Denmark—air mail—as an object. Used.

For form's sake, he said she was insane. But he shouldn't have done that. He was simply throwing her glove back in her face.

She calls up and asks if it is her fault that Nils is in the closed ward, just because she never wrote to him from the time he was twelve and they sent him away to boarding school.

I think she believed she could buy off the gods with her sex—wherever she got that idea. . . .

5 "Just Be Natural."

There are males who, without arousing any particular indignation on the part of their fellow citizens, wander freely through the streets of many towns dressed as women and heavily made up. These are the transvestite hijras, who belong to the lowest castes. They play an undeniable social role as male prostitutes. Sometimes they even become eunuchs by surgical means. They are the counterpole to the holy men in that they destroy Indian social barriers in a downward direction, just as Sadhu eliminates them upward, toward heaven. Now and then one sees them putting their uninhibited lusts on display—in a manner that becomes too much for decent citizens. These then attempt to inspire greater modesty in the hijras by dealing out more plentiful alms.

MEDARD BOSS
Indienfahrt eines Psykiaters

He had removed his hips and put them on the dresser, along with the summer dress and the crinoline. The sun was shining through the window, for it was a clear blue summer day. The furniture stood pushed together in the middle of the room under a plastic drop cloth because I was having some work done on the apartment. But this was Sunday, and I lay in bed rubbing Solvej's bony back —a little absentmindedly but interested too. The heavy odor—heavy for *him*, anyway—of Miss Dior hung a little too sweetly in the air, and I could taste the Mary Quant on his lips. It tasted odd, even though I used it myself. But what with the furniture in such a strange state, and Solvej's plastic earrings dangling against my cheeks, and his red-checkered cotton breasts pressed against my own more ordinary ones, I had the feeling I had set out on some fantastic journey—and had landed at some peculiar station along the way.

As I lay there that whole afternoon holding Solvej in my arms—not too hard, for I was afraid of knocking off his wig, but carefully, the way one does something with misgivings . . . well, why *was* I lying there?

Of course I could wave my arms and declare that this was MY homage to "more sensitive natures," my greeting to imaginative chromosomes. But that sounds so pious it's almost a lie. No, I was merely curious, and then too there had developed such a physical intensity that it was either cuddle up or cut and run. And if I had run away, I would have despised myself. For it would have been because he was dressed up like a girl, and how could I decently reject anyone on those grounds? They say that appearances deceive. But it's probably the other way around. Appearances reveal our real identities, and so it ought to be perfectly safe to give oneself to a man in woman's clothes.

And still it was strange. I think I lay there indulging myself with charming notions that in reality would have required a great deal of imagination to live up to. In fact I was utterly confused and had no idea where I stood. At one point Solvej grabbed me teasingly around the waist and accused me—not without sarcasm—of being hopelessly confused. It must have been then that the devil got into me and gave me the strength not to waver.

When I was in Thailand, transvestites moved about freely. In any case, they were not surrounded by special moralistic value judgments. For that matter, it was hard to tell the difference—women and transvestites looked the same. With their slender wrists, delicate hands, and lovely ivory bodies, Thai men can pass for women without much trouble. What used to fascinate me were the offended bitchy expressions on the faces of the white men when they would discover, in the early-morning hours at some crummy waterfront bar, that the woman they'd been warming up all night at great expense in hopes of finally screwing had the same kind of screwdriver and the same proclivities. When these "women," with their cool swan fingers, played an accompaniment to "Why Does the Sun Keep on Shining?" on the big necks of white sailors, and when, by and by, their own erections began to press against the bulging flies of the white men, it was regarded as an insult, an outrage even, whereas it could just as well have been viewed for what it was—an additional attribute. I guess I wouldn't have begrudged the sailors a more suitable means of satisfaction, but when it was a question of bureaucrats and East Asia Company officials, my laughter was raw, and no more than they deserved.

I mustn't forget Peggy of Pisserend—although there's no danger that I will. He had a long, white, fox coat, with special snaps so he could make it into an evening fur when he wanted. He showed me how it worked. When I saw him for the first time, he was sitting on a tall stool in a gay bar—a violent affront to all known sexes. I guess I was a little dumbfounded. In any case I asked my escort to excuse me—there was something I just had to look into a little more closely—and I moved over next to Peggy.

He was wearing a thick, streaked, Kay Kendall-style wig and a heavy sweater dress of silver lamé, and his voice was hoarse, yes, enchanting, if I may say so. Peggy sat there on his pedestal at night and radiated VAMP. He was magnificent. Nothing commonplace could touch Peggy. If he turned up before some magistrate, the fine would always be dismissed in return for a promise never to show himself off publicly again. It couldn't be any other way, I told myself as I sat there dreamily mimicking his movements, inhaling deeply when he inhaled, exhaling when he exhaled, even though I had no cigarette. (I simply didn't have time to smoke.) My eyes were glued to the striking, slightly prominent jaw, the greedy, muscular throat that could devour anything, the shameless Adam's apple that made light of every illusion. There was something in him that I relished. I'd like to call it strength, because that's what I long for in women. Maybe he wasn't strong at all, but he was a woman, and I was struck by the thought that it might actually be necessary to go to a man like Peggy in order to understand women. My lips quavered dumbly to the exaggerated swaying of his dark red lips, and the palms of my hands tingled with a desire to capture his supercilious gestures in midflight. Peggy was outrageous, although I couldn't say just why. I stared so intently at his long, fluttering, steel-wire lashes that I forgot to blink myself. I suddenly realized—in a flash—that in his desire to play the feminine role, to act it out to its logical extreme, he was laying it bare. That is something a person may not do, I saw that clearly. A person may not expose the feminine role. Later, I also began to work out why.

If a man dresses up as a woman, he is risking the loss of his house and home and daily bread. Can a bus driver pretend he's a woman, or a cashier? Of course the tendency is not very widespread, but being a woman is obviously such a serious matter that no one is allowed to poke fun. It's forbidden. Exposing the feminine role is an affront to public decency and a threat to law and order. We are all perfectly free to *discuss* the feminine role. We are perfectly free to hold meetings, give lectures, organize study groups, and discuss the subject backward and forward, using masculine jargon. But anyone who lays bare the feminine role in action, the way transvestites do, is going to be fined. And if they persist in pretending to be women, they will be locked up.

Of course we can make fun of women, but there's fun and there's fun. Permissible fun must conform to what the male culture finds funny. All laughter-producing amusement entertains in direct proportion to the degree to which it supports known feminine polarities: ignorance/cunning, inferiority/dominance, wife/whore, and so forth. The permissible woman jokes are: mother-in-law jokes, extravagant-wife jokes, woman-driver jokes, woman-on-a-diet jokes, dumb-blonde-secretary jokes—"All right now, this is called a typewriter," and so forth. This kind of joke is considered very entertaining. But when transvestites unmask the whole woman for what she has become, a role—and a grotesque role at that—it is both awesome and unlawful. The female role is so intimately bound up with our social well-being that society must protect itself against any real exposure of it. When a man dresses up as a woman, it is regarded in the moral sense—and punished—as being subversive activity, which is exactly what it is.

As I sat there devouring Peggy with my eyes, beginning to see that it was not Peggy that was a poor actor but rather the feminine role that was poorly written, Peggy must have conceived an affection for my person. In any event, we began chatting the way girl friends will and complimenting one another's outfits (I was wearing only a simple gray dress). On the way out he even acquainted me with the finer points of his fox coat, whereupon we took our leave and threw each other kisses.

I can see quite clearly that being a transvestite is no joy, but on the other hand, neither is it a tragedy to be despised. I was struck by the heady thought that transvestites are in fact the guerrillas of the war between the sexes. Transvestites are the real partisans in the battle against sexual roles, because for the moment they are the only ones who pay the price and risk their lives. Transvestites are without compromise, the only women who cannot be bought. For their psychological makeup is such that they could not possibly suspend their subversive activities even if the death penalty were introduced. These men function only as women, and no matter what happens—barring a whole new culture—they will and must continue to demonstrate woman's grotesque situation. Transvestites are way out in the sexual front lines where very few people venture. They are harassed and humiliated and have to sneak along in the shadows of buildings in broad daylight. But they persist in their demands for a new culture, because they have no roles to fall back upon. Transvestites have revolutionary chromosomes—they cannot be rehabilitated.

As a transvestite, a person cannot become a clerk of the court or a policeman or a teacher, which in itself speaks for the revolutionary structure of transvestite chromosomes. The world is such a petty place that transvestites are not even allowed to be clerks in flower shops. Indeed they cannot be integrated into the working world at all, which is both their strength and their weakness. Like all other guerrillas, transvestites must attend to their real business after closing hours, when the sun has gone down.

But even if I march down the street with "sex warriors of all nations" on my lips, it is still the transvestites who pay the price. It is the transvestites who risk their lives in order to open our eyes to an arbitrary sexual idea, an ideology based on a genital mystique, a system only the benighted can live with. There are even people who call this system Mother Nature. I call it an *idée fixe*. Transvestites proclaim woman to be just that—a concept, an idea. Their crime consists in presenting a clear picture of that idea and in not confusing it with nature.

For the sake of my dreams, I give transvestites a halo of heroic martyrdom and assign them a crucial sexual role with which most of them would have a hard time identifying. I am acquainted with the hackneyed observation that all deviates want nothing more than to throw off their crosses and be normal, if they only could. But there is this about real heros and real stars, that they never bother to explain themselves, who and what they are, they just stick to their task—to shine. And when I fell in love with Peggy and saw the way he shed light on the feminine role simply by playing it clearly, I realized that I too have wanted to unmask the female role. Not as an expression of courage or of enlightened consciousness; in my case too it may be nothing but an innate propensity.

"Naturalness" has always filled me with horror. I knew instinctively that what was "natural" was very dangerous, a terrible trap, and my fear was confirmed by the discovery that being "natural" was considered the most important thing in the world. A sweet, natural girl . . . It didn't matter if you were unmusical, cruel, and incompetent, as long as you were "natural." So what if you couldn't do magic tricks or ride a horse or make pancakes, the most important thing was being "natural."

As a twelve-year-old, I had no very clear picture of what being natural was supposed to conceal. I didn't realize that naturalness was a justification for a lack of skills and that it meant, "You must not try anything new!"

Nevertheless, I dissociated myself from naturalness by ostentatiously painting my whole head with color crayons —from purple around my eyes to flaming orange cheeks and luminous white lips. The crayons were poisonous, but I couldn't help that. In fact when I was told that I looked alarming, it made me feel very secure and self-satisfied. But things went badly for me at school, particularly at examination time, for my painted face upset the outside examiners. A kind teacher put his arm around my shoulders and told me that I was making life difficult for myself by not looking natural—the examiners had expressed distaste and fright. He also advised me to put aside the war paint at future examinations, which surprised me a little since our teachers didn't usually urge us to be devious.

Later I did shelve the crayons, for variety is the spice of life. But I stuck to the strategy. A lot of people hoped that this childish nonsense was just a passing phase, but quite the contrary, I struggled harder and harder against "naturalness"—determined to meet violence with violence. And, like all martyrs, I registered as victories the innumerable defeats brought about by my increasingly terroristic methods. At school, I was called in for a private chat with the headmistress. She said things could not go on the way they were . . . that it was dreadful to look at me . . . and then she stopped. I asked what it was that was so dreadful, and she answered that whenever anyone looked at me they always got the "wrong" idea—and that that was a shame, since at heart I was such a "natural" girl. Since neither one of us was qualified to say what "naturalness" might mean, I settled for a polite and apologetic shrug of the shoulders and an assurance that I would see what I could do. My *esprit de l'escalier* told me that I should have said, "There you are quite wrong, madame, because if you have eyes in your head you can see that I am not the least bit natural. And I can assure you that I have no 'at heart.' I am precisely what I appear to be." But there are a lot of such things that we never do say, and "naturalness" continued to haunt me. I would be invited out, if only I would promise to look natural. The judgment of middle-class men and their wives echoed through my life: "Nothing personal, of course, but why do you always have to be different? Why don't you just be natural?" For them, naturalness was whatever was most decorative, conventional, and undisturbing. But the worst part was that since their ideal was for women to be natural, then we must conclude that in their eyes it was also natural to be a woman.

And by God that was where they lost me. It is one thing to be gracious and agree to play the feminine role without a gun in your purse. But to have to pretend that the feminine role is natural! They'd like that! But that would be treachery, for is there anything more grotesque and unnatural than the feminine role?

It is time to report that there *is* no such thing as a natural woman—or if so, she is in a psychiatric ward—because naturalness in women is a mutation that our cultural history has so far refrained from encouraging. A natural woman today would be an anachronism. Moreover, it is probably a waste of time to place so much importance on being natural, since no one knows what that means. For the time being, all we know is that natural women do not exist today, no more than natural polar bears exist on Strøget or natural giraffes on the Common. If people had eyes in their heads or nerves in their skin, they would be SHOCKED at the sight of a woman, or at least upset, just as they would at the sight of a legless veteran or a eunuch who was seven inches tall. But what women get instead is a clammy pat on the cheek and a, "Why don't you just be natural?" A woman is not allowed to shit, or play the drums, but that's okay as long as she is "natural."

The only honest way of being a woman today is to play

the role to the hilt—or, for that matter, to play *all* the feminine roles if one is not enough, but on no account to take them seriously and confuse them with nature. For once you accept the middle-class *idée fixe* that women are a natural phenomenon, you have sold your soul.

And so I must continue to wear a parrot feather in my hair and a chrysanthemum in my bum—the way transvestites do. We must give offense, for God's sake. History's real transvestites are all the women who have accepted their disfigurement as normal, and who earn their living by disguising the madness and looking natural. "My" transvestites, the ones who are out at night, lay the madness bare.

I guess it was after meeting Peggy that I decided I wanted to interview a transvestite. Something like: "My dear friend, the papers are full of the oppression of women, so how does it happen that you go rushing headlong into the street in women's clothes? What is it that's so wonderful about being a woman?" I suspected that a man who lived both parts might have a significant point of view on the whole problem of sexual roles. Also, I suspected that it was not so much the feminine role that was attractive as it was the masculine role that was forbidding. When a man disguises himself as a woman, it is not so much in order to *become* a woman as it is to illustrate and epitomize a "No" to the male world. But even though Solvej was now lying in my bed, and even though I regarded his behavior as the expression of a sensible head and an educated heart, still I was no wiser. For it is not necessarily the man in the front lines who can best explain the war.

Solvej had said on the phone that it would be nice to have a cup of tea and some good girl talk. I wondered what that might be—girl talk—and whether I could handle it. At the same time, I was overwhelmed with his joy at being able to "dress up." Myself, I didn't have the strength to do the whole number. I was in the process of whitewashing the bathroom ceiling, so he would have to take me as I was—or whatever it's called. I was very nervous waiting for him to arrive and kept going to the kitchen window to get a glimpse of him—just a glimpse to have something to get used to before he rang the bell.

A gigantic woman twisted out of a Morris Mascot. A dark-haired girl in a summery dress, I noticed, as he walked toward the steps. I knew he was married and had children, and that in everyday life he was some kind of a professional man. But the woman who came up the stairs was not his wife or his sister or his mother, not a member of his family at all, but someone quite different whom I couldn't immediately place.

The bell rang, and I put some water on to boil and opened the door. I think he must have been six feet three —the kind of girl who tries very hard to be SWEET—like a bakery clerk on her day off or a very young tobacconist's assistant. He had a short, slightly rumpled, cinnamon wig, big cinnamon lips, large cinnamon fingernails on a pair of powerful fists, and a little, light-blue summer dress with puffed sleeves, ruffles, and a crinoline. I couldn't help thinking that transvestites are always twenty years behind the fashion. We gave each other our hands and smiled.

No sooner had I made a mental note of his SWEETNESS than he was standing in the kitchen telling me how he had recently come across one of my articles while he was lying under his car fixing something in the motor. He had been using the newspaper to wipe up oil. Solvej explained that he was an amateur auto mechanic, an amateur in a thousand fields, but had a hard time sticking to anything. He had very sweet, starry, light-blue eyes that went well with his dress, and he stood there blinking them the whole time I made tea—probably to indicate that a couple of compliments on his outfit would not be out of place. I told him he looked very smart, but I did add that his dress was out of fashion and that I couldn't understand why transvestites absolutely had to be twenty years behind the times.

"Well, but that's not so strange," he said. "It's because we identify with our boyhood sexual objects. And so when we finally get our bearings when we're more mature, it's the old dreams that rise to the surface."

I was glad he hadn't taken it personally, and I served him tea on the bed—the only available piece of furniture in the room. The disorder was not conducive to serious discussion, much less girl talk, but Solvej didn't seem to mind. Solvej was beaming. It was his dress-up day.

Interview with Solvej

Have you gradually learned the tricks of playing the feminine role?

"I really blew it in Tivoli yesterday, when this guy stepped on my toe. I forgot I was being a girl and said, 'Oh, that's all right!' But I know perfectly well that I should have looked insulted, stepped back a couple of steps, and waited for a complete apology—that was my mistake. I am well aware of the fact that there are a lot of things a person can't do as a woman—look people in the eye, for example. It's been hard to break myself of the habit, because I'm a very inquisitive person. But now I try to look down, or straight ahead, as unencouragingly as I can, because otherwise you can get into a hell of a lot of trouble. I make a fool of myself all the time—and those starving foreigners are especially bad, because they take the merest glance to mean that . . . well, that you're BAIT. You can get burned real bad. Strøget has come to be out of the question. I was accosted there the other day, pawed and everything, it was really gross. . . . Well, like the eel said, you have to learn to wiggle. . . . And nevertheless I feel freer as a woman, though I can WELL understand the women's libbers."

How so?

"I don't like the way men are always chasing women. All you have to do is ask directions or the time of day, and there's genitalia in the air. Of course that can be a lot of fun if you're in the mood, but it gets to be irritating in the long run when it's just an automatic reflex."

The streets would seem strange if women didn't try to look pretty.

"I just have the feeling it's a whole different thing, because the ways for a man to make himself attractive are so limited. I notice how interest grows the moment I put something on my face, because makeup simply makes you more exciting. Most people accept it, too, as long as they haven't smelled a rat in advance. It's a frightening thought, if they're not ready for it."

How do women perceive you?

"There's a lot of coldness in the female world, even if I do like to think of it as a world of elves and flowers because it's so far from the world of the businessman. But I can't let myself look a girl in the eye—as a girl—the same way I can—as a man. They know right away something's wrong. Women have their own secret language among themselves. Looks that touch and measure. I really noticed it in the beginning, when I was so badly dressed. Nothing was right. I looked awful: I'm sure it was a giveaway. Men don't know those looks. But it's unmistakable when women meet on the street—one of them just throws a GLANCE at the other, but she's seen everything, clothing, makeup . . . If one shoe needs shining, she's seen it; if the dress is a little out of style, she's seen that too. It all feeds right into the computer, and she walks right on. . . . There's something very cold about it. I have the impression they're all fighting to be the loveliest thing on the market."

There's also something called "masculine vanity"—you know . . . which you're not supposed to offend.

"Oh, that! I've never had any use for that. I've always let people offend mine just as freely and fiercely as they wanted. But of course that spoiled their fun. I've never felt at ease in the male world. I want to be beautiful, but in the male world, the part of me you might call the "girlish" side has no real right to exist. I feel as if I'm being squeezed into something I never asked for. If a man is going to get ahead in the male world, he has to play a game that I can't stand. He never tells the truth, only something that points in that direction . . . and then you have to guess what the truth really is. If he tells the whole truth, then people think there must be something else behind it. It's very unpleasant. The same thing's true in business. You play a few cards and then watch to see what the others do. You can't just say, 'Here's the way it is.' The very essence of the male world is that you're a hero if you live against your own inclinations and do what you least want to do, because it's your goddamned duty. Oh, and men's clothes are so dull, and I can't wear makeup and move gracefully, and so forth and so on."

Do you move differently in different surroundings?

"I try to act girlish when I'm wearing girls' clothes so I won't give myself away—since after all I am sort of rough and craggy. But the funny part is that when you put on a dress and heels, you actually WALK differently. There IS something to the saying that clothes make the man. Women live much more with their bodies. That was one of the first things I noticed when I walked in a dress—the way it warmed my legs, I could suddenly feel them. . . . God knows what's *really* masculine and what's *really* feminine. There's nothing to say it's feminine to wear a dress or masculine to have short hair. I have the feeling we invented most of it for ourselves. There's a group of islands in the Philippines where it's considered terribly feminine to have a moustache. Women have moustaches tattooed on, while the men shave theirs off. It's easy to imagine the moustache becoming a feminine sex symbol if you're surrounded by women with moustaches, don't you think?

"The men and women alive today never decided their own sex. They never had any say in the matter at all! The whole pattern of your life from the day you're born, all your dreams and ideals and prejudices, are all predetermined—on the basis of one single sex. That is strange, isn't it?

"In one way I'd like to have all the restrictions removed. Abolished. And then again I don't think I would. By pretending to be a girl, I'm just jumping the fence at its lowest point. But I have the feeling I'm living two lives and taking something from another world that I'm not entitled to. And yet, at the same time, I *am* entitled. Because I've been cheated. I have the feeling I've been tricked out of something, something broader. . . . In *Daphnis and Chloë*, he puts on her clothes so that he can sort of understand her completely. . . . I know just how he feels. Changing sexes is terribly exciting. I've always been fascinated by the idea of living life as a girl. Identification is very fundamental, and I have the impression—both from my own experience and from other transvestites—that our sexual identity has been uncertain right from the start. When I was a child, I knew perfectly well that I was a boy. But I didn't know which world I belonged to—the boys' or the girls'. Did you see *Death in Venice*? The pretty blond boy, the angel of death? That's what I was like."

When did you start dressing up as a girl?

"I've been doing it all my life. When I was little, we used to play we were great ladies. I just kept on, that's all.

But if the male role weren't so limited, and if I could dress the way I wanted to, I don't think I'd be sitting here with a dress on now. . . ."

No?

"I don't think so. I have an idea that even if I wanted to, I wouldn't do it, because it wouldn't be so necessary. The way things are, if I want to act out my feelings, I have to play the female role one hundred percent—there's no middle ground. And I don't have anything against that. But it irritates the hell out of me that I can't be myself as a man. . . ."

It still hurts where the rib is missing?

"Yes, something like that."

Aren't you afraid of being discovered when you walk through the garden gate and pass the neighbors?

"Yes. But that's a small worry in comparison to the experience."

Then it must be a terrific thing!

"Besides, I think I play the part pretty well, if I do say so myself. . . ."

Hmm.

"Don't you think so? What did you think when you saw me? Tell me what you thought. Were you the least little bit surprised?"

Oh, a little bit I guess . . .

"Haven't you ever seen a man in women's clothes?"

Oh, yes, with feather boas and long cigarette holders and gold lamé . . . But I've never had the bell ring on a sunny day and when I open the door, there stands a man in a perfectly ordinary summer dress.

I could tell I wasn't going to get much more out of this interview, and it was my own fault, because I couldn't concentrate. I was sexually confused. In the end we just sat there and talked.

"Are you wearing artificial hips, or is that just a crinoline?"

"Both. I've got a crinoline, but I had to put in something extra on the sides. . . ."

"You're wearing panty hose, aren't you? Why don't you have a garter belt? I thought that was what transvestites usually . . ."

"Because they're so impractical—I've outgrown that stage! But I do think transvestites and fetishists have a lot in common. It's erotically stimulating to put on women's clothes, even though very few people will admit it."

"Is it?"

"Yes, I love to seduce girls when I'm wearing a dress. I'm much more relaxed and in the mood. I just like it that way. I don't know if it's because of the dress or because I'm pretending I'm a girl or just because I'm enjoying myself. I can't tell which, but I just feel fantastically free. . . ."

"You must be a lesbian!"

He laughs.

We sit there for a long time in silence. It's almost more than I can stand. I'm not feeling very free. Solvej looks me right in the eye. I look down. I'm ashamed of myself in a way—my uncertainty doesn't become me. It wasn't just his sex that confused me, it was also the way he talked, which didn't suit the bakery girl he was pretending to be. How can anyone wearing puffed sleeves and ruffles talk about genitalia and the predetermination of the sexes? That sort of thing usually goes with an entirely different uniform.

"What DID you think when you saw me? How . . . how did I look to you?" asks the bakery girl eagerly, shifting his weight on the bed.

"I was mostly wondering if we'd be able to talk to each other. . . ."

I'm lying. I haven't thought about much of anything

except the fact that there is a man disguised as a woman in my room. Or a bakery girl who talks like a psychologist.

Solvej is sitting straight and painted and silent like a figure in Madame Tussaud's wax museum. She is resting, looking through me.

"Of course it is a little bit upsetting, you know. . . . Because you do think about it. . . ."

I'm stammering. What I want to say is, "Because you can't stop thinking about it." But that would sound too strong, might even hurt his feelings. Because his happiness depends on making the illusion complete. And so I let it go at "You do think about it." But still I haven't really said very much.

"Yes, I know what you mean. I feel the same way. But I think I got over it. I'm not thinking about it anymore. . . ."

He says that to reassure me.

"I'm not thinking about it so much anymore myself," I say, to reassure Solvej—and myself. But I know I'm lying and I have to explain what I mean—and fill up the silence. . . .

"It's sort of like trying to talk serious business to a businessman, and he's got part of a pea stuck to one of his teeth, you know, and you just can't get anywhere, if you know what I mean. . . ."

"What do you see like that about me?"

"Oh, nothing at all . . ." I stare down at the bedspread.

"I guess what you mean is that sex is something that comes from down inside, right? And right at the moment you're perfectly well aware that you're sitting here with a man, is that it?"

I was not perfectly well aware of anything. But when Solvej grabbed me around the waist and declared that I was hopelessly confused, I got up and took off my clothes in order to achieve a little clarity and a little self-respect.

Solvej asked me if he should take off his wig.

"No," I said. "For God's sake, leave it on."

A month later—summer was now on the wane—I was on my way to Rådhuspladsen at five o'clock in the morning to catch the night bus home. On the flagstones in the distance I saw something gleaming, long and white. I was so exhausted that morning I felt as if my guts were on the outside of my clothes, so to speak, and at first I thought it was some sort of luminous natural phenomenon, and on second thought I decided it must be a ghost. But when I came to the kiosk to buy the morning papers, it was Peggy, out in his fox coat, long and white, let down to formal length. I saw him bend down toward a little man who came up to his bosom and give him a kiss on the cheek. I didn't even have time to wish Peggy good morning before he had swept into a taxi like a silver bow. I had been making love to Ulla and Ina and Balthazar that night, and I was feeling so lighthearted that I waved to him without caring at all whether he recognized me or remembered me or even saw me. But he waved back, with his long white gloves!

I trundled on to my bus stop with the morning papers under my arm. And as I stood there waiting, a taxi came backing down the street toward me. It was irritating that a person couldn't stand there in peace and quiet and enjoy the morning. But it turned out to be Peggy, and he offered me a lift! I jumped in happily, and we lit each other's cigarettes. I felt safe with him, as he talked about various forms of flagellation and the decline of pleasure. People had no appreciation for anything but the vulgar anymore. I don't even know if he was going my way, but it seemed natural for us to share a cab. We drove off together in the blue morning light. We didn't talk the whole time, we were both too tired. But I felt a great closeness, even when all we did was stare straight ahead. As we drove by the telephone building, he mentioned in passing that he was actually a man. I nodded wearily. It had no significance that morning. I mean, he might just as well have told me that his name wasn't ACTUALLY Pedersen with a *T* but merely with a *D*.

When I got out, I gave my strong, white, wombless vixen girl friend a kiss on his bright red lips. The taxi turned and drove off in the opposite direction as I walked into my building, and I felt the way his stubble had been peeking through his makeup—as if the morning sun were prickling his skin.

6 Of Something Feminine and Something Masculine

They say that anyone not conversant with three thousand years of history is only living from hand to mouth. But no one can accuse Karen Blixen of that, for it is reckoned in high quarters that she is nearly three thousand years old herself, give or take a few hundred. This relatively great age is of course an advantage for a person like Karen Blixen, who likes to range back and forth in time at will. We say of a man who has lost his memory that he doesn't know who he is—and it wouldn't surprise me if the same thing applied to a woman.

Who the woman is is one of the themes Blixen plays with in two of her essays, "Daguerreotypes" and "A Fire Speech" (Copyright © Rungstedlund Foundation). And since the question of woman's nature is being taken up everywhere with renewed energy, it might be useful to turn to someone three thousand years of age whose memory is in order. Not so much to lean back as to push on from a sound, objective starting point.

Daguerre was the man who invented photography. It was not supposed to be an art, but merely a means of picturing things exactly the way they were. And *things* are always interesting, because we sense some connection between an era's millinery and its ideals, between its davenports and dreams. What makes Blixen so modern in this context is that she depicts woman not so much as a natural thing, but as an idea. A concept. A concept that women have taken as their ultimate mission to represent as well as possible. Blixen uses her daguerreotypes to portray the way people—that is, men, and particularly gentlemen—thought, and to show us how traumatic was the cultural revolution unleashed when women began to ride bicycles.

My first daguerreotype is in the form of a pronouncement. I heard it uttered sometime around the turn of the century by my old uncle, my father's brother, Chamberlain Dinesen of Katholm. . . .

People of his kind simply do not exist any longer. I could tell many stories about him. His whole life was colored by the fact that as a twenty-two-year-old officer in the Guards he was sent to Russia as attendant cavalier to Princess Dagmar on the occasion of her betrothal to the Grand Duke and heir to the throne, later Czar Alexander III. As my uncle had neither title nor much money, I am forced to conclude that he was chosen for this exalted mission because of his very uncommon beauty. My father, his younger brother, said of him that he was the only completely beautiful man he had ever seen in his life. . . . He was a blusterer and a domestic tyrant, whom pretty women and clever old servants could twist around their little fingers. I could tell as many stories about his good heart as about his prejudices.

Somehow the talk that summer afternoon must have

come around to bicycles, which at that time can hardly have been a new invention but which were just then winning rapid acceptance in all social circles and even among women. It was this last circumstance which angered and upset my uncle. He began by saying that it was a damned shame to see women on bicycles. He was opposed—which he did not tolerate easily—and he worked himself into a rage. In the end he struck his knee with his fist and declared, in his most ringing officerial tone, "When I see a woman on a bicycle, I reckon, by God, I've got the right to slap her on the bum."

I was so young myself that I didn't dare reply. I had just been given my first bicycle, but I swallowed down my burning indignation in silence. However, I had two pretty young cousins, ten or twelve years older than I, who rode bicycles very smartly and who stood their ground more firmly. In clear high voices they leaped intrepidly to the defense of their bicycles. They were no match for my uncle, but toward the end of the discussion one of them did get off a good remark. "Yes, but you simply couldn't, Uncle," she said, "because in the first place she'd be riding away from you, and in the second place she would be sitting on it!" My uncle was a little taken aback and could not come up with an immediate reply. "No," he said then, with great importance, with the profound conviction of the righteous, "No, but the right—by God I'd have the right."

Late that evening up in the tower and the guest room beside it, we young people continued the debate among ourselves. My two cousins were still quite hot beneath the collar. "Right!" they cried. "What kind of a right is it Uncle thinks he has? I really wish someone would explain me that!"

And that is what I would like to try to do now, some fifty years later.

Karen Blixen explains her old uncle's right to give the lady cyclist a slap on the bum with the myth that says a woman must be a woman in order for a man to be a man. A man's education, a gentleman's upbringing, cost a lot of money and entailed rigid self-discipline in submission to the ideals of the age. And if a woman then climbed up on a bicycle, thus revealing that she also consisted of two parts below the waist, she not only put those ideals to shame, she held up the man's education and all he had learned to ridicule. Yes, she questioned his very identity. For a woman's secret power lay in mystery. Such was the belief in the best circles, and since not *all* women could have secrets, it became a sound and easily comprehensible rule to keep the *body* secret, from the waist downward—since all women did at least have bodies. But by riding on a bicycle, a woman surrendered her secret power, which is to say, all the power and being that she had. She ceased to be a woman, which meant that a man could no longer be a man. And then what would become of world order? People had always feared that someday it would come to naught because of some whim of fashion. In this connection, Karen Blixen provides us with a valuable commentary on PANTS.

It may be even more difficult to explain to the people of this day and age how the skirt—that is, floor-length clothing—came to be such an important, indeed a crucial symbol of woman's dignity, and how her legs became the one sacrosanct taboo. The women of that time were not stingy about showing their charms above the belt. But from the waistline to the ground they were mysteries, sacred riddles.

Personally, I think the explanation can be found in the fact that pants are a doubtful garment, a garment that lacks dignity. Even for men, the age of daguerreotypes referred to them euphemistically as "unmentionables" or "permissions." Or perhaps it can be found in the fact that it is actually disquieting for a fully-clothed human being to have two legs. It is often said that pants are unbecoming to women, and I can concur in that judgment, although I must add that they are also unbecoming to men. When I remember the robes worn by my acquaintances among the Arabs and Somalis, and when I think of the dignity and expressiveness they lent the movements of those slim creatures, I can only pity our European men in their trousers. One time in Berlin I saw King Lear step onto the stage in tight pants and realized immediately that it was impossible to perform the role of the great mad king in that outfit. A flow of folds must follow his powerful outbursts and gestures. The great scenes of antiquity—the death of Socrates, Caesar's murder on the Capitol—are incompatible with any hint of pants. Moses could never have struck water from the rock dressed in trousers.

In any event, things were as they were, and long skirts were the holiest attribute of feminine dignity.

The English author Samuel Butler tells the story of a little boy whose universe collapses when, in the course of a holiday on which he shares a room with two young aunts, he sees them step out of their crinolines, long-legged and bipartite, whereas until that moment he had believed that women continued in one piece from the belt down to the ground.

In those days, when it was far better to say of a woman that many men had suffered for her sake than that she had made many men happy, women were divided roughly into three groups: guardian angels, housewives, and harlots. There are less attractive words for this last category, but harlots at least had the distinction of possessing legs—two shapely ones as a rule—since after all they had to live on them. The guardian angel and the housewife had no legs, but they did have one thing in common with the harlot—*a price*. Woman's price is a central theme in Blixen's work, just as woman's price is fundamental to the view of women that has prevailed since the Renaissance—that is, since capitalism, the nuclear family, and patriarchal culture as a whole gained their foothold. The housewife and the guardian angel have never been wild about the whore, and yet it has always been a source of satisfaction to them to know that the concept "femininity" could be made to pay in dollars and cents.

> My old friend Mr. Bulplett, who had in perfectly good conscience ruined himself on a courtesan—La belle Otéro—has told me many times about the great cocottes who played such a prominent role in France during the Second Empire and up to the turn of the century. Millions of francs passed through their hands every year. Like Zola's Nana, they drove to the races in a coach and four, and their jewels outshone those of both the guardian angel and the housewife. Gaby Deslys, he said, had been the last of the real cocottes. When I asked him the reason for their almost complete disappearance, he answered, after having thought it over, "There are too many amateurs these days."

Even though many women seem on the surface to have grown more liberated—or more amateurish—and have begun to display themselves in a manner that would make a person think for all the world that they were free, nevertheless it seems to me that the tendency on the female market—a tendency set by the *avant-garde*—is in the direction of *higher* prices. And there is talk of prices that very few men can or will pay. I don't think women have ever been as expensive as they are right now; no women have ever cost those around them as much as the ones now trying to liberate themselves from the roles and patterns they were born into by virtue of anatomy and mythology. I myself am not especially inclined to accept that inheritance with all of its assets and liabilities, but I definitely think it is a mistake to raise the price, for that will serve only to perpetuate the market economy and the dehumanization that must be eliminated before there is liberation of any kind. I don't think there is any alternative but to be completely free of charge, for if we're to believe Karen Blixen, the old witch, why, woman's price is so bound up with world order—or the status quo, if you prefer—that the woman who simply waives her price will lead the world straight into misery. Of course that doesn't sound very pleasant, but why should the world be pleasant? Unfortunately, I don't think there is any way around the misery that the women with no price are going to inflict upon us. But I do have the feeling that there is comfort to be found among the witches, for they have always been gratis and have managed anyway—independently of men and the market. The witch has always lived with her center of gravity within herself, and in purely strategic terms there is much to be said for the suggestion that our present-day sisters, with all their solidarity, should be meeting on heaths and commons under the waning moon instead of sitting on subcommittees and writing articles.

The witch has played a greater or lesser role in every age, but she has never disappeared completely. Presumably, most men take the view that a woman who can do without men can obviously also do without God, that a woman who does not want to be possessed by men must necessarily be possessed by the devil. The witch has no scruples about showing her legs, she brazenly straddles her broomstick and flies away into the air. . . .

I once had a conversation on this subject—also in Africa—with an old Frenchwoman who was a friend of mine. She expressed her firm conviction that all men without exception believed in witches. There was merely a certain difference in the degree to which they feared them. "The more of a man a man is, my dear," she said, "the more freely he will admit that he believes in witches, but the less he will actually hate or fear them. Seamen will admit to having known more than one witch in their lives, but they will take a fairly kindly attitude toward them, and now and then they will even confess to being in their debt. Bookish men are not eager to admit the existence of witches, but the fear of witches is deep in their blood. And those men who wear long clothing themselves—the priests—they hate and fear the witch more than they hate and fear her Lord and Master."

And if learned gentlemen feel their masculine dignity offended at the thought that she prefers the devil to a man, why the layman and the outdoorsman will find some redress in another consideration: the basis, yes, the condition for the entire practice of witchcraft lies in the fact that the devil is masculine.

In "A Fire Speech" Karen Blixen takes up feminism from the point of view of a newcomer and in her wonderfully systematic way begins to speculate as to why we have two sexes in the first place. . . . Those who think about nothing else will already have guessed the reason, of course. And what a boon it is that we have advanced so far beyond the animals that our mating season lasts all year. A society where the attractive power of the two sexes was limited to a definite brief period would become curiously meager, according to Mrs. Blixen. She finds that what is most advantageous about the division into two sexes is the mutual inspiration—in the sense of an interaction—that we today call the sexual dialectic. How *great* a division and what *kind* of a division is required for this mutual inspiration to take place, however, is difficult to judge. In any event, this wonderful interaction must originally have depended on some notion of a division of labor, where the female sex saw to the propagation and sustenance of the race and the male sex to its development and progress. And I believe that this notion was a very good one, that is, until the development and progress of the male sex had brought us to the point where we are today, when there is no longer any justification for the female sex to propagate or carry on the race. The former conditions for life no longer exist, which people can figure out for themselves with about ten minutes thought. And so so much for the division of labor, even though it was a good idea.

Another idea that Blixen advances is Kaiser Wilhelm's three Ks—Kinder, Kirche, Küche—and that too was a good idea, if only it had been taken seriously. But it WASN'T. For the Church was given no female priests, and the Kinder program was limited to nipples and diapers, while the schools and the whole educational sector stayed under the supervision of men (which is why the world has come to look the way it does). And as for the Kitchen, there too it was male taste that came to dominate (what with all the heavy food), and the most famous cooks were men. So there have been a lot of good ideas. But as I understand Karen Blixen, it would seem that even if we have stripped the sexes of their cultural functions, we are still left with one crucial sexual difference that does not depend on anatomy alone. For, she says, "Man's center of gravity, the substance of his being, lies in what he accomplishes and performs in his life, while woman's lies in what she IS." Therefore competition must be a waste of time, since each sex has its own path to follow—as a bishop and a knight in chess, which as everyone knows are of equal value in their separate ways. Woman's real work should be to expand her being.

> And if we go still higher, to the woman who all through history has meant more than anyone else, who has inspired the most great works of art, who has most deeply gripped and moved our souls and most powerfully altered our minds and manners, if we go to the Virgin Mary—whether we believe that she really existed or not—then the same truth applies. She has her power by virtue of what she IS. God created the heaven and the earth. Christ redeemed mankind. But the Virgin Mary performed no great work beyond this—to give birth quite passively to Jesus, to surrender her whole being to God's incarnation as man. Nor do people expect or desire anything more of her. I have the impression from my travels in more southerly countries that the Virgin Mary is the only heavenly being in our time who is really loved by millions. But I believe that these same millions would react with incomprehension, perhaps even with indignation, if I tried to tell them that the Virgin Mary had produced an important invention, solved difficult mathematical problems, or brilliantly organized and administered a housewives' union in Nazareth. No, she is quite simply supposed to BE there. The queen of heaven expands her being to reach all

mankind and all the earth. She undertakes no flights to the moon but stands quite still upon it.

Over the course of the last five hundred years, woman has been assigned all sorts of innate qualities—partly as compensation for her lack of knowledge, and partly to make the whole thing add up or to compensate for the fact that our addition has been wrong—for mankind has always been the advocate of harmony.

But if a woman KNOWS nothing, and if she doesn't just happen to BE the Virgin Mary or someone similar, it can be painful and feeble amusement to *expand* her being, unless against her own good judgment she subscribes to the view that a naught is worth more when it is written large.

No, I don't believe in this difference between men and women, and I was pretty close to losing my belief in Karen Blixen. But when dealing with the late lamented baroness, in the end you always yield. For although she does talk about masculine and feminine qualities, or powers—the masculine "to know" and the feminine "to be"—she says nothing, nor is there any indication, that these masculine and feminine attributes must be distributed rigidly between men and women respectively. Her writing suggests instead that there are many more than two sexes—a whole confusion of them. Karen Blixen is herself a sexual mixture. In an essay called "On Mottoes" she writes, "I have been very strong, unusually strong for a woman, capable of walking or riding farther than most men. I have drawn a Masai bow, and in the ecstasy of the moment have felt I was related to Odysseus." She acknowledges her debt to the old champions of women's rights who now lie in their graves, but she feels that women today—having made their way inside the walls of masculine institutions in disguise, in mental and physical male dress—can now raise the visors on their knightly armor and reveal that they are women.

The masculine "to know" can perfectly well be a female quality just as the feminine "to be" is not the sole property of women and artists. The feminine "to be" is latent within masculine society's male functions:

> For those who have held that femininity would be out of place in the pulpit and on the bench, it is worth pointing out that the male experts who so matter-of-factly occupy these positions do willingly—as if driven by some special instinct—alter their appearance toward the feminine. The priestly gown with its white collar is an attractive and a dignified woman's dress. The smocks of doctors and housewives have much in common, and when exercising their office, high court judges wear flowing robes, and in some countries augment their dignity with long, curly wigs.
>
> Maybe the really orthodox feminists will still insist that I express disdain for woman by assuming, or agreeing, that she cannot accomplish as much here in life as man, that she cannot perform feats that are as great nor exhibit results that are as concrete as his.
>
> And so to conclude I will quote a wiser person than myself and submit the following reflection by Meir Goldschmidt. "Scholars assume that what for man is ideal is for woman nature. Woman is in many ways more perfect than man. On seeing her, one does not ask her name or status or accomplishment, for she is herself, a woman, and contains within herself everything essential. But let a man appear, even the most distinguished—indeed the more distinguished he is, the more we will ask: In what way?"
>
> And from deep personal conviction I would add that

our particular society—in which mankind has come so far in what it can accomplish and in the concrete results it can show—has need of people who ARE. Yes, our very age might be said to need to shift its ambition from accomplishment to BEING.

Of course Blixen's "A Fire Speech" has been considered reactionary within the inner circles of orthodox feminism. But in an age when decadence and darkness characterize both sexes and when neither men nor women can be said to have much being or much substance left, it is interesting to note that it is women who are most persistent about finding an identity—which may be said to support Blixen's theory. Women have not yet lost heart quite as much as men have, and their search has to be regarded as an expression of the fact that in spite of everything they still retain a little of their memory and some sense of their being.

The lack of being is the ultimate but logical consequence of patriarchal culture. Humanity has become wholly and completely a means of knowing. Therefore we expect a great deal of the feminine—not in the form of a guardian angel, and certainly not in the form of an absolute sex, but as a sense of being in whatever sexes may exist. And this is what "A Fire Speech" is all about, at least the way I read it. Perhaps it deals with the matriarchy of the future:

> A person who has no independent substance—or who lacks allegiance to such a substance—cannot create. I have not meant to say that the women are the trees and the men the motors, for I would lay this to the heart of today's women as well as its men—Not merely to think about what they will accomplish, but deep down to know what they are.

For we have need, I think, of craftsmen who not only amaze the world with what they can produce, but who are craftsmen. . . .

We have need of people who not only can achieve record crop yields with their tractors and harvesting machines, but who ARE farmers. Who can not only sail to America in record time, but who ARE sailors. Who have not only passed major examinations and have all sorts of knowledge at their fingertips, but who ARE teachers. Who can not only write a piece of literature, but who ARE poets.

7 Rape

I was sitting at a restaurant with some friends. In fact we were ready to go home, but hadn't quite pulled ourselves together to get up and leave. The chair beside me was empty, and a dark-haired man came over and asked me if he could sit down. Yes, of course he could. We got to talking a little, he and I, and after about ten minutes I stood up and said, "Well, we have to be going. . . ." It was only then he discovered that I was not alone, and when he saw me going out with my friends, he kicked the leg of the table and snarled, "Why the hell didn't you say so!"

His anger was so spontaneous and his kick at the table so staggering that I couldn't help speculating on what it was I should have said when he came over and asked if the chair beside me was taken. He obviously felt that he'd been cheated and deceived and made a fool of, because it had looked as if I were by myself. But what was it I should have said to protect the poor man from such a setback? Should I have said, "No, the chair is not taken, but I have no intention of going to bed with you"? He would have thought I had lost my mind. "Crazy bitches. You ask if you can sit down in a chair, and all of a sudden they get ideas. . . ."

And it's true enough—women are gradually beginning to get ideas. They are beginning to talk to each other, to analyze their relations to men, and to compare experiences. They are beginning to realize that their disappointments and defeats are not necessarily the result of their inadequacy or their anatomy. Women are beginning to see that some of the most fundamental, if intangible, patterns of sexual behavior are based on myths. And that those myths must be demystified, no matter how hard that may be to accomplish.

We need the answers to some simple questions, one of which has been asked by Germaine Greer. Suppose, she says, that a man at a party complains of having nowhere to sleep, and that some woman at the party offers him a bed in an extra room and supplies him with towels and pajamas and then goes to bed herself, whereupon he steals into her room in the middle of the night and penetrates her against her will. Why is it that, in popular parlance, she is said to have "asked for it"?

Men's incontestable right to deprive women of their freedom of choice is bound up, of course, with the fact that for centuries women have shrunk from formulating their own desires, so that men have not been able to figure out what women were actually thinking or dreaming. "What do women want?" Freud never found an answer to his famous question, because in fact it only serves to make woman's "nature" even more obscure.

For me, the question is fairly simple, because all I want is to decide for myself how I will live as well as with whom I will copulate.

In an article in *Playboy* called "Seduction Is a Four-Letter Word," Germaine Greer struck at "the art of seduction" as being a legitimate form of rape in disguise. False promises, false tenderness, everything goes when it's a question of getting it up. The premise is that even if the woman isn't in the mood, why, by God, she will be. He's man enough to see to that.

The essence of rape, as I see it, lies not in the degree of psychological and physical force associated with the involuntary act (whatever it may be), but in the very *attitude* toward women that makes disguised and undisguised rape possible. The same attitude that requires a woman to be dead, or at least a bloody mess, before she has earned the right to be considered a victim at all.

In America, a woman who has been raped will be advised against pressing charges, even if the case is good, if she wants to live the rest of her life without psychological scars. And why? Well, because it is assumed that she was asking for it, and if she is unfortunate enough to have the reputation of being "erotically inclined," the situation is hopeless, because then "she probably liked it." If a woman lives alone without a man, she has to "watch her step." If she is molested or raped anyway, why then by the very nature of things she must have done something foolish. She shouldn't have walked down a dark street by herself. She should have had an extra lock on the door. She shouldn't have such large, provocative breasts or go around without a bra. She shouldn't talk openly and freely about sex. She shouldn't go out with a man and let him buy her an expensive meal. She shouldn't have bedroom eyes. In short, she shouldn't be a woman, for women get raped if they're not careful. And unless they're killed in the process, they must have been asking for it.

It's a strange anxiety to live with. Strange because it's intangible, and because our culture concentrates so hard on genitalia that all the disguised rape offenses are simply never counted. It is only the genital aspect that stirs people up, for most people are so alienated, their egos so ravaged, that they are not disturbed by the contempt for humanity, the hatred for women, and the scorn for personal freedom that a rape victim (always female) is exposed to—exclusively because of her sex. It is not especially sensational to be raped, it is merely embarrassing.

It is a rainy night in Amsterdam and I have lost my way and don't dare stop to look at my map for fear some man will come slinking up to help me, and if I tell him where I'm going then I'll just be asking for it. . . . Asking for him to come with me and asking for whatever comes next. So I just walk along in any old direction, I don't know where. I have to keep my eyes on the ground or up in the air, because if I look straight ahead and watch where I'm going, and if a man should suddenly appear in my field of vision, then I'm asking for it. "Hi, there, sweetie . . ." Well, I guess that can't kill me. And yet the tone is humiliating and contemptuous and actually means, "How about some pussy, you little piece of ass." Because when I don't respond, he goes on in the same breath, ". . . you tight-assed bitch." I am really not provocatively dressed. A long dress like a tent, and a scarf covering my head. But I'm out alone at night, so I'm asking for aggressive treatment. It is the aggressiveness that is "natural." What is "unnatural" is to be walking in the rain alone at night. If the lady doesn't want anyone to speak to her, she can always stay at home.

Of course I'm paranoid, but if I relax and say the hell with it and glance at the people I pass as usual, then the obscenities will start. And I'll have them coming to me. My shoes splash in the puddles, because the straps have slipped off. But I don't dare stop and bend down to put them on again, for that would be taken as an invitation. I step right in the path of a car as I cross a street down by the canal—I didn't dare look around, because I heard footsteps and I was afraid my eyes might meet those of the man behind me, and then of course . . .

It is simply not in my nature to feel hunted. But then I don't feel I represent my true nature out on the street at night. I'm walking like a sex, not like a person—a sex that shouldn't be here if it wants to stay out of trouble. My sex is a lower caste, I can see that very clearly. It used to be the case in India that if the shadow of a person of lower caste fell on a person of higher caste, the latter had the right to execute the former. And the person of lower caste had it coming to him, just as I have it coming to me if my eyes should meet those of some strange man.

I am beginning to whimper from exhaustion and frustration. I don't dare stop to figure out which way I should go, and therefore I'm getting lost. And I'm whimpering from anger at having to follow the rules of this sexual game in order to avoid unpleasantness. This much can be said in favor of masculine civilization, that if a woman follows the rules set down by the male society, she will be rewarded by not being raped or molested. But conversely, if she *is* molested, that is her punishment for not having behaved properly.

If a strange man says, "Evening, sweetie, rotten weather," it is in my nature to answer, "Good evening, yes it is." But of course I wouldn't dream of being true to my nature on the streets of Amsterdam at night. I stare obediently at the pavement, as I must if I'm not to be spoken to.

"Come on, little lady, let's come down to earth. What's so bad about being spoken to? Are you made of glass?"

What's "bad" is that it doesn't feel natural not to answer, but if I do answer, I'm helping to start a "dialogue" that will develop entirely on his conditions, which means that I will either have to accept them (go with him) or become openly hostile in order to neutralize his camouflaged aggression. "Well, so you're out cruising, you little whorecock!" I might say. "And you do it free! So you can't be very fucking good!" And so forth. But that macho line doesn't appeal to me, and anyway, I'm a friendly soul, and I'd like to continue to be. But if I answer, "Yes, the weather is unpleasant," why that means (in the classic situation) that *I* am going to have to give *him* an explanation for why I won't *copulate* with him. He has created the situation and indirectly set forth his terms, which dictate my subsequent behavior and reactions. All I can do is *react*. I have to come up with an explanation that *he* will accept. An explanation of why I don't want to fuck, once I've said good evening or told him that a chair was not taken.

It's like someone stealing your watch and then forcing you to tell him precisely what time it is.

It makes no sense in my opinion. But our behavior is dictated much more by public opinion and by generally acknowledged but unwritten laws than it is by the ones on the books.

One of the written laws says, "Thou shalt not covet thy neighbor's wife." But its unwritten counterpart speaks to the woman and is far more effective: "It's up to *you* not to be coveted by your neighbor's husband" (or there'll be hell to pay).

But if you try to decipher the code: "Evening, sweetie, rotten weather," and reply—not to the code but to the real content of the speech—"Yes, it is unpleasant weather, but I don't want to go to bed with you," it sounds so crazy that it might *make* you crazy. But if a woman can't say good evening without risking her freedom, then that woman isn't free. For that matter, neither is the man who can't say good evening without thinking of his genitalia.

As I walked along in the rain, raging at these unwritten

laws, a car came driving up beside me, from behind. A man stuck his head out the window and announced that it was raining (and offered me a lift), to which I now responded, bravely, "Yes, you're absolutely right, it is raining," and, nose in the air, I sloshed furiously on through the puddles. The man persisted, driving along behind me and calling out, "It's raining." This weather report hardly came as a surprise, since I was soaking wet. I was angry at having to accept the social convention that says you can't get into a strange man's car at night unless you're prepared either to accept his conditions or else to kick and scream and spit in his face. Neither alternative was terribly appealing. I was haunted by Emmanuelle's story—the one she published in *Partisans* magazine.

One evening in Paris, about eight o'clock, Emmanuelle was walking along the Rue du Four toward the Metro, on her way home. As she crossed the street she caught sight of a man on the other side—respectably dressed, law-student type, glasses with gold-filled rims. He stood there and studied her, waited for her and approached her. "Excuse me, miss, it's a lovely evening. How about a cup of coffee? Careful, miss, if you walk too fast you'll just trip and fall," and so forth. He followed her down the street. . . .

Being spoken to on the street would not be a problem if the relations between the sexes were different. But at the moment, street contact is not "as good a way as any other" to make someone's acquaintance, because it is a way that necessarily makes the woman an object. In most cases, a man who accosts a woman is utterly indifferent to whether she shows any sign of wanting to talk to him—or even if she sees him. A man will often start talking to a woman before he has even seen her face, hail her from *behind* and strike up a conversation with her ass.

The man (whose name was Marc, so be warned) kept

on and on about the coffee, and his persuasiveness, combined with her loneliness, finally led her to accept. She realized that she really would like to talk to someone, almost anyone at all. But now there is no one to help her, and the ball is rolling, for he knows a café "in the neighborhood," and pretty soon they're standing by his car. He holds the door for her "politely," but without asking if she wants to get in. And, theoretically, she CAN refuse, but women are so used to this kind of small-scale coercion that they simply don't think about it. But when he opens the door to his car and expects her to get in without having asked her first, he is infringing her freedom of choice. His gesture does not differ in *kind* from rape, but only in degree. She can't really be said to have any freedom in this situation, for if she doesn't get in, it's because she is not free to do so without risk. And if her only choice is between cutting herself off from companionship or accepting it along with the risk that her freedom will not be respected, then she is not free.

At first she protests. "No, let's find someplace nearby, it's easier," and so forth. She pretends that in the present situation the car is simply impractical. But by not giving her real reasons, she is spontaneously accepting a set of social rules. When she says that the car is "impractical," she is in fact making use of a *code,* which the man understands very well, for he answers, "You don't mean to say you're afraid? Do you think maybe I'm going to eat you up?"

On reconstructing the course of the rape, it is perfectly evident that "eating her up" was precisely what he had in mind from the moment he spoke to her. But he too uses the code, which explicitly excludes any infringement of her freedom but implicitly guarantees that she will be raped. What Emmanuelle is afraid of—with good reason—is that getting into the car will be interpreted as a sexual invitation, or, to be exact, that he will *pretend* to interpret it that way in order to make it easier to justify or deny any subsequent sexual aggression. Her fear is governed by a social convention according to which women are never viewed as victims but as accessories. A convention that tries to deny that women are, by definition, sexual objects. Conversely, men often use the illusion of a woman's freedom to extort additional concessions that will confine her even further. In Emmanuelle's case, the lawyer's extortion consists of ridiculing her fear of being regarded as a sexual object. "I'm not going to eat you up," that is, "It's only little girls who are afraid; you're too grown up to believe in child molesters; you're a free, mature woman, and if you don't get into the car, you'll be doing violence to your own freedom by letting yourself be affected by stupid, old-fashioned taboos," and so on.

Like all women in this predicament, it is Emmanuelle who is the "guilty" party. If she resists a temporary liaison, she is being "middle class and prudish"; and if she becomes the victim of a temporary liaison, she is equally at fault, because she should have been more careful. In this way, the lawyer makes two attacks on Emmanuelle's naïveté. Before the rape, because she hesitates to get into the car with him. After the rape, because she shouldn't have.

There is really no worse racism than sexism, because it includes half of the world's population, which is humiliated, terrorized, subjected to constant pressure, and denied its elementary right to self-determination on account of its "color." And sexism is especially outrageous because it is expressed in codes, tacitly accepted rules of conduct between the sexes which are only revealed on being overstepped.

Emmanuelle got into the car—partially because she was lonely, but mostly because she *wanted* to be free, or to act as if she were. At that moment she chose to ignore the social convention that says you cannot climb into a strange man's car and mean to have nothing but a cup of coffee.

Suddenly he enters an expressway.

"What in the world . . . ?"

He knows "a café in the neighborhood."

He asks her various questions of a sexual nature. She is not embarrassed to begin with, but then he switches to direct obscenity—another form of sexual aggression that is no different in kind from rape. It puts Emmanuelle in the position of having to come up with an explanation (that he can accept) of why she won't answer his questions.

She asks to be let out of the car. But it's too late, he says. "We'll be there in a minute."

It is now clear to Emmanuelle that he doesn't intend to leave her in peace, but it still hasn't occurred to her that she is actually going to be raped.

He finally pulls up in front of an isolated house. She goes in with him and begs him to drive her back. (Oh, how naïve, little Emmanuelle! You deserve what you're going to get . . .) And he puts on a record and pours a whiskey and places his hand classically on her knee.

She removes his hand, classically.

"Why not?" asks the specimen. "Don't you want to have some fun?"

"Well, no, that wasn't what I had in mind," she answers "stupidly," for he immediately delivers another classic line: "But then why in the world did you come?"

Emmanuelle bursts into a fit of rage and for a moment the lawyer removes his paws and tries to calm her down. "All right, all right, now let's not get excited. Come sit over here on the bed by me."

Emmanuelle sits down defiantly on the bed. She knows it's a stupid thing to do, but I understand her perfectly. She does it as a kind of magic gesture meant to defy fate.

Then too she may be hoping to cool his sense of power by disguising her anxiety.

But he worked out this whole project long ago, so that whatever she thinks and feels and does from now on really makes no difference whatsoever.

The instant she sits on the bed he falls upon her and forces his mouth into contact with hers. That is, he tries to kiss her. It is an insanely grotesque gesture, of course, but the man himself is probably unaware of how much he loathes women. Emmanuelle tries to break free, but he holds her down forcibly, still trying to kiss her, and so she bites his thumb. Wronged and furious, he leaps up from the bed and stares at his bleeding hand.

"You little shit! What's wrong with you?"

She explains (!) that she was only trying to defend herself—once again, the code that gives the aggressor the right to demand an explanation of why his aggression is unacceptable.

"You don't have any right!" he says. "I haven't done anything to you. I haven't done you any harm. . . ."

He grumbles over his thumb and sits and sucks it for a while. With his free hand he starts battering her head. "Well, honey, if you put up a fight you're going to have to pay the price, 'cause it's Daddy who makes the decisions around here."

He affirms his power with a blow to the jaw. "You just do what I tell you. Don't forget I could burn a hole in your cheek with my cigarette here, or I could give you sleeping pills. I'm in command around here."

Emmanuelle starts crying.

The law student tells her it isn't going to do her any good.

Emmanuelle gets a grip on herself. In her desperation she tries to talk morality to him, to get him to see that it just isn't nice to make "love" to a woman this way. (Observe the interesting phenomenon of a woman taking the trouble to view the rape from the *man's* point of view and consider *his* interests in order to get him to leave her alone.)

But it doesn't help. Our young law student decided to have her the moment he saw her. And since Emmanuelle has no desire to go home with bruises or some other memento of a fight, and since she doesn't dare provoke him for fear of his running amok, why, she submits (the little slut).

His labors take him thirty seconds.

Emmanuelle has told the story and written it, and a lot of men have asked her, in all seriousness, if she had an orgasm, which can only mean that most men do not distinguish between rape and love. This is true of any man who can get an erection with a woman who has no desire, and of any man who complains about a frigid wife but at the same time forces her to perform her "marital duty." All the women who copulate to keep peace in the house are the victims of rape. All our grandmothers who just "let it happen" were essentially force-fucked all their lives.

The truth of all this is confirmed by the fact that we now have two generations of men who are conscious of this violence syndrome, and who compensate for it by constantly *asking* what the woman wants. This is a very odd form of consideration, but it couldn't be otherwise. The explanation is that most men are so alienated from women and from their own femininity, that is, from themselves and their own sexual drives, that they must constantly ask (with the best of intentions) what they ought to do next, as if they were solving some kind of Chinese puzzle. They must constantly be assured that their performance is satisfactory. They must be allowed to believe in their ability. However, sex is not a matter of believing, but of knowing. Not of being able, but of being. The sexual significance of our patriarchal culture is that both sexes have become such strangers to each other and to their own sexual drives (that is, to themselves) that they spend their whole lives asking each other for advice. Is it better like this, or like that? To which the only logical answer is, "You know that as well as I." Nonalienated eroticism is to exist someplace beyond "positions" where there is only free and weightless movement in space and a complete and inescapable insight into one another. That is what's so wonderful about it. And you don't have to have known each other for five years. Five minutes can be sufficient, and miraculous. That's why eroticism was invented. Everything else, from rape to sex education, is alienated eroticism. The motives of the sexologists—to make the best of the worst possible culture—inspire more confidence than the miserable theory that we must slaughter one another in a bloody revolution before we can find love. Nevertheless, it is obvious that all the sex books in the world can't teach us how to achieve the reunification of our selves and our sexual drives, which, we hope, lie vibrating someplace out in the erossphere, waiting for us to come to our senses.

But back to our epic. After the climax of the rape, our law student hero is distressed and disappointed, for, after several inquiries, he discovers that he is not the best fuck his victim has ever had. "You mean you really didn't think it was great?" asks Marc in amazement. And then, when she has cautiously inquired if she might go, he has the infuriating gall to ask if she wouldn't like to SLEEP with him all night. Once again, a code designed to deny the fact that there has been a *rape*.

What Emmanuelle really wants, of course, is to lash out and spit in his face, but she is in no position to give way to such an impulse.

On their way into town, the law student praises himself for being man enough to drive her home. No one can say he isn't a gentleman. He politely regrets the fact that she was not completely satisfied. All of his previous experiences with women he met this same way were entirely satisfactory. Most women accept his "manner," he tells her. In fact, "they like it."

When Emmanuelle gets out of the car, she is too paralyzed even to slam the door.

In Uzbekistan I met a lovely young man who looked like a cross between a boxer and a Persian prince. He helped me set up various interviews. One day in the middle of Karl Marx Prospekt he presented me with an orange and I sat right down on a bench with him and ate it. He had blue, blue eyes that a person could simply float away in, which I immediately did—only to find myself up the creek.

I don't know if it is God's intention that those who are humiliated also shall be raped, or that social losers shall lose more with every step they take, or that those with the dullest work shall have the lowest pay while money shall come to those who have it already. But if God is going to laugh at us, then we had better laugh back, just to rectify a bit of the injustice.

My own rape story, which deserves a title such as "The Prickly Path to Humiliation" is in the nature of a morality play in ten acts.

The moral to the first act is easy enough. It reads: do not travel alone in Soviet Asia nor eat a strange man's orange unless you want to be raped.

Act II

The young man with the blue eyes, my prince, invites me to dinner at a cafeteria and says he would like to kiss me good night. That makes me happy. But he doesn't want to come up to my hotel room with me, for there is a babushka on every floor keeping track of the people and he is nervous (about his career). He's afraid we'll be "discovered." Well, all right. It occurs to me that as the foreigner in this situation, I ought to show some consideration for his career. He suggests that we go for a walk, and he buys me a rose down at the corner. In front of Tashkent Party Headquarters—a concrete building full of brown oil portraits of the national notables—there is a park full of statues of Lenin, Lenin petting a cat, Lenin giving an apple to a boy (the apples are much larger since the Revolution), and so forth. It is dark by now, and I notice a rustling and a rummaging behind the bushes. There are people crawling in and out, brushing leaves from their clothes. Well, I think to myself, so this is where they do it in Tashkent. When in Rome . . . Their apartments are too small and crowded, so they build a lot of parks. The Tashkent brochures boast of the greatest number of People's Parks of any city in the world, and presumably they were designed to compensate for the crowded living conditions. People go to the parks to be alone. And so I do the same. (You silly little tramp.)

Moral: Do not go into a park with a man unless you want to be raped.

Act III

Under a bush in the dark I put my head down on the stomach of my blue-eyed prince and slip his manhood into my mouth. Every now and then I whisper "moy golubchik," for those are the only loving words I can think of. But it suits him, being called "my little dove," for pretty soon the two of us are fairly floating in the air.

Moral: Do not float in the air unless you want to be raped.

Act IV

For suddenly we are surrounded by boots with men in them, and the men are shouting and blowing little boy scout whistles so that more men arrive with more boots and more whistles. Of course they want to know what we're doing, but I refuse to answer silly questions. I just lie there with my eyes closed, hiding like an ostrich in his stomach. I still have his sex in my mouth, of course, because I think it would be unbecoming to reveal his shame to the view of strangers, or, to be exact, because I don't know what to do and so I just lie there and do nothing.

The policemen kick us to our feet.

I throw my panty hose up in a tree, because I'm too shy to put them on in front of ten policemen.

There follows an extended parley between the ten to twelve policemen and my blue-eyed hero. It is conducted in Uzbek, a Turkish dialect that I do not understand. I'm dying for a cigarette, but I remember all the times I've been told in this country that "nice" girls don't smoke, and right at the moment I had better try to be nice. . . . A disgusting little policeman in plain clothes, a creepy little cop, circles me with a sly grin and pinches my nipples, but what can I do? I can't call the police. I just stand there and note the fact that he is pinching me. I'm upset, I'm boiling, but I'm incapable of reacting, for he acts as if he is perfectly within his rights.

Moral: If someone pinches your nipples, you must have been asking for it.

Act V

The man with the blue eyes pulls me aside and whispers that we're going to jail, and that when they start to question me, whatever I do I mustn't tell them who I am.

"Who am I then?" I'm eager to know.

"Tell them you're from Riga."

I can tell from his urgency how important it is that I not give myself away, but in the confusion I don't understand why.

And now I am really in a panic. For who am I, if I am not myself? It's not enough just to be from Riga. What is the girl from Riga like? I am also worried about my accent.

But in the course of the interrogation it gradually dawns on me that the girl from Riga is a whore (I am greatly relieved), for decent Soviet working girls don't lie around in parks sucking cocks. And what's more, an upstanding Soviet citizen always carries her identity papers on her. I do not. All I have are some dollars and a press card, which the object of my passion takes care to remove from my handbag so the police won't suspect anything. They ask me a lot of silly questions, but even though I am relieved to have a role to play, I am so dumbstruck that my Russian fails—the man with the blue eyes has to keep heaving me aside to tell me what to say. It is a great mistake to give up my original identity so easily, but holding on to it doesn't cross my mind, since I assume instinctively that the man with the blue eyes knows the local circumstances and customs better than I.

But it is naïve of me to put my faith in him.

Moral: If you're naïve, you're simply asking to be raped.

Act VI

The police declare us under arrest.

I dread the proceedings to come. Partly because I know what to expect from any bureaucracy—that is, waiting—but also because I'm afraid they will punish me more severely when they find out I've lied and am not a whore from Riga. I ask the man with the eyes (in a capitalist whisper) if we couldn't give them my dollars. But he's already tried that, he confides. For a moment I'm staggered to realize he's tried to buy them off with my money, without asking me, but what the hell?

"You don't really mean we're going to jail?"

"Yes," he says. "There's nothing we can do." His blue eyes have turned black.

"Yes, but, my God . . ."

"There's nothing we can do," he repeats. "But if you'll give that fellow over there a kiss, they'll let us go. . . ." He points to the little toad who's been pinching my breasts.

"You're kidding!"

Naturally I would prefer to go to the police station and get the whole thing out in the open, but they stand there yapping away in Uzbek, and I can't assess the situation because I don't know what being arrested might involve. Siberia is what's at the back of my mind. At the same time, I'm both overwhelmed and outraged by this exotic offer. Imagine getting free with a kiss, like in some fairy tale. But it would be better than Siberia, even if it is too nasty to be true. For how can any man who's shown such enormous contempt for my person want a kiss? But of course that too is naïve, for you have to realize that contempt and sexuality go together. If you are ignorant of something as fundamental as the nature of the male animal, then rape is all you deserve. They said a "kiss," and to me a kiss was a kiss. But:

Moral: It won't do you any good to play innocent, my fine friend.

Act VII

As the minutes go by I grow more and more disposed to seize this fairy tale expedient so as to get out of the hands of the law as quickly as I can. I pull the fellow to a bench a few steps off and sit down and prepare my lips for a kiss. Come ahead, Comrade! But the boy sneers at me, jerks me up from the bench, shoves me into some bushes and down a steep clay slope, down to some wet, marshy ground that lies at the bottom in pitch-darkness. Presumably one of the police department's private places.

The boy opens his pants.

"Do the same thing to me you did to him!"

I am speechless. So speechless that I might almost start laughing, if I weren't simultaneously furious. And scared. There's absolutely no question of a choice, for I can't get away, and it doesn't even occur to me to start a fight with a man in this dark swamp (or whatever this moisture may be). I ask him if I can definitely go afterward.

The boy nods impatiently.

I ask for his WORD OF HONOR. Yes, I do (how naïve can a woman be?), and he gives it to me eagerly. I am about to bind him further with a few phrases from Pravda about his representing Communism and the Friendly Russian People, but it occurs to me that a whore from Riga would hardly come up with anything like that.

To tell the truth, the erection in my throat is the least of it. In fact I find him pathetic and ridiculous. The manipulation of his genitals is at least something I'm familiar with, and therefore sort of a "relief" in comparison with the basic situation, where I'm being deprived of my identity and my freedom of choice and made the object of transactions in a language I do not understand. But on the other hand it makes me mad. It fills me with such loathing that my whole body trembles, which makes it hard for me to accomplish my task.

I feel as if I were being forced to scratch Hitler's back—for ten minutes—for a nickel. It's not the back I can't stand, and it's not that the price is too low, it's the WHOLE

THING PUT TOGETHER. And the kid won't come. It's as if he's determined to make it last forever. I also have the feeling it's an unspoken accusation—I'm not letting myself be raped good enough. My mouth is completely numb, as if it weren't my own anymore. I try using my hand instead, but he pulls my hair. I'm forced to go to the trouble of putting "feeling" into it, in order to make him come. That is the worst part of all, for it is a tacit acceptance of the situation. And when I pretend to like it, then he comes. I spit his semen out into the swamp—there has to be some limit. To my amazement—maybe because I've been so rude—he throws himself on top of me and tries to force his way in. But he is attempting the maneuver on a steep, slippery bank, and I manage to shove him down toward the mud.

Then comes the sound of a whistle from the park above and another policeman comes sliding down the slope with his prick out of his pants and a boy scout whistle in his mouth. "Do the same thing to me you did to him!"

Moral: Once you've let yourself be raped by number 1, why surely you won't mind being raped by number 2 as well.

Act VIII

It was my own fault that I'd done it to the first one. And so it was my own fault that I did it to the second. And now to the third. There were ten or twelve policemen altogether. I started to cry. But my crying didn't seem to interfere with his lechery. He sat on the bank with his legs spread apart and masturbated to my sobs.

"Come on now, let's get started. . . ." He wasn't unfriendly in the least. He seemed to be in a rather pleasant mood.

"But I CAN'T. I DID. And he said I could go." I wanted

to say something about how it was a gentleman's agreement, but I couldn't think of the words.

"That kid, he's only eighteen, he's not a policeman. But I am. I'm a sergeant. . . ." He smiled at me sweetly with his glistening Mongol face. (Of course it had been naïve of me not to realize that the police force in Uzbekistan didn't recruit eighteen-year-olds.)

"I don't WANT to."

"But why not?" he asked in bewilderment. "You did it to the others!"

I couldn't explain why I didn't want to. I couldn't think of a valid argument. He grabbed me by the scruff of the neck and pushed me down toward his groin—like a cat toward a hunk of meat. He stank of some greasy rice dish. Naturally I've wondered why I didn't bite it off, or tear his balls with my teeth. But it simply didn't occur to me. I am utterly incapable of physical aggression, and when I was little I was always scared that the boys would hit me or wash my face in snow. I used to take long detours to avoid running into the mean ones. And I have always been afraid of gymnastics and ball games and used to hide in the changing room and howl with rage when I was discovered and dragged in to an exercise horse.

Moral: If you don't even resist, you can hardly expect them not to rape you.

Act IX

When the policeman's insanity was spent—and I had dried him off with my hand-embroidered handkerchief (in a moment of demented delicacy)—he vanished into the darkness.

I had no idea how I was going to get away, since as I said I have no athletic talents. But in the end I stuck my shoes in my shoulder bag (which I still had) and dug into the mud with my toes and fingers. Crawled up, slid down, crawled up again. At the top, a couple of policemen appeared and grabbed me by the arms. I was under arrest, they announced—and you can hardly blame them, considering my lascivious behavior. They dragged me away by the arms, while one of them held my mouth, because I had begun to scream. I wanted to scream out who I was, but they hit me in the face. Then we came to a path, with lights, and there was the man with the eyes. The two policemen took off.

Moral: Don't breathe more easily just because the rapists have run away.

Act X

He came trotting toward me, and when he saw I was covered with mud, he asked what in the world I'd been up to all that time.

I gave him an account of my activities.

He stared at me in amazement and contempt.

"How could you make yourself do anything so filthy?"

He began sniveling, as if my behavior was an insult to his pride. To think that "his" girl could have done such a thing . . . the girl he had wasted a dinner on. . . . Or else maybe he was only terrified that I would tell someone.

I gave him my wet hand-embroidered handkerchief to dry his eyes with. I am absolutely convinced that the whole transaction was his doing, his way of keeping his good name and reputation from being posted on the public notice board for hooligans and drunks. But he went on: "How could you make yourself do it? I just figured you must have gone back to the hotel."

I couldn't explain how I'd been able "to make myself do such a thing." I told him I was tired and would like to go to bed.

"But you can't show yourself at the hotel looking like that."

I walked away from him.

He ran after me. He wanted to say he was sorry. Sorry that this had happened in his country, in the Uzbek Soviet Republic. And he wanted me to promise never to tell anyone.

Moral: None.

Early the next morning I slipped down to Intourist wearing sunglasses, canceled my trip to Kazakhstan, Tadzhikistan, and Kirgizia, and took a seat behind a glass partition in the section for foreigners to await the first departure for Afghanistan. I was wearing my capitalistic jeans and T-shirt and had fortified myself behind a battery of cameras and a tape recorder of Western manufacture.

Outside the glass partition stood the policemen from the park who stared . . .

I knew who they were, but I'm not sure they realized I was the whore from Riga. I did look just like her, but here I was sitting in the Foreign Section, and a section *is* a section, after all. I sat and fiddled with my cameras so they would know they were mine. They couldn't arrest an alien woman for creating a disturbance in the park. Nor did they try. They just stood outside the glass partition in their brown uniforms and gazed at me with their brown eyes as the hours crept by. I didn't dare venture outside the glass wall to get something to eat. I sat there and filled a notebook with "I am so scared, I am so scared, I am so scared."

From Afghanistan I wrote the paper some lie about how the other Central Asian Republics were "without interest and not worth visiting." The worst part of the whole experience, almost, was having to give up an assignment in advance, but I was scared to death of staying in the USSR and I couldn't explain that I'd been raped. For there's nothing quite so embarrassing and ridiculous. If you get raped, you're obviously not qualified to be sent abroad, you're not man enough for the assignment. (Moral: A person who gets raped is not a good journalist.)

In the years that followed, I wrote maybe eight versions of the story, trying to make sense out of what had happened. For a long time I couldn't figure it out myself. I mean, what are the sexual mechanisms that make it possible for rape to occur in the first place? And yet even more important than making sense out of the episode was taking the mystery out of the sexual aspect, by making it seem comic. In the first place, it *was* comic. A man comes running along with his tongue hanging out of his pants and a whistle in his mouth in order to assert himself. A woman would look funny, too, if she came rushing along with her pants around her ankles, blowing a whistle, in order to get a man. And in the second place, I cannot—not in my wildest dreams—let myself be terrified by genitalia. Conversely, I am paralyzed by the tacit codes and myths that make rape not only possible, but, for most men, an exciting idea. For me, the explicit sexual character of these codes is, and always has been, secondary.

Five years later I published the story as a rape report, in the conviction that rape can't be a private matter. I wrote it for an international underground paper called *Suck*, edited by Germaine Greer, because no commercial paper would print a rape report on my terms. To illustrate the text, I had myself photographed naked, I wanted to defy my own embarrassment and anxiety. But even more than that, I wanted to make it clear that what scared me wasn't sex but rather the sexual fixation that the whole concept of rape reflects and that serves to legitimize all the other forms of rape to which women are constantly subjected.

But of course I couldn't change the genitocentric madness of our male society. One of the morning papers stole the story and the picture, against my will (obviously) and behind my back, and presented them as a good old-fashioned dirty story, which can hardly come to anyone's surprise. But here is the strange part: Having been raped (and no doubt having "asked for it") and having asked for the story to be stolen and twisted (by being naïve enough to publish it in the first place, since if you're raped you're supposed to keep your mouth shut), I was to be humiliated further by having the violence itself obscured in favor of the version that goes, "By God, she loved it." For the fact is that any woman who does not fear and adore MANHOOD has this additional insult coming to her. And yet one of the fundamental conditions for the very existence of rape is precisely this fear of the male organs. So if you defy the rules of the game and say, "It's not your cocks I'm scared of, it's your culture," then the shit hits the fan. For it is obviously more urgent for men to preserve an unchallenged respect for their sex than for their culture. The culture can go to hell, which, by the way, is where they're busily sending it.

Maybe it doesn't make any difference whether a society is masculine or feminine, as long as it functions. Very well, but the masculine society is no longer functioning. Quite aside from what they have done to women, men have raped the earth, exhausted its resources and thus its generosity. Giant phallic skyscrapers have been erected mindlessly into the clear blue sky where neither men nor women nor children can exist.

There is a penalty for taking the mystery out of the rape syndrome. Rape must always be viewed in genital terms, so that the other forms of rape can continue to go unpunished. The male genitalia must always be the center of world order and make their claim to fear and/or adoration. Women are expected to be so terrified, so panic-stricken at the sight of them that they will scream and holler and let themselves be strangled in hysteria. Once they are dead, society will reward them with respect and regret, for after all it was a DREADFUL thing. But if you have the gall not to die of terror, why then you must have liked it. Everyone knows you can't rape a woman "unless she wants it"—one more figure of speech designed to deny and disguise violence. Our genitocentric male society punishes a neutral view of the masculine organs. Total pain or total pleasure. It doesn't seem possible that anyone might be indifferent to the male sexual parts in and of themselves.

But once you've put your foot in it by showing your lack of respect for "world order," you at least get a chance to confirm your theory about how our culture equates lewdness with violence. For after the rape story was printed, I got innumerable phone calls à la "Have you really done all those filthy things?" Streams of panting, masturbating men rang my doorbell because they took my story as an invitation. Just like the Uzbek policemen—she does it to other men, she can do it to me. I got letters that began, "In response to your advertisement . . ."

One newspaper put me on its blacklist. Because, obviously, any woman "who can get herself to do things like that" has disqualified herself as a correspondent.

But it would be futile to try and diagnose the malignant cancer of masculine society in all its hopeless detail. Someday we must reach the point where we find it more urgent to ask: What is it about a woman that makes it absolutely necessary to rape her? Is it the female anatomy that makes her especially suitable as an object of violence? Or is rape, instead, bound up with male myths and patriarchal culture (and thus with the female *psyche*)? The answer to this is immediately apparent when we ask the question: Why are MEN never raped?

This is a question to which most women shrug their shoulders, but which, in my experience, makes most men leer. For make no mistake—men would love to be raped. Violence and dehumanization are so profoundly and passionately bound up with masculine culture that they would not have the slightest objection to being raped—and that may be the most horrible part of all.

Rape is not necessarily associated with anatomy or biology, as most men would like to believe. When one sex is raped and another sex is not, it has to do with the different myths and ideas we associate with the respective sexes. If men lived in constant fear of being raped, they would be raped. In a female society where women had the power and the prestige and the money (and used them in a masculine manner), men would be raped. They would not be able to resist the power structure. They would be asking to be raped, simply because they were men.

Malinowski describes the rape of a Melanesian man as follows:

> The man is the fair game of women for all that sexual violence, obscene cruelty, filthy pollution and rough handling can do to him. Thus first they pull off and tear up his pubic leaf, the protection of his modesty, and, to a native, the symbol of his manly dignity. Then, by masturbatory practices and exhibitionism, they try to produce an erection in their victim and, when their maneuvers have brought about the desired result, one of them squats over him and inserts his penis into her vagina. After the first ejaculation he may be treated in the same manner by another woman. Worse things are to follow. Some of the women will defecate and micturate all over his body, paying special attention to his

face, which they pollute as thoroughly as they can. "A man will vomit, and vomit, and vomit," said a sympathetic informant.

(*Sexual Life of Savages in North-Western Melanesia*, New York: Harcourt Brace Jovanovich, 1962)

One of the early signs that something is happening to the sexual perceptions of our own culture—although the phenomenon is difficult to analyze in the field—is represented by "groupies" and the way they attack a pop idol in his dressing room after a concert. In many cases, these incidents amount to rape. For even if the pop singer does produce an erection, after the groupies have rubbed up against him and pawed his groin, that does not necessarily mean that he has the desire. In many cases his passivity, the casual mechanical nature of his sexual feelings, is merely an expression of the fact that he has sold his soul to his fans, and that his identity stands and falls with the popularity level represented by these girls. Whether he gets an erection or not, he is a rape victim the moment he seeks ego confirmation outside himself, in his fans.

Here again, the significant aspect of the rape is not its genital character but rather the violence committed against a person's ego and dignity. Women are subjected to this kind of violence almost daily, but it is permitted to rage on because it is fired by the myth of feminine sexual inferiority.

The victim of a rape always suffers additional humiliation as the victim of the prejudice by which "you can take a woman anywhere but never at her word." "A woman never says what she means," and a nice girl is expected to say no when deep down she means yes, and under no circumstances to say yes right away, even if she wants to. As a result, judges often have a hard time distinguishing between cases where the decision to copulate was mutual and cases where the man enjoyed his partner's favors by force. But women didn't think up these cunning rules all by themselves, just for the fun of it. They are organically bound up with the masculine culture that has shrouded woman in mystery in order to hold her in check. In Western Europe's most famous erotic work, Ovid writes, without blushing, ". . . and when I beg you to say 'yes,' say 'no.' Then let me lie outside your bolted door . . . So Love grows strong . . ."

It is possible that it does grow strong, this kind of love. But since Ovid's day it has occurred to some people that the curious expression of love that Ovid had in mind—and God knows it has been eagerly advertised—is fatal to any loving relationship, because it builds on a feminine mystique that no woman can live up to. And it wouldn't help if she could. On the contrary.

It is popularly believed that rapists are more or less (temporarily) insane. This belief is meant to conceal all the other forms of rape, the legitimate forms, but it has no scientific basis. According to Menachem Amir's study of 646 rapes in Philadelphia, *Patterns in Forcible Rape* (Chicago: University of Chicago Press, 1971), the men who commit forcible rape are not psychologically deviant or in any other way abnormal.

> Studies indicate that sex offenders don't constitute a unique or psycho-pathological type; nor are they as a group invariably more disturbed than the control groups to which they are compared.

The fact that rape is committed by normal men could put us on the track of yet another male myth, namely, that if it weren't for socially acquired inhibitions, all men would run around raping—that is, that rape is "natural" behavior, as in the cartoon of the Stone Age man dragging his prey by the hair to the nearest cave.

Not-to-rape has to be learned . . .

But this is a distorted truth, or at least it is not a universal truth. (The truth is really the reverse; it is rape that must be *learned.* The fact that rape is against the law hardly proves that our culture does not encourage it.) For example, Margaret Mead describes a society in *Sex and Temperament* that does not share our view. "The Arapesh do not . . . have any conception of the male nature that might make rape understandable to them."

Professor Amir's study also shows that rape is not a matter of impulsive, spontaneous behavior, but that most rape attempts are planned. This undermines the myth that the rapist is a man who is very much sexually aroused, a man who is suddenly overcome by lusts that society will not permit him to satisfy in any other way.

Sex cannot be viewed in isolation from the rest of the culture, and it is alarming to realize how deeply male sexuality is associated with power. Power on all levels, from invisible, shadowy power to that which is blatant and coarse, from rough patriarchal authority to the more spectacular refinements of violence. From the nuclear family to nuclear weapons.

The capacity to fire a machine gun and the capacity to make love don't appear to have any connection, and yet there is something suspiciously feminine about pacifism. It was Malraux who wrote that childbirth for a woman is the illuminating experience of standing face-to-face with death.

In his study of the relationship of sex crimes to the legalization of pornography in Denmark, Berl Kutschinsky shows that "indecency toward young girls" has declined by 60 percent since the repeal of visual censorship, whereas crimes of rape do not appear to have been affected. "Indecency" is a matter of fear and impotence, with little girls substituting for the older women such men do not dare approach. This substitute can easily be replaced by another, that is, passive pornography.

On the other hand, it does not appear that violent sex crimes can be replaced by peaceful reading—or by anything else, either. This must mean that a man who finds his gratification by raping women enjoys the violence and his own sense of power more, if possible, than the simple pleasures of the flesh. Of course coitus is never an isolated phenomenon, plucked out of thin air. Wind and weather, the alcohol and sugar content of the blood, as well as attitudes, fantasies, and ideas, that is, the condition of the world at large—all have their effect on a man's ability to achieve orgasm. On a woman's too, of course. But if a man can ejaculate after terrorizing and humiliating the object of his passion and perhaps even hurting her, then we must suppose that it gives him pleasure to give pain. If a man can get an erection and reach a climax with a woman who has shown no indication of desire, then we must conclude that he is totally alienated—not only from the woman, but from himself and all real being.

Chivalry was invented to give men a civilized veneer, and to protect women against all the "other" rapists. But in practice it became one more form of blackmail against the woman, because chivalry demanded that in return for its protection the woman should live up to—or down to—the concept of womanhood. And chivalry drove the man to a state of sexual schizophrenia. He had to be capable of rape in order to retain his manliness, but at the same time he had to show gentlemanliness toward the woman (his) who was destined to be raped by all those other men unless he took care of her. In other words, the woman was not granted the man's chivalrous protection for the sake of her pretty blue eyes. Classical sexual politics required her to subdue her behavior and suppress her sexuality in order to make herself worthy of protection. The price she paid for common civility was chastity and monogamy.

In the United States today, a woman who is known to have been unfaithful to her husband, or who has a lover, or who is an "unwed mother" hasn't a chance in hell of bringing charges against a rapist and winning her case. Because in the first place, a "loose" woman cannot be raped (since she is lascivious by nature), and in the second place, a woman who breaks the unwritten sexual rules has no claim to protection. This leads us to the not unreasonable suspicion that society is more interested in controlling the woman's behavior than the man's.

Femininity is an ideal that women have had to live up to in order to expect any sort of chivalrous treatment (not being raped), or even common courtesy. But femininity is at the same time an unwritten law that makes women the consummate victims of sexual aggression. Femininity is wearing shoes that make it difficult to run, skirts that inhibit movement, and underclothes that interfere with blood circulation. It can hardly be coincidental that the clothes men find most flattering on a woman are precisely those that make it most difficult for her to defend herself against aggression.

Maybe that is why the women one meets on the street have cold eyes and hard faces. They have lost the polygamous capacities with which they were originally equipped. By the time she is ten or twelve years old, a girl has learned not to meet men's eyes if she wants to be left in peace. She has learned that her behavior must be different from a boy's and that she must always be feminine. In this way she will come to doubt her own sensuality, and thus her own spirituality as well. She learns to deny her own feelings and not to act on them. She learns to fear herself. This is the essence of passivity. But a woman's passivity is not only sexual, it is a fundamental unconscious attitude that prevents her from expressing herself in all of life's proceedings.

Considering that most women are constantly on the defensive and have grown accustomed to living in daily fear of being confronted, if not with rape in its most blatantly sexual form, why at least with pressures and intrusions on their freedom of choice, then why is there so astonishingly little written on the subject? One might almost suspect a masculine conspiracy. For even if very few men commit forcible rape, most of them nevertheless accept its occurrence because of the way it indirectly confirms their virility. The fact is that most men identify with the rapist, not the victim, and it is presumably for the entertainment of this armchair rapist that the media give us such detailed accounts of the rapes that do occur.

In a film like Hitchcock's *Frenzy,* where women are raped in a steady stream and then strangled with a variety of pretty neckties, the criminal is finally captured. But the expected conclusion is nothing but conventional Hollywood pseudomorality, teaching us once again that crime, in this case rape, does not pay. Because all of the unidentified rapists in the audience, all the petty, small-time rapists in the crowd, know perfectly well in their hearts that rape pays very well indeed. They know that rape is a part—a not unexciting part—of everyday life. And in fact that *real* moral of the film is quite a different one, namely, that a woman needs a man to protect her. If you are alone, good woman, then lock yourself in. Put an extra bar across the door. Keep yourself in hiding. Be discreet. For a solitary woman is an invitation.

In the Arab countries, a woman has no autonomous existence—her identity is dependent entirely on a man.

A woman is "sister of Bechir," "daughter of Mustafa," or "mother of Ahmed." And so a woman without family relations is an outcast and has, theoretically, no identity at all. She belongs to no one, which in practice means that she is common property.

It wouldn't surprise me if even in the West most women get married because marriage is the only protection, the only hands-off arrangement that all the other rapists more or less respect. Married women aren't treated as crudely as single women, or, to be exact, crudity is harder to justify in the case of a married woman. Although even an honest rapist can make a mistake. If a married woman walks down the street provocatively dressed, it is natural to suppose that she is single, for the assumption is that no man would let his wife display herself that way. If she is married, consequently, a woman can both have her cake and eat it too. She can wander around turning men on and still remain forbidden fruit. "You're making a mistake, young man, I am a married woman." Which means—my body belongs to someone else.

But provocative female dress should not be dismissed as if it were merely a feint. Provocative dress is terribly important—not as a challenge to masculine potency, but as a challenge to masculine culture. Broby Johansen has this to say on the subject:

> Dress is armor, a tightly sealed costume with a gas mask to complete it. Heavy, tightly fitting clothing is war dress, for we are cold when we are afraid. The clothing of peace is open. Women's dress as it has developed in the period of women's liberation, with its explicit tendency toward nakedness, is the expression of an alternative—and now pay attention, for this is the point—to the determined preparations being made by our male-directed civilization for the heroic suicide of

all mankind in a global Götterdämmerung. . . . This is where male government with all of its stupid, puerile ideals has brought us.

I think it is important for women to hold their ground and not to disguise themselves in psychological or physical male dress, even though it is tempting to try and neutralize the "differentness" that is the necessary object of violence and insult. But if women put on men's clothing, with everything that implies, they will have abandoned themselves to male culture. And with that, they can abandon hope.

If women do not become sexually aware, they will continue to be raped. Even if they do, there will still be men who lead them up the garden path. Therefore it is essential for women to join forces and use every possible means to publicize all of the "private" situations where they are raped or subjected to other forms of extortion.

Germaine Greer delivers a warning in her *Playboy* article. "How would you feel if a video tape of your last fuck were playing at the Feminist Guerrilla Cinema?"

Sex is also politics. And therefore being humiliated is no longer a private matter—not even if we're used to it.

A film called *Bluebeard,* with Richard Burton, is playing at the Imperial—"a hilarious thriller about the famous lady-killer and his victims," it says in the ad. The reviewer writes, "Edward Dmytryk does not exactly have a delicate touch, and yet he has undertaken to make an amusing two-hour Gothic thriller spoof about a man who murders six women. By gunshot, drowning, guillotine, impalement on tusks, burial alive, and an attack by falcons. It's a laugh riot."

8 Dorotea

I have sent a girl over for the second time to get the poems from Dorotea. Blue tissue paper bound in two pieces of faded green suede. After all, they weren't to her. The message I'd instructed the girl to take was, in its harrowing simplicity, "Suzanne would like to have the poems back. You're welcome to keep them if you like, so long as you clearly understand that they weren't to you." But I can just imagine the way she'll go galumphing in and mess it up. "You've got some poems of Suzanne's and she says they're not yours, or something." How do I know what she'll say? Maybe after all I should have written it down for her—no, by God.

I purposely put in that part about how she was more than welcome to keep them so long as she clearly understood—emphasis on CLEARLY—that I hadn't written them to her. That was about the cruelest thing I could think of, and it isn't the fever alone—even though illness does make a person especially disposed to mental blocks and clumsy cunning and malignant schemes. . . . The darkness and the cold sweats—and anyway, isn't it her fault that I'm sick in the first place? I might die!

I drop the thought as unfit for further malice. It wouldn't bother her, just me, and for me it's bad enough to have been in bed with a fever for a month, on account of something as silly as what we commonly call love. But here I am! The doctor fills me with penicillin every day and talks about a virus. But it's the world; it's too rotten for me to get well again.

I had very carefully figured out—it seemed to me—that if I said she was welcome to keep the poems (which I had written to her one hundred years before) so long as she clearly understood that they weren't to her, I would be presenting her with a difficult choice and precipitating an identity crisis. Because who was she? Trash! The question was whether I could get her to decide if she was the person I'd written the poems to or the person who had betrayed me. For me they were not the same. She had shown me the only form of faithlessness that I can grasp. She had betrayed that part of herself to which I was particularly attached and which I loved, and had become another person. But that too was nonsense, for what I had particularly loved—and loved Dorotea for—her moral laxity, was the very thing that made it so easy for her to betray me. It was logical enough, but that didn't make it any easier to take.

I lay there and tried to imagine how she would react. Deep down, I was hoping she would come over and see me *herself*—without the poems (it didn't matter who they were to) and without a word—just put her hand on my brow. Not to pretend that everything was like before—I wasn't born yesterday—but just to put a cooling hand on my fever. It is possible that we could have laughed together for a moment, just for a moment—it's just possible.

Difficult choice, identity crisis, ha! Dorotea and difficult choice and identity crisis? Come off it! Not that concepts of that kind were irrelevant in Dorotea's case, no, on the contrary. It was just that Dorotea was not very aware, least of all of herself, poor thing. Well, for that matter, that was how I'd managed to seduce her in the first place. So I shouldn't complain. Come to think of it, was it I who seduced her? I wonder.

No, obviously I didn't think she was going to come over here herself. The worst part was that I knew perfectly well that my most malicious cunning, my thoroughly premeditated judgment: "keep them but they're not to you," would have no effect at all. It didn't matter what sort of ornate cruelty I might think up, it would go right over her head. And if I turned to more tangible particulars, threatened her with anything as particular, say, as a knife, she would simply run away. Not even come over and embrace me, the pig. She was as common as they came, and she had simply thrown me over, whisked me away with a flick of the finger like a worm on her sleeve. Period. For of course there had been no explanation. So we couldn't even go through love's final "voluptuous" phase, where all the "truths" must out. And she was right, the little bitch, because she wasn't stupid, or rather, she had her intuition and she knew she'd get the short end of any discussion. There was no question but what I could convince her that she loved me more than anything else in the world, that she just didn't realize it. . . . Was it true that I stifled her, injected too much of myself into her? But I didn't mean to, I swear. Of course I could write her a letter and tell her what she's REALLY like; I could take her "true self" (the one I couldn't trust) and shove it in her face, twenty-five pages, be my guest! Disgusting little tramp! But she was very much mistaken if she thought SHE could get twenty-five pages out of ME to bask in! Heaven forbid! So it was more elegant to say, "You can keep them, but they're not to you." Brief and blunt. Right?

I knew very well that the most I could hope for from her side would be some slight vexation at having to part with the poems. Because aside from the fact that the paper and the leather were exquisite and would grace any table, they were love poems written to her, and as we know, no one can ever have too many love poems, not even silly D. Of course they were all about Mnadsidiki and Bilitis of Pamphylien, maenads and naiads, young courtesans in tunics and sandals, breasts like young birds bathed in milk, perfumed armpits, and that sort of thing. But they were written to Dorotea, and since she was sentimental enough to keep withered rose petals and velvet bows, she would definitely want to hold on to the poems "in memory." Bah! In memory of a youth spent at a boarding school, a bewildering, bittersweet (ugh) time when she (ah, fond memories) still didn't know her ass from her elbow. I fancied I myself could tell the difference between asses and elbows, thank you, even if it wasn't always that important, thank God.

In any case my love for her wasn't for lack of something better, even though at the moment I was lying there trying to tell myself I didn't REALLY love her. Loving a woman is always doubly narcissistic—is it the other person or yourself that you love most? There's no telling. It is—doubly wonderful. I pulled out a comforting thought from the back of my brain—there are X many billions of people in the world, why should I suffer because of a single one of them—a girl at a boarding school? It isn't the schoolgirl that's ridiculous, but suffering as a criterion for (love's) earnestness. This love could not possibly be natural. Not that I am especially interested in what is "natural," only in what is love. And I lay there and told myself again and again that love in confinement always became distorted.

The absence of a look could take on monstrous proportions. It was suddenly hard to tell what you really felt, because, in confinement, other people's feelings were forced upon you. But there I lay, loving Dorotea, or hating her—an unworthy form of love that I do not choose to examine further.

No one came to see me for a month. By "no one," I mean the girls Dorotea and I surrounded ourselves with. Now they have all joined forces around Dorotea—so I've heard—and it may be my imagination, but I have the feeling they are gloating. Dorotea is spared further demoralization. Everyone knows that love between girls must end badly. The burden of disproof rests on me, and I lie here sick and full of hate. . . .

To show them a little understanding—and I like to be charitable—I think they are relieved that the cooing nucleus of love we represented has been broken up. They found it both exhilarating and unbearable, because it was closed to them but gave the two of us such a surplus of light that we could draw them into our aura with a smile, when it suited us. They were fascinated, but as soon as they attempted any real approach, we barred the way and sent them out into the darkness. No wonder they were curious, angry, and envious—for I am convinced that they were. But undoubtedly everything is better for them now, for once again there's nothing new under the sun: girls who go to bed together are perverse and come to a bad end.

There was Else, for example, who would be delighted to come to any sort of end at all, no matter how bad, if only she could be *in* on things. Even before I got to know Dorotea, Else had tried to arouse my interest by rubbing up against me in an unambiguous manner. I have never been especially interested in women sexually, nor especially uninterested, merely interested in a general sort of way. The fact that I haven't cultivated women to any great extent is because I have the feeling I would be taking on an unreasonable responsibility. They have to be supported hand and foot, or at least they let you do it. You have to nurse even their consciences and their hangovers and, if possible, stand ready with some sterling philosophy of life that tells them they haven't sinned but rather accomplished something virtually heroic by recognizing something new within themselves. They always have to be pioneers in some sort of cause in order to get onto speaking terms with their own sexuality—with their own being. And that can become exhausting. I lay there and promised myself I would never again make love to a woman—unless she suggested it herself, or gave some indication.

Of course Else had given more than an indication. But the trouble with Else was that I couldn't stand her breasts. Heavy cream teats fat with milk. That kind of breasts can probably be a lot of fun, but it was the WAY she used them that I couldn't take. She let them carry her through life, that is to say, through school, as if her whole person had been pumped into these balloons and lay there ready to pounce. When she was examined on Charles XII, she laughed her ready "woman's" laugh and stuck out her boobs as if they could talk. Someone may have breasts that can, I don't rule out the possibility. But hers could not, and so it embarrassed me. And it wasn't that I was envious because she got away with it and passed. I just felt she had cheated. It isn't particularly nice to admit, but I had the most revolting fantasies of kneading those teats until they were pulpy, putting my hands in them and mashing them like lumps of liver, letting them squish through my fingers—or of tying them up crisscross with strips of linen. Do you suppose I have put my finger on some unhealthy tendency? Once several of us attacked a naked girl with wet towels, but right at the moment I don't remember if it was Else. All I can remember is a body with its rear end up in the air, the face turned away. Come to think of it, I don't believe it was Else.

Dorotea was as esthetic to me as Else was crude. Now I know well enough that beauty is a code and a fashion, and I am grateful that there are people who sit around and try to figure out what sort of capitalist swindle the whole thing is based on. But all I wanted was to run my tongue over Dorotea's entire body, set my teeth daintily in the curve where her thighs crept up and became a waist, hold her wriggling loins tightly in one hand, nibble her earlobe, cradle her head with the other, and let her eyelashes flutter against my cheek and inhale her breath.

Of course she was supposed to have something to say about it too, even though I don't remember ever asking for permission. But certain women just "let it happen" as they say, and that is what Dorotea did—to my infinite delight! I never want that kind of woman again. For the trouble with women who simply let it happen is that suddenly it simply has happened.

She had what I loved—large hips and thighs and a frantically tiny waist, pliant and flexible, oh, my. Her torso was smooth and lovely, and her breasts were very small—you could easily flatten them out with your hands as she lay pushing up with her pussycat (as we called it), which was damp, tight, triangular, and black—not too wet. With her long, heavy hips and legs and her slim waist and torso, she was everything at once, full and trim. Like certain of Modigliani's mistresses. I must add: shoulder-length brown hair, blue eyes, straight nose, thin lips. Like Bilitis or Mnadsidiki? I used to call her okapi now and then because of her thighs, and she called me giraffe on account of a light birthmark on my stomach. Of course it was a dream world, even though I can't stand the way everything has to be called a dream just because it's wonderful.

Before we had ever kissed—oh, that light playful tongue—we talked mostly about men. Pricks. Backward and forward and in and out for months. Sitting at opposite ends of the dining room, Dorotea would pick up her knife and fondle it with the tips of her fingers in such an unmistakable manner that we giggled so hard we were almost in tears. For that matter, a wax candle was enough to break us up.

I had the good fortune at that time to have a lover in Tokyo, who had just sent me a most ingenious phallus in a lemonwood box. In its dry, shriveled state it resembled a twig, but when soaked in lukewarm water for ten minutes in accordance with the directions (in five major languages), it swelled up. Of course it was slightly irritating to have to stand and wait for an empty sink while the other girls brushed their teeth and washed their feet, but patience is a well-known virtue.

Was it calculating of me to tell Dorotea about it? Honestly. We were absolutely sober. We were sitting in the dark red parlor with forty other girls one Sunday evening doing our embroidery, while the headmaster read aloud from *The Art of Life Without Philosophy.* And I whispered to Dorotea about the phallus. I insist that it wasn't calculating, that I didn't make it sound any better than it was. Right away Dorotea wanted to know if she could see it, and I told her to come to my room after lights out. Lights out was at ten o'clock, but we always hung a blanket over the door so the proctor wouldn't get suspicious.

Whether it was I she came for, or the phallus, doesn't matter at all. At ten-thirty, Dorotea was standing in my room. I threw the quilt aside and she lay down beside me, calmly—and trustingly, I think. There is nothing as easy as women. The first time you lie there body to body, your breasts pressed together, your legs intertwined, there's no limit to your pleasure. It's you yourself you feel, and no woman can resist that—unless she simply finds herself disgusting.

She had the kind of temperament that could just as well fall for a man with $25,000 a year and the prospect of a Deepfreeze. Not that she was particularly interested in money or appliances, but she was never the sort of person who was on her way, she always just WAS somewhere. Right at the moment she was with me. She had many small talents, musical ones among others, but most of them seemed to be superficial appendages—in my opinion because she never took them to heart. She had a somewhat awkward charm that I fell very much in love with. When she got into bed, for example, she would first step up on the mattress with both feet, then sink to her haunches, whereupon she let herself fall with a little bump. But most of all, I suppose, she radiated a need to be "taken care of," and when a girl of seventeen is afflicted with a helplessness that is ungainly but not "unfortunate," there will always be someone to give her what she needs. Right at the moment it was I.

What I loved about her was a flowerlike quality. Flowers do not choose where to grow or whether to live by the light of the sun or the moon—they blossom all the same. Dorotea was like that. Or should I say that she was like a piece of paper on which a person could make things up? Since she made no demands on herself, I came to define her more and more. I really don't think I dominated her. After a few days I told her to throw away her brassiere, but wasn't that for the good of her own breasts? Maybe, too, I filled her with all sorts of theories, mostly about love, but that was because they engrossed me, and no one said she had to take them as gospel.

At one point, a Peruvian lover announced his arrival in our provincial town. Since he had come all the way from Lima to Jutland, it seemed to me that I ought to see him. I had had two wonderful days with him in Paris once. I took Dorotea with me to his hotel room. This was partly because I always wanted to be with her, but also because I didn't feel my relationship with him was intimate enough that I wanted to be alone with him. Dorotea was a little upset by this triangle, and I know just how she felt. He was more mechanical than I remembered him. But maybe he was flustered that there were two of us. It was probably too much to spring on him, he may have felt like a sex object. But that night Dorotea menstruated, and I distinctly remember that Antonio took it as a personal affront. And so then we had him to vilify for a month or two. We composed a nasty song about him and allowed our ladies-in-waiting to join in on the chorus. It was a stupid song, but so what?

I don't remember what Dorotea and I did with ourselves during the next year and a half. School and lessons took most of our time—and the nights together wore us out. There were walks on the heath, though usually with the other girls who wanted to come along. We had adequate adoration and felt that spectators were good for our love, within certain limits.

The Japanese phallus had worn out long ago. Then I got the idea of buying a cucumber, just for a lark. So one winter day we walked down to the store and asked for a cucumber. Dorotea did it, I didn't have the nerve. When the grocer said it wasn't CUCUMBER SEASON, I turned quite pale. I didn't know there was such a thing, and I was about to walk out. But Dorotea was quick as lightning. "Then we'll have a carrot, please!"

She was wonderful. I could hardly breathe, myself. It felt practically as though the grocer and I were having intercourse right there on our feet, and I was afraid he'd hear the throbbing in my guts.

I can never remember what lovers do with each other, but the high points were the quiet afternoons, Saturday and Sunday, when the school was empty and the girls gone for the weekend. Those who stayed behind were allowed to use the record player—otherwise it was against the rules to use electricity—and we played Mozart: clarinet and piano concertos. Dorotea would lie with her legs apart and I would put my cheek against the inside of her thigh and count her hairs for fun. We did hairdos on each other, rubbed each other with lotions, tickled each other between the thighs with a cotton ball dampened with eau de cologne and blew on it and drank white wine and all that sort of thing.

But I wouldn't say I dominated her in these things either. She would straddle me, and scratch my neck and down along my sides, and fuck me lustily with whatever was in season.

I had some ideas—or dreams—about how love is not diminished by being "shared," but increased. Dorotea could have told me that was a lot of bull, but she didn't. On the contrary, she insisted that I visit her lover; in fact she was quite fired up at the idea. I ought to get to know him, she said, it was only natural. If I had known it would hurt her, I wouldn't have done it, for I loved her more than my dreams.

Nor did she say anything when I came back from Easter vacation and told her about it. We didn't talk about it a great deal. For me it had been lovely and uncomplicated. Partly because he and I had so much to talk about—Dorotea. It seemed beautiful that the two of us loved her together, dear Dorotea.

Summer vacation came. I went east and Dorotea went to the beach with a family. We wrote to each other, long reports about okapis and giraffes on the savanna. Or rather I wrote, and she stopped writing. I was terrified she had fallen ill and couldn't wait to get back to school, prison of all prisons.

She was not on the train, and not waiting at the station. The first time I saw her again, she was walking across the schoolyard. I ran over with my arms spread wide to embrace her. She kept right on walking. I might have run after her, of course, and asked what was the matter, but I couldn't. I just couldn't. Her face had been turned away, her eyes had been focused on something in the distance—so what would I ask?

Later that day, Else came over to tell me that Dorotea was engaged to a lawyer. I said I didn't see why that should keep us from speaking—even though I was about to throw up, not about Dorotea or the lawyer, but, oh, how do I know? "What changed her so much?" I said.

"Just leave Dorotea alone. Besides, she visited her uncle over the vacation, and I guess she told him about your relationship, because he explained to her how dangerous bisexuality can be. He's a doctor, you know, so you can't honestly blame her. You've forced yourself on her enough."

I have retreated and asked no questions. I have only asked to have my poems back. The most painful part is this feeling that my love is up against something that isn't Dorotea.

She has returned the poems.

9 Monogamy: the Cannibalism of Our Time

(What you don't know can't hurt you.)

I have a bone to pick with Elizabeth Taylor—which I believe is Aristotle's fault. I think he was the first to promulgate the principles of Western logic—the identity axiom, for example, which implies among other things that we can love only one person at a time, since "It is impossible for a given phenomenon at a given time both to belong and not to belong to another given phenomenon." Further to the East they would say—and do say—"That which is one is one. That which is not-one is also one." But such a paradox would probably have confused Aristotle, who never would have agreed, either, with the proposition that a person is perhaps most alone when he or she is most united, or that by belonging to one human being, a person belongs to all human beings and at the same time to no one at all. Aristotle might be left to rest in peace if it weren't for all of his absolutist, cannibal descendants. We will never have any peace from them.

When, 2320 years later, a great gorgeous lump like Elizabeth Taylor says, "I'll knock his block off if he cheats on me," and by "he" she is referring not just to some man on the street but to her beloved husband, she is building on grim old Aristotelian logic: If he loves me he can't simultaneously love others. And clearly he cannot, without throwing overboard all of Western thought, and he is hardly interested in doing that unless he wants to get his block knocked off.

Elizabeth Taylor is a very dangerous person. She is a potential murderess. A murderess at large. She is more dangerous than Nixon and Brezhnev and the whole bunch, for when the powerful preach murder, we turn against the idea, at least for the sake of appearances. But when Elizabeth Taylor declares that she could seriously consider murdering her beloved husband, we all clap our little hands together and get tears in our eyes, knowing that this is true love and great passion.

Monogamy is the dogma of love as principle. But what is more ridiculous than principles? For thousands of years we have put logical thought on a pedestal as an intellectual principle, while in practice we have punished most severely the "cynical" murderers who planned and thought out their crimes and let those who committed impassioned and unpremeditated murders off more easily. But in terms of pure logic we must ask ourselves: What's the matter with a well-planned murder? It ought to be better than a thoughtless one. . . . Monogamy is love as a commandment: Thou shalt love thy neighbor. But in practice it comes out: Thou shalt love thy neighbor, but not too much or I'll knock your block off.

If that's the way it's going to work, then it seems to me we might just as well abolish love. At least we'd be free of all that cruelty.

In *L'Amour et l'Occident*, Denis de Rougement writes that half of mankind's misery could be summed up under the heading "infidelity." He wrote that in 1938. Thirty-five years later we find that the world has changed. The other sources of misery, such as hunger and material want, have been greatly reduced in the West, while a growing share of unhappiness seems to be left for infidelity. Contrary to what one might expect of a younger generation whose job it is to revise the values handed down to it, most young people are preparing for even more difficult lives than their parents had. This can be seen from the divorce statistics. Today people separate at the slightest provocation: infidelity. It has become a greater source of anxiety than ever before. The utterly absurd situation where a man is forced to choose between "her" and "her" with a knife at his throat is an everyday phenomenon. "*Either* it's her *or* it's me," is the watchword, and when the man (I say "the man" because at the moment men are more polygamous than women) finally makes a choice, it is taken to be an indication of maturity. Particularly, of course, if he has chosen his wife. As if anyone could ever choose between human beings, all of whom are equal in their own ways. But to choose between human beings is the most famous choice that human beings make, and when they have chosen to love one person, they have as a rule betrayed all the others. This is called love.

Yes, but if everyone is as good as everyone else, are we simply not going to have couples anymore?

Oh, yes, indeed. One of the best reasons for grouping ourselves into couples is that this is by far the best way of coupling. But to go on from there and map out the whole universe and organize the whole planet and all of existence in accordance with our sex lives, it seems to me that's going too far. It is quite unnecessary to relate to other people from a genital point of view now that we no longer need to populate the earth as quickly as we can. Institutionalized heterosexual monogamy is the moral and philosophical consequence of the fact that once, at the dawn of time, we were forced to get on with the job of peopling the planet, while at the same time we were knocked out by the mysterious discovery that every now and then two people can become one. We've never really gotten over that. And so we have cultivated this thing—called love—and the result has been that these two people who sometimes become one very quickly become zero—whenever love becomes an exclusive program.

How many married people are there who maintain strong, independent relationships outside their marriages? In most close-knit marriages, the wife has a right to only one relationship—her husband. If one of the partners does have meaningful relationships on the side, it is regarded as disloyal or unnatural, because "that simply shouldn't be necessary." Meaningless outside relationships are perfectly all right. But if the relationships mean anything at all, then what they mean is trouble. The less other people mean to your wife or your husband, the better. Outsiders have no business in a loving marriage, for what if someone fell in love? That would be the end of love. Life and love are both threatening. They should both be avoided as far as possible, and to this end we have developed institutionalized cannibalism, that is, monogamy.

The cultivation of love as a principle—Thou shalt love thy neighbor (but God help you if you do, you bastard, I'll murder you)—pays homage to the dualism between body and soul, the conflict between Agape and Eros. God only knows how we are able to figure out from infancy *how much we may love*. . . . It seems to me that adapting love to the rules of society in this way represents an extremely sophisticated computation. And if love is going to be like that, then the hell with it.

I no longer care to read philosophers who write about love but who seem to be unloving. Marcuse strikes me as nonerotic because he thinks mechanistically, so he might just as well spare himself the inconvenience. I don't care to read writers at all, male or female, unless I'm in love with them. As Elishama says, "Either I'm in love or I'm bored to death."

Erich Fromm, now, seems very loving when he writes:

> Love is not primarily a relationship to a specific person; it is an *attitude,* an *orientation* of *character* which determines the relatedness of a person to the world as a whole, not toward one "object" of love. If a person loves only one other person and is indifferent to the rest of his fellow men, his love is not love but a symbiotic attachment, or an enlarged egotism. Yet, most people believe that love is constituted by the object, not by the faculty. In fact, they even believe that it is a proof of the intensity of their love when they do not love anybody except the "loved" person. . . . If I can say to somebody else, "I love you," I must be able to say, "I love in you everybody, I love through you the world, I love in you also myself."
> (*The Art of Loving,* New York: Harper Colophon, 1974)

Although Plato cannot escape responsibility for having contributed to a repressive definition of Eros, nevertheless the *Symposium* does contain a tribute to spirit and flesh as one and the same thing. For as I recall, Eros's desire for one beautiful body leads to another . . . and finally to all beautiful bodies, for "beauty in one body is related to beauty in another," and it would be silly to deny that "beauty in all bodies is one and the same."

It would also be dumb to go around believing that love is like an apple pie or some other measurable quantity, so that you only have as much to give as will just fit into a pie pan, for that implies that you have no more to give when you have given all. In practice, the famous apple pie theory just doesn't hold. In real life the truth is just the opposite. The more you give, the more you have to give. Love breeds love, it is a force that produces love. One of the proofs of this is that we instantly fall in love with people who are in love, because they are so attractive. But since it is forbidden to fall in love with someone who is in love already (it is interpreted as a desire to "destroy" something), we pull in our feelers. Otherwise, it would only mean trouble. We are only allowed to fall in love with people who are not in love with anyone else, for there has to be some order in things. This "order" is institutionalized cannibalism. In our culture, every one of us, in the course of our lives, has the right to eat at least one other person, provided only that we eat every last morsel and not just nibble.

Behind the desire to unite with another person, the desire for love, lies our curiosity about "the secret" that is hidden beneath the surface. The fact that we cannot see this secret with the naked eye, or weigh it and measure it, but only occasionally sense it by means of love, misleads us into believing that love is a very mystical and irrational thing that gives the green light to all sorts of irrational feelings such as jealousy and selfishness, not to mention murder. The most widespread method of learning this secret is to leap upon another person and tear him to pieces, limb from limb, in the name of love. But the secret will always elude the cannibals, just as scientists will never know everything about the snake they cut into thin slices. The more irrational we make love, the greater the chances of disaster. Wiser people than I—Albert Schweitzer, for example—have also pointed out that love, the desire for union with another human being, or, religiously, with God, is by no means irrational, but rather the boldest and most radical consequence of the rational position. Love is the purest cynicism, for it is based on an understanding of the limits of knowledge and on an insight into the fact that we will never grasp all the secrets of the universe or of mankind, except, occasionally, through love. Psychology has its limits as a science, and just as the logical extension of theology is mysticism, so the furthest extension of psychology is love. So actually there would be nothing more to discuss . . . if it weren't for the fact that the most widespread of all life-styles, monogamy, excludes this rationalistic insight, and thus also excludes love.

Our moral fundament cannot entertain even a suggestion of life-styles other than monogamy. But if we must talk about morality, then all I can say is: only that which contributes to our mutual isolation is morally reprehensible, and only that which strengthens human solidarity is morally correct. People who feel they must challenge the limits—and that is the fashion—operate with serial monogamy, consuming other people as if they were commodities, replacing one with the next in the best consumer style, although during the process of ingestion they are usually completely "faithful." First we are "faithful" (to what?) and then it's over. There is a thing called "it's over." It exists in our language. But either it's just the meal that's over, because we have eaten each other up, or else what's over never existed. Conforming to the rules, we go from one passion to the next, from "I love him so much I couldn't live without him" to "I hate him so much I never want to see him again." The antipsychiatrist David Cooper puts it another way. "The only evil of divorce," he writes, "is the prior evil of marriage." (David Cooper, *The Death of the Family)*

There is something very unloving and arrogant about the monogamy principle, according to which we are to be someone else's entire joy, or, failing that, his or her entire misery. In the name of love, we place the beloved "object" in a position where he or she must meet all of our needs. No one can do that. We have to accept people for what they are. As Karen Blixen's old baron says: "If my chef succeeds in making me a good omelet, I don't bother much whether he loves me or not." That is a cynical remark, of course, but as I said earlier, love is the purest cynicism. We have to make the best of people, we cannot demand both love and omelets from one and the same individual. If we nevertheless insist, in the face of all reason, upon having all of our needs satisfied by the cook, or whoever it is we happen to love, then one-to-one relationships become pure business arrangements in which neuroses intermesh and the best a person can figure on is "fair" treatment: "I'll give you exactly as much as you give me—and not another crumb."

According to many of the operating instructions for a happy marriage, the goal is to become a smoothly functioning team. The "lovers" are to become functionaries in an enterprise where love is on the prospectus and vitality is an investment, meant to yield the greatest possible return under current market conditions. If the enterprise should fail, or fail to function smoothly, you replace your partner with a new one, acquired in accordance with the current market value of your own personality stock.

Under present market conditions, love is not only a threat to this arrangement, but the social equivalent of subversion and terrorism. As long as love is an exchange of wares between vending machines, an exchange of personality merchandise, where the best we can hope for is a square deal, society can function. But if people are in love, they won't be able to meet their quotas. Nor, in their wildest dreams, will they be able to figure out why they should, or what the quotas are good for.

Erich Fromm writes:

> Modern capitalism needs men who co-operate smoothly and in large numbers; who want to consume

more and more; and whose tastes are standardized and can be easily influenced and anticipated. It needs men who feel free and independent, not subject to any authority or principle or conscience—yet willing to be commanded, to do what is expected of them, to fit into the social machine without friction; who can be guided without force, led without leaders, prompted without aim—except the one to make good, to be on the move, to function, to go ahead.

(*The Art of Loving*)

Obviously, if the monogamous life-style had never been invented, we would appoint a commission of wise men to invent it. For if the object of life is to stimulate production, it is hard to imagine a better solution. Unless it were to be an out-and-out labor camp with barbed wire and machine guns, but after all that sort of thing does smack a little too much of constraint. No, the ideal conditions for production today are provided by a life-style that appears to be based on love (so that no one can come along and say the essentials are missing) but that is in reality a refined form of cannibalism. A life-style crowned by the promise of fidelity, in order to prevent love from forcing its way in from the outside. In this way monogamy gives people armor-plated protection against real life and thrusts them into the working world without their perceiving it as coercion but, at the very most, as necessity. And life is necessary, after all. Life must go on, as people say, by which they mean that there's nothing new under the sun.

In 1910, a lifelong marriage lasted about twenty-eight years. In 1970, it lasted forty-two. Lifetime relationships last longer and longer, and I'm all in favor of that, so long as they *are* relationships. But as a rule they are not, not when love has become a monogamous principle that precludes closeness and intimacy with everyone outside. As for middle-class social life, I would call that the most effective possible means of exclusion, a trivial form of pornography—a mockery of our longing for union.

On the subject of love as a threat to our way of life, David Cooper writes:

> The appearance of love is subversive to any good social ordering of our lives. Far more than being statistically abnormal, love is dangerous, it might even spread through the aseptic shield that we each get each other to erect around ourselves. What we are socially conditioned to need and expect is not love, but security. . . . A man marries a woman whom he will never leave, and because she knows that he will never leave her, she will never leave him. She accepts the conditionality of her situation because there is a social bribe built into it, in the sense that her husband can only opt out of the conditional system if he, as the apparent initiator of the whole scene, accepts guilt that may be lethal or nearly lethal to him.
>
> (*The Death of the Family*)

But if monogamy is an agonizing experience for the man, who must always bear his guilt (since very few men enter into marriage or any other lasting relationship with the intention of remaining monogamous), the experience is even more agonizing for the woman. For monogamy is somehow a thing that a woman has to deal with all alone, a thing she is beaten over the head with as a part of her "nature." In one way it doesn't matter if the husband is getting a *lot* or a *little* on the side (the most common, of course, is somewhere in the middle—middle-class infidelity). The main thing is that the world stands open to a man quite differently from the way it does to a woman. For a woman, the world is—a man. But when a man walks into a large room filled with people, he is automatically interested in them (especially the women) because he knows that he can spend time with them under more intimate circumstances. It is this possibility, exploited or not, that makes social life exciting. But when a woman enters the same room, she thinks, as a rule, Now how shall I say No this time? For her, it is much more a question of how she is going to *avoid* advances—real or imaginary. She gives off negative vibrations because she already belongs to her husband—and that is her "nature." Women are a priori on the defensive. And it is characteristic of this defensive posture that sex becomes no more than a weapon—which the woman can use either to assert herself or to put pressure on her dear husband in order to have her market price confirmed. Of course it is said, all too often, that a woman who loves her husband has no *desire* to be with other men. And that is very likely, but all it tells us is something about a woman's broken antennae, for if promiscuity is nice for a man, why shouldn't it be nice for a woman? Perhaps it isn't nice for either men or women, but let's at least try to find out. In every field except the erotic, we regard experience as a valuable thing. But in the question of female erotic potential, we hold fast to the principle of pious ignorance. A person can perfectly well *choose* to be monogamous. Just as it is possible to perceive totality in a fragment, so it is theoretically possible for someone to experience love through one single other person. But since the majority of men do not do so, we can't say that women have a free choice in the matter, based upon their experience. What they do have is a need to conform, and a fear of overstepping accepted norms. Moreover, women are as a rule more practical than men and they know it cannot pay to offend male property rights. The average woman is happy to pay the price of monogamy for her moral power over men. She can use man's so-called "swinish" nature to put feathers in her cap and money in her bank account. She is often prepared to let all other people glide past her life unnoticed if only she can get one single man to recognize his fundamental guilt. Theoretically, there may be any number of monogamous superwomen who do not use abstinence as a means of exerting pressure. But as a general rule, this technique turns the monogamous housewife into a whore, repressing her real nature and desires in order to use love as a means to power.

If it can be demonstrated that the monogamous lifestyle has become woman's nature, then I think she will come to realize that it is in her interest to transform nature, at least to the extent that it is an impediment to love. Studies of the most common of all sexual disorders—female frigidity—show that it is not ignorance about the body that makes it difficult for women to experience love and surrender, but rather hate and fear of the so-called opposite sex. The latest major study of female sexuality, Seymour Fisher's *The Female Orgasm* (New York: Basic Books, 1973), settles accounts with the purely technical explanations of female frigidity and comes to the tentative conclusion (we know next to nothing about female sexuality) that the only common denominator for all low-orgastic women (a little over one-third of the study's three hundred women) is an unconscious anxiety at being dependent on the husband and a fear of losing him. (This includes a fear of losing things, and the fear of abandoning oneself to pleasure and thus losing sight of one's concrete surroundings.)

If this kind of symbiotic attachment to the man is

supposed to be woman's nature, then her nature is tragic, and must be combated. When so many women have placed their identities outside themselves and are afraid of surrendering themselves and thereby becoming themselves, because of the risk of losing their men, and when so many women have unconsciously castrated themselves and killed their own sensuality in order to hold onto their men, then the monogamous life-style cannot even be justified on moral grounds—it is pure insanity. Woman's threshold of happiness in the monogamy she's been stuck with can be measured only on a negative, and, as a rule, progressively diminishing scale:

"I'm happy as long as he doesn't cheat on me."

"I'm happy as long as I don't know about it."

"I'm happy as long as he doesn't leave me."

"I'm happy as long as he comes home for meals."

"I'm happy as long as he comes home now and then and doesn't make a scene."

"I'm happy as long as he doesn't beat me."

As long as he doesn't stick a knife in my eye, well, as long as he doesn't twist it, life is still worth living.

Thus, as Madame de Staël put it, love is "the story of a woman's life, and an episode in a man's." But men get more out of their simple episodes than most women get out of a whole long life. It doesn't make a damned bit of difference at the moment whether men are monogamous or not. But it is absolutely essential that women not be.

If women began to realize their erotic potential—in other words, if they began to develop a forthright relationship to the world—we would know a little more about how things stand between the sexes. For the time being, the man's "positive" sexuality depends entirely on the woman's negative attitude toward herself and her own possibilities.

If women began to realize their erotic potential, we would for the first time learn something about male sexuality. Because men are very twisted, but they will never realize it as long as women fail to challenge them.

If women began to realize their erotic potential, many men would be frightened and take it as a threat, but at least we would move a few steps in the right direction. We could finally separate the men from the boys and the lovers from the chauvinists.

It turns out—predictably enough—that men have far more difficulty adapting to "open marriage" than women do. There is nothing so surprising about this, for women have always been expected to live with male infidelity, while men are not used to having their property rights violated in the same way. It seems that women have less trouble swallowing their jealousy, because they are used to living with it. Whatever we may think of "open marriage" as the last hope for the nuclear family, it is at least a step in the direction of sexual equality—and a step away from monogamous cannibalism.

But there remains the fear of change. Love always alters us in a microcosmic sense, and it is a hard thing to bear that it never alters us together or at the same time or in the same way. Therefore we are always alone—and yet united—which Aristotle never would have been willing to concede. Aristotelian logic has led to everything from dogma to science, from the Catholic Church to atomic energy.

And even though atomic physicists have long since abandoned this mode of thinking, we still use it as the basis for our ideas on love, in that love excludes love, and by loving one we exclude others. If we accept the notion that it has come to be our nature to behave this way, then

I see no alternative but to remake nature. For the sake of our survival, if nothing else.

Once upon a time there were some hungry birds who found deep holes in the moor that were especially rich in microscopic animals. They were so ravenous and greedy that they bored deeper and deeper into these holes until they had eaten their fill. They stopped caring about everything else around them. Because the holes were so deep, their beaks grew longer and longer. The ones with short beaks gradually died off, until only the long-beaked birds were left. But one day there was a fire on the moor and all the long-beaked birds were killed, for their beaks were so heavy that they could no longer fly.

This is a story about overspecialization, always a threat to survival. *Monogamy is overspecialization in love*, if anything ever was. And as Buckminster Fuller points out in *Operating Manual for Spaceship Earth*, overspecialization has always meant ruin for cultures as well as for species. It spells anthropological as well as biological disaster.

I believe that at the moment, our goals with regard to love should be dilettantism, naïveté, and superficiality, and that we should strive to achieve them in whatever way we can.

> L'amour est toujours contre nature. Il est anti-nature absolue. Il est le crime, l'insurrection par excellence contre l'ordre de l'univers, la fausse note dans la musique des spheres. Il est l'homme, c'est-à-dire qu'il s'est echappé du paradis terrestre en pouffant de rire. Il est l'échec des plans de Dieu.
>
> EMMANUELLE ARSAN
> (*Emmanuelle*, Paris:
> Eric Losfeld, 1971)

Yesterday I called Jørgen.

"Hi, love, why don't you come on over and play Mah-Jongg?"

"No, thanks. I'm writing a love letter."

"Who to?"

"That's what I'm sitting here trying to decide."

10 Why Do People Have Children?

A lush I know has a son.
He's a problem child, he says.
"How so?" I ask.
"He keeps hiding my beer . . ."

It is hardly a decent question to ask, I know that well enough. In the first place, of course, why people have children is a private matter, and anyway it's perfectly natural to want to contribute to the propagation of the race. Where people get the courage to take so formidable a step as to reproduce is an almost impossible question to answer. It is only people who have *no* children who have a ready answer, since it is natural to demand an explanation of those who do not do the natural thing. But those who do the natural thing cannot really explain it. "We didn't plan it." "It just happened." "To bring us closer together." "So we wouldn't be alone." "It just seemed like the thing to do." "To make me feel grown up." "In order to have something of his." "Just to try it—being a mother and all." Those are the answers I got when I asked the question at a ladies' luncheon.

Little children would simply not be brought into the world if people gave it any thought. But the little children keep on coming, because reproductive behavior has never depended upon logical argument. Bearing children is one of the most beautiful things in the world, it gives meaning to all our lives, particularly a woman's, and if all of a sudden we have to come up with a valid excuse for doing what comes naturally . . . Do we really need permission just to be here?

The problem is that children don't really *have* permission to be here, and I suspect that the survival of mankind—at least in our part of the world—became a doubtful business the moment we could even ask the question as to whether or not we should have children. It's not the question that's crazy, but the situation.

It ought to be everyone's right—if not her duty—to bring children into the world. Otherwise to hell with it. And yet I'm afraid that hell is exactly where we find ourselves when we can no longer regard the natural thing as being entirely natural.

In the first place, conception has become an act of will and is no longer the natural consequence of the act of copulation. In the second place, demographic analysis and the development of modern weaponry have turned the question of how many people the earth can support—if it can support any at all—into a subject of critical importance. In the third place, most children are born products of the monogamous nuclear family, which in the best of cases has nothing to offer the child but love. And finally one of the most compelling reasons why it is no longer entirely natural to have children: children no longer have any natural function in society. Supposing for the moment that society does function, then it does so in spite of children. The social mechanism would not tremble in the slightest if no children existed. And this is probably the heaviest charge one can bring against a society in the long run—and even in the short. For one criterion of a society's viability must center on what it can offer its children—on whether it has the capacity to integrate its children into its vital functions.

The late American anthropologist Jules Henry wrote a study of the family called *Pathways to Madness.* It is a detailed description of the everyday life of five normal American families, families that have only one thing in common: a psychotic or autistic child. In it he writes:

> In the course of evolution only those cultures could have survived in which mothers or their surrogates were adequately available to infants. Societies must disappear which place such burdens on people that there is not enough time for sufficient interaction with infants to make them human; hence today only those remain which achieved the proper balance.
> (*Pathways to Madness,* New York: Random House, 1965)

Cultures that must depend on family relationships like those Jules Henry describes in *Pathways to Madness*—and everything considered, these families are what we would call completely normal—will not survive. Not because the children will starve to death, but because they will go insane. The quality of the childhood offered children in this society, where they are completely excluded from public life and all the processes that make a society function, is entirely dependent on love. And therefore the recurrent question is, Why do people have children? Out of an overabundance of love, do you suppose?

We know that in certain specific places there are certain

specific buttons that could put an end to the discussion in a matter of seconds. Thanks to empirical-analytical science, the "to be or not to be" of the whole human race has become a question that anyone can go around asking without looking stupid, whereas the question "to breed or not to breed" is thought to be an unnecessary abstraction, since having children is regarded as private and instinctive behavior.

And it is a very important instinct, if it *is* an instinct at all. The paternal instinct is easily dispensed with—anthropologists discovered a long time ago that it does not exist. Being a father appears to be a more or less important function, but men never die of not being fathers, and there is nothing to indicate that men suffer psychological disorders from being childless all their lives. The maternal instinct is another story, and a more mysterious one. It does exist. But the instinct doesn't appear until the child is lying in the mother's arms, and sometimes it doesn't appear even then, which can be very sad. If the maternal instinct really is an instinct, then it is certainly an odd one, for a woman can satisfy it whenever it suits her, or not satisfy it at all, at her own discretion. The word "instinct" implies that she would let herself be fertilized from the moment she began to ovulate. But nowadays some women get educations and put off childbearing until they have their degree and have been to Katmandu and lived "life." Many women have their first child when they are twenty-five or thirty or thirty-five years old, at an age when they have been running around with fertile eggs for up to twenty years—without becoming ill or out of sorts because of it. The maternal instinct is a capacity or disposition that a woman can pull out of the bureau drawer whenever she doesn't know what else to wear, when the financial situation is right, when she wants to be cared for or has some other use for it. If women do get "sick" or "strange" from not bearing children, it is because they see the maternal role not simply as one possibility among many others, but as their destiny. For the maternal instinct is socially conditioned in the sense that up to now it had been a woman's only real test of maturity. A childless woman is no real woman, she is "cold" and a little "masculine."

Childbearing can also serve to fill a person's life. I remember reading that every time Picasso's ex-wife Françoise began to get aggressive and speculate about the meaning of it all, Picasso would say, "You need a baby, my girl." And he was right. It helped every time. A maternal instinct would immediately rise up in her bosom and push everything else into the background. The maternal instinct has been used for a lot of purposes down through the ages, among them to push women more or less voluntarily into the background. Hence the myth of a woman's "secret" power—a power that lacked any direct outlet and therefore gave women a taste for intrigue, which in turn became the male pretext for keeping women even further from the decision-making process and positions of real power, the clever bitches.

Having children is natural all over the world. But of all the great religions, Christianity is alone in presenting the myth behind feminine power in the form of a mother. Mary, the most famous woman in our culture, never undertook to do anything at all except to give birth to Jesus. She is no goddess, she has no independent power, her divinity is not her own but rests in motherhood.

Since the dawn of time, bearing and raising children have been considered an important task, perhaps the greatest task in life. Most women still look upon it as a lifetime mission, to which they devote their complete attention for about twenty years. But the average life expectancy of a woman today is over seventy, and childbearing suddenly seems a peculiar lifetime mission when it stops short in the middle of life.

The most obvious explanation of the fact that motherhood today has taken on the character of a tour de force is that women and the nuclear family are isolated from the functions of society, from the world outside their doors.

Women are not trained to be mothers in our society—nor in any society. But in other, more primitive cultures, families are less isolated from one another, and childrearing is carried on much more publicly and openly, which gives mothers a chance to learn new tricks, or, as the psychologists like to say, to experience other frames of reference.

The fact that society provides formal training for virtually every occupation makes motherhood seem all the more archaic and atypical, since mothers still learn by trial and error. A new mother is expected to act on instinct, and this expectation puts women in a special category. The expectation that instinct alone will enable her to perform her maternal function successfully suggests that women operate on a level which, if not lower, is at least more *primitive* than what is considered normal in the world outside the nursery. As a result, the maternal role is very much marked by Kafkaesque scruples: "Am I failing where all other women naturally succeed?" "What sort of children will I raise?" "What sort of adults will they become?" These questions demand answers from the world at large—the world from which, as a rule, the mother is cut off. You might say that this is just as well, everything considered. . . . But in the long run, and even in the short, the isolation of women and children from the centers of power, from the decision-making process, and from the world of production, may well prove to be fatal.

The work that a woman turns out at home (cookies, knitting, and so on) no longer has any economic value from society's point of view. It may be personally satisfying, but its meaning and significance have changed, and many women have a hard time enjoying productivity in a vacuum. Housewives can assess the fruits of their labor and the meaningfulness of their lives only on the basis of personal emotional value, which need not be a misfortune in itself. But as Elizabeth Janeway writes in *Man's World, Woman's Place: A Study in Social Mythology:*

> When the outer world is totally excluded it becomes impossible to imagine it. If this is the case, the sheltered being may develop quite inappropriate, even fantastic, reactions to any given situation. Some nitwits, in short, are born; but others are produced by lack of contact with anything real.

Women are supposed to condition their children for a society whose norms and ideals they often find questionable—morally unjustifiable and emotionally unsatisfying. This task of preparing children for the outside world is expected to take place with the help of instinct alone and without regard to all other social and economic processes. The mother is expected to perform a marvelous feat of balance by ensuring the security of the child's emotional relationships while at the same time giving it the opportunity to escape those relationships and grow out into a world with which the nuclear family has only tenuous connections. And she is expected to accomplish this task guided by instinct alone! Whether or not people actually possess the supernatural powers that motherhood appears to require, they usually bear one or two children anyway—1.8 on the average in Denmark. They do so, as a rule, because they want to, because it gives them joy, because it is a piece of real life that they can touch and feel (not an area where they've been exactly spoiled). It can also be a great delight for a man to give a woman a child, a meaning to life, a bouquet of flowers. . . . They can also give a child to each other, to put magic back into their relationship. Yes, there are any number of uses for a child. . . . Children have lost their fundamental social function and have become a private concern.

In the Middle Ages, there was no such thing as "childhood," writes Shulamith Firestone in a chapter called "Down with Childhood" in *The Dialectic of Sex*. There were no such things as children's clothing, toys, or baby talk. These "aberrations" did not appear until the Renaissance, in conjunction with the spread of the nuclear family. Before that, children were "grown-ups" right from the start—only smaller. They were servants and they were apprentices, because of course they didn't know as much as the adults and so had a lot to learn. But right from the start they were completely integrated into the world of productive labor. The children were members of the household but they were not indispensable to the emotional well-being of the parents. They were nursed by a wet nurse (an outsider) and later, from the ages of seven to fourteen, they were sent on to other households as apprentices. Because people raised other people's children, children were not private possessions, and there could be no question of an exclusive, dependent relationship to the parents, who were responsible only for the child's purely physical well-being. The crucial factor was not that parents *wanted* their children, but that the children themselves were aware from the very beginning that *they were of some use to the world,* that they had vital functions to perform—and that is another thing entirely.

The situation today is just the reverse. Parents want the

fun of having children, but the world outside has no use for them. We feel we have taken a step forward in eliminating children from the work force and saving them from factories, coal mines, and idiot drudgery. Now all that remains is to save the adults. But as long as that does not happen, and as long as children cannot be integrated into the adult world, that world has condemned itself. As long as "progress" is dependent on processes and transactions that children haven't the remotest possibility of taking part in—or even of finding out about—then progress no longer serves mankind. As dear old Charles Fourier wrote, "The touchstone must be whether or not the work attracts children, who feel a much greater distaste than their parents for everything that offends the promptings of nature." But children today are born for no earthly purpose. Children today are born because their parents want to satisfy a metaphysical, existential need. But if I were a child today, I would rather go down in a coal mine than be given the task of filling in someone's existential blanks, for that can drive you insane, which is worse than mere exhaustion.

But of course there is no choice. Almost all children are born into nuclear families as the culmination of some couple's efforts. A child is often indispensable if a relationship between two adults is to function and come to resemble what we—mistakenly—call a family. Two young people moving in together buy a lot of *things,* because things symbolize their having become a family. And in the same way that they buy a washing machine, they produce a child. The child symbolizes fellowship and family. The child is the marriage's justification and at the same time its hostage. It is used to create the illusion of family, although neither 2.8 nor 3.8 people can ever be a family. The child is offered up to an idea, an idea that says that the world has not changed and that the family pattern is divinely unalterable and eternal. The child is used to piece together a relationship or to give one (new) meaning. A child immediately lowers a veil of forgetfulness over the monotony of a two-person relationship. People have a child in order to produce a (happy) event. It is easily done. It requires no great creative talent, and yet the event is possibly the greatest in human existence. The only thing lacking is some handbook for the child: "How to survive and retain your sanity as an event."

The child is born, whatever the reasons, and we are father and mother. Naturally the child shall live where the rest of us live, in the suburban house or three-room apartment with kitchen and bath. Any expert can tell us that the child should have its own room from the age of two weeks, which is very interesting from a purely geographical point of view. It means that father and mother are supposed to live glued to each other in roughly the same space as the ten-inch child. A separate room for the new color TV is the more usual arrangement.

From the very first day of the child's life a remarkable relationship develops between the parents and the child—probably because we were once in a crowd, and now for the first time we are alone. We have produced a happy event to distract us from the daily grind. And how strange it is to see the two parents before the inarticulate infant, gooing and gurgling. . . . Two grown people taking the first available opportunity to fall back into childhood's patty-cake, and enjoying it inordinately. For there can be no doubt that the new toy enriches both their lives, just like a new appliance that everyone has to go over and touch—a wonderful novelty in the home. The parents have improved their lives. The child has no function as a separate individual. It has its identity and its right to existence only by virtue of the relationship its parents have to one another—or fail to have, a failing the child is now going to correct. The child is predestined to a labor of Sisyphus.

This worshipful, voyeuristic attitude of the parents toward the child is only partially the result of their being left alone with it. It is also due to the fact that from the moment mankind established nuclear families and entered the world of capitalism, we killed childhood in ourselves and did away with *homo ludens* once and for all. The adult, who has ceased to play, invariably elevates children to membership in a specially chosen, fanciful, elfin class. All adults want to give their children an unforgettably happy childhood so that they will have something to fall back upon—a thing they usually proceed to do. But every attempt to create this kind of an artificial paradise for the child is based on the parents' conviction that being an adult is hell. Whereas the child wants to grow up and make itself useful as quickly as possible (unless of course it has already discovered that it doesn't pay to be realistic), the parents, on the other hand, have a nostalgic desire to relive their own childhood, that whole golden age of innocence when the nipple was never far away and beefsteaks came floating through the air. As Shulamith Firestone writes in *The Dialectic of Sex*, "It is clear that the myth of childhood happiness flourishes so wildly not because it satisfies the needs of children but because it satisfies the needs of adults." Children are smothered in toys, kisses, and artificial consideration "because they're so sweet." The principle is that of camouflaged oppression or repressive tolerance, which women also experience. RESPECT for children (and women) is a curious phenomenon. It originated around the time of the Renaissance, and it was a necessity, once women and children were no longer naturally included in the functions of daily life. Little by little, they had come to comprise a special group, cut off from the activities of society. Thus we see the first children's clothing toward the end of the sixteenth century, while toys first appear in the seventeenth century. And baby talk—"patty-cake," "choochoo," "bowwow," "kittycat," "moo-cow," and so forth—arose in the same manner, in conjunction with the growth of the bourgeosie. Before the rise of the middle class, there were no bowwows and moo-cows and kittycats. There were only dogs and cows and cats—for adults and children alike.

"Childhood" became an ideology, whose purpose was to demonstrate that children were different from adults—not just in age, but in kind. Now that women and children had been separated from life functions, they became somehow "purer" than men, and as such they came to stand on a pedestal where they could lay claim to particular respect. To this day the news makes special mention of "women and children" in reporting accidents and acts of war, as if "women and children" were a particularly innocent race with some claim to exemption from the world's concerns. The My Lai massacre would never have appealed so strongly to world public opinion had it not involved "women and children."

This ideology of childhood, or philosophy of innocence—which also implied that children had a special, privileged affinity with God by virtue of their tender years (the little angels)—was in reality an expression of the fact that there was no longer anything *concrete* for children to do in the adult world, and that therefore their mere existence had to be ascribed some metaphysical significance. But the pat on the head that was to keep children three steps removed from life also meant, of course, that this little race had to consist of asexual creatures—just as women were supposed to be asexual. To acknowledge sexuality in children would be to hasten their entry into the adult world, and this transition had to be postponed at any cost, since society did not and still does not have any use for them. Children have no function and no legal rights, even though it is always the adult, of course, who is put behind bars for having a relationship with a minor. But this is because we refuse to regard children as seductive, or to recognize that they are capable of surviving a variety of "perverse" relationships without any particular injury aside from the trauma caused by hysterical adults. It is adults who have a use for the "purity" and "innocence" of children, for adults have lost the ability to conjoin with anything outside themselves.

Jules Henry has this to say about our culture's innocence-nostalgia:

> Helplessness, vulnerability, weakness, innocence, incomprehension and subjection to overwhelming urges seem to inhere in the biology of infancy (throughout history, somewhat the same characteristics have been attributed to women in our culture), but it does not follow that what looks inherent to us need be accepted by all people. (*Pathways to Madness*)

There are cultures, for example, where infants are considered veritable devils with cannibalistic tendencies, and where it is not good form to protect them. On the contrary, it is considered essential to drive out the evil spirits harbored by the little monsters!

Clearly, the adult attitude toward infants determines what sort of adults those infants will become. And the metaphysical point of view that defines children in our culture includes "incomprehension" as a fundamental element. A child understands nothing, and this infantile stupidity implies that a child can do no evil. We also believe that an infant is incapable of understanding our motives. The infant develops its image of our culture out of this particular type of confrontation with adults. Thus childhood is not merely a biological stage in the development of the organism but also a biosocial phenomenon subject to certain educational principles. These principles, which we absorb without realizing it, require the child to view the adult world in a certain way. If these principles are overstepped, we are beside ourselves. If we see a mother reasoning with her infant, it upsets us. "What in the world is wrong with her? She's talking to that baby as if it could understand. . . ."

This metaphysic of innocence has become a fundamental part of our ethical perspective and helps to define our relationships to people and nations. Expressions such as "aggression," "small defenseless country," and "aid to less fortunate nations" are all dependent on the innocence metaphysic. For several hundred years we have plundered "the helpless." "But they don't realize we're taking their gold," we say, or, "But they don't know what to do with it themselves." And now the big strong countries are afraid the little helpless countries will get hold of atom bombs, because "Are they capable of handling them properly?" The implication being that "*We* are adult enough to know what atom bombs are used for."

The mother has a remarkable power over the helpless child, which in turn becomes totally dependent on a person who is, as a rule, cut off from the rest of the world. Children learn their "place" in the universe from the people who care for them as infants. Here the foundation is laid for everything that will come later.

A mother whose authority is limited to the nursery will attach a greater emotional value to everything that happens within it than will the woman who also works outside the home, or the woman who, in years past, has had control of hired hands and servants and thus of recognized productive processes. A mother's power lies partially in the fact that she can disappoint her children more than they can disappoint her, that she can manipulate them, frighten them, and alter them to a greater degree than she can be forced to alter herself. This is the essence of all power, and for many women this power is not less attractive for being "secret."

But power is too dangerous a thing to leave in the hands of the powerful. It is forbidden to attack the traditional maternal role, but today we cannot even speak of a traditional maternal role, for it has been isolated from all other social roles, and the bond to the child occurs at the expense of all other outward bonds. Shulamith Firestone writes:

> The mother who wants to kill her child for what she has had to sacrifice for it (a common desire) learns to love that same child only when she understands that it is as helpless, as oppressed as she is, and by the same oppressor: then her hatred is directed outward, and "mother love" is born.
>
> (*The Dialectic of Sex*)

And:

> The child . . . senses that his mother is halfway between authority and helplessness. He can run to his father if his mother tries anything unjust; but if his father beats him there is little his mother can offer except tea and sympathy.

The socially castrated mother manipulates the child because she has a need to live vicariously, and, as Elizabeth Janeway points out,

> So many women come to see their families, or others to whom they are connected by bonds or affection, not as people but as implements to gain satisfactions that are purely selfish, satisfactions they cannot lay hands on honestly and directly if they are unable to act and feel for themselves. And if that is all they see, that is what they will teach their children. (*Man's World, Woman's Place*)

And then there is the father, not to be forgotten. He can always relieve the misery a bit—if he's around. But working and living conditions for a middle-class, nuclear-family father are such that he is not worth much when he gets home. Whereas the child always has a mother, of sorts, it must somehow struggle to achieve any sort of closeness with its father. This struggle is expressed in a variety of tactical maneuvers ranging from protest to terrified attempts to become invisible so as not to irritate the exhausted breadwinner. In little girls, the favorite tactic is usually to mount an offensive with erotic charm. The tragedy is that the children who never learn the proper tactics simply lose their fathers. And they cannot learn because their father's unavailability makes them angry and desperate, which in turn puts the father even further out of reach. The middle-class father is the alligator in the glass cage that we throw coins at in a desperate attempt to get a reaction. And even if not all the children of alligator fathers become mentally deranged, nevertheless Jules Henry suggests an intrinsic connection between unavailable, unresponsive fathers and their autistic children. The father, with his psychological absence, represents the autistic *idea*, and the child reacts by becoming unresponsive itself—once and for all. There is nothing we can upbraid the father with; we cannot even claim that he has failed, for there is some question as to whether it is even possible to be a father in our culture.

Jules Henry puts it this way:

> How can any middle-class man in our culture build a life for his family? Aren't there middle-class men oriented toward *death-in-a-career* instead? Aren't business and the professions mostly a matter of dog-eat-dog or, at best, a matter of getting ahead while dying to one's self? . . . So, since our society seems to create the conditions for separation of the middle-class father and child rather than for their union, the relationship of these fathers to their children puzzles me, and though there are many "warm, good" fathers, they seem improbable.
> (*Pathways to Madness*)

Just as Homo sapiens is an improbable result of all the chemical processes that produced life on earth, so too all the factors required to create a *father* are of such a nature that in our culture a good one must appear unlikely.

It is not only their careers, but also the very "ideology" of the nuclear family—if we can speak of such a thing—that keeps good fathers from coming into being. Career and nuclear family are so closely connected that they tread on one another's heels, for the business of "caring for your family" is regarded as an absolutely watertight and noble excuse for raking in all the money you can lay your hands on. Greed may be a sin, and exploiting other human beings or having unduly sharpened elbows is no longer thought to be a pretty sight, but who can blame a man for wanting to do "the best he can for his children"? Thus providing for the nuclear family serves to justify, in fact to catalyze, the psychological atomization of the husband, which in its extreme form prevents any kind of family life worth mentioning. The degree to which material satisfaction is linked to love in our culture is remarkable. The man who cannot provide for his family cannot love his family. We occasionally acknowledge that the family is held together by bonds that are stronger than loyalty and devotion, that is, bonds of economic necessity—which every woman knows already. Expressions such as "family solidarity" and "security" are clichés and are used very loosely. Eventually it becomes difficult for most people to tell the difference between love and money. But when we cut through the security talk, we can usually spot a fat bank account, two cars in the garage, and a house with a garden and a hedge. If you talk to an unemployed man or to a woman from the slums, the "security of family life" takes on a rather different meaning.

I don't say that all fathers and mothers are worthless. No two are alike, and heaven knows a lot of them are very nice people. I say only that all of them have one thing in common—the same cultural conditioning. And neither the mother's isolation nor the father's profession promotes the love that has now become the whole basis for the child's upbringing. And what's worse: simple love is not good enough—it has been turned into an educational program. We are constantly being told that "a child must have love to feel secure," or that some child "did not receive the love he needed from his parents" and so became a bank robber or a lesbian or a schizophrenic—or, I almost said, a Jew. Love and tenderness have come to have the same significance as vitamins, or a course in child care, or the university education we ought to get, or the latest film we ought to see. If only we are given adequate doses of security, knowledge, and love, then mankind will be happy and life will involve no risks. But in that case, if that's the way life's going to be, then deliver us from love. For my own part, I would rather have a hit on the head.

Fortunately, however, this is a kind of love that very

few children are given. For adults have become so powerless in their confrontation with the technocracy that of all the people they come into regular contact with, only children seem to be weaker than they are themselves. And so it has become normal for parents to fight their children—without meaning to, of course—out of pure desperation at never being able to struggle with the forces that hold them down. There is no reason to elaborate on the outright cruelties that parents perpetrate on their children—mothers who give them baths in boiling water or choke them with mashed potatoes, and so on. We need only point out that in this society, which depends so heavily on cruelty and repression and which finds rational grounds for training soldiers and fighter pilots, it would be pure *coincidence* if cruelty were not also found within the four walls of the home.

The problem is not so much the cruelty in itself, but the fact that cruelty is in conflict with our ideals, with our expectation that parents will love their children. This conflict affects the middle class in particular and leads inevitably to hypocrisy, because very few middle-class parents are prepared to admit that they do not love their children. I have seen working-class parents throw stones at their children, but I don't think those kids necessarily suffer as much as the middle-class youngsters who are the constant victims of hypocrisy. Jules Henry writes that ". . . when parents do not love a child and conceal this fact while trying to act as if they did love him, a condition is given for madness. This takes us into the deep underground of sham." (*Pathways to Madness*) And also, "To get along in life without too much misery one must at every moment be able to manage sham; this is the essence of being middle-class."

Sham, he says,

> is the expression in action of alienated vulnerability between people who cannot get away from each other. . . .
>
> A culture like ours, which heavily rewards the capacity for sham, must also produce a pathology of sham, whose symptoms range from the smiling masks of the perfectly normal people next door ("You never know *what* Mrs. Figbert is thinking") to schizophrenia. In between are the uncountable miserable ones who "don't know who or what they are."

This is, roughly speaking, the psychological climate of the nuclear family, the child's starting point in life. We don't know what to do with our children, but fortunately it's not up to us, for the educators tell us that children ought to be free to determine their own lives. What a relief! Today's children pass directly from the gurgling distraction, plaything, happy-event stage to a stage called "You work that out for yourself, you're a big boy (girl) now."

The old farm family we're so tired of hearing about could offer contact with eighteen or twenty people, large areas to move in, and work just as soon as the child showed the first signs of being able to handle it. Children's abilities were turned to the interests of the group, so that right from the outset they had some idea of what they were living for. The family gave them a destiny. Many people in the course of history have turned down this destiny, of course. And this has led, among other things, to industrialization and the spread of the wage-earning class, which has turned the family into a 3.8-person, four-hundred-square-foot battlefield without central values, where children are born without purpose, without fellowship, without freedom of movement, and without a destiny.

True, the society at large offers children more things

than ever before—movies, exciting streets, and later on the genius of science and technology. Theoretically, too, children have a chance to learn about the world they live in, but only within the family do they learn about THEMSELVES. Even their experience of the world outside seems, in practice, to be problematic, for as a rule children have no opportunity to observe the world directly but are relegated to having it explained by their mothers, who often know very little about it. Even when their fathers help, there is no natural, relaxed way for children to learn about the world of work—the world their fathers are shunted into every morning. In the old days, work was carried on publicly. A smithy, a shipyard, a farm, and so forth, were places where work was performed as well as demonstrated. Nowadays, most work is "secret." A child can't simply run down to Burmeister & Wain and be initiated into the secrets of technology. (Maybe this is because the machines are too dangerous, but in that case adults shouldn't have to deal with them either.) Even if your father takes you along to the office one day, your experience of the working world remains pretty abstract. The child is not only isolated *from* one world, it is isolated *into* another. All of the tasks given to a child relate exclusively to the home. Straighten up your room, pick up your toys, help with the wash, take out the garbage, and so on.

But then at some point comes the blessing known as SCHOOL. Parents are delighted, of course, for what would they do with their children otherwise?

School as we know it today arose in conjunction with the invention of childhood, and it became the institution that was to confirm the segregation of children as a separate race. Medieval schools gave individual instruction on the apprentice principle, in all practical subjects, and they were open to people of all ages. The establishment of

The children don't really have one either, al-
looks that way to the parents. In reality it is
war between two persons, between the wage
l his children. And the only place they got to
other—was in the family.
ıeration gap is as old as Methuselah and Tur-
t all the previous youthful rebellions in history
:ed by a desire to *go into society* and alter it.
er from the old, yes, indeed, but not stand out-
shoot at Father and Mother—that would be
ıt that level of absurdity has now been reached.
oday slam the door and set out to battle Mom
It's an odd phenomenon. . . . They turn to drugs,
ə, to flying saucers—it makes no difference—for
how they choose to become "delinquent," their
s an unequivocal symptom of the nuclear fam-
petence at raising kids.
claim that people should stop having children.
say that the nuclear family is incapable of pre-
ldren for the world—because it does not know

ldren of wage earners have been liberated from
er destiny, which lay in the soil, and have been
ir "freedom" instead. But this freedom would
əal if we lived in small, airtight plastic cabins.
em is that we still live together—more or less.
reality behind this facade of freedom is *imper-
hority and the absence of all individuality*. A
acher wrote this letter to a mother:

ıot getting along too well at school. He holds his
cely in several areas, but his social adjustment
been as good as it ought to be. He is in the habit
ing with one or two friends—and now and then
ıs to enjoy being by himself. . . .

modern schools, the kind we have today, suggests a systematic devaluation of children's capacities.

But even though some teachers today are terribly clever, and even though school has a positive function for many children in that it gives them a chance to get away from home, the fact remains that any child's most important learning period occurs *prior* to its fifth birthday. And during this period the child is consigned, as a rule, to the nuclear family. The child can learn about the world later on, but it learns what it IS within the intimate framework of the family, which exercises no conscious influence because it has nothing concrete on its mind, neither work nor ideas, but which involves emotional bonds that are exclusive and absolute, even when they can't be satisfied. The child's attitude toward the mighty world outside is entirely dependent on what the family can offer in the way of excitement, and it can usually do no more than report that the gross national product has risen by 2.4 percent in such and such a period. And no one can live on that. In the final analysis, we derive a certain happiness in having a purpose in life, and here the nuclear family can only offer itself as a goal. And then the parents are surprised when the kid drops out of the whole mess and decides to become, say, a dope addict. (Since we think of children as innocent victims, we refuse to believe that they can become addicts on purpose—another underestimation of their insight and understanding.)

All right, but is childhood in the minifamily really THAT awful? It is quite possible that twelve-year-olds could not tell us if we asked them, for they know no other childhood and have no experience of any other life-style. But we do get the hint of an answer from the way these children who grew up in the 3.8-person battleground behave later on, when they have slammed the door and left home.

We call it youthful rebellion and the generation gap.

Most children, of course, will get through life on middle-class terms, with hyprocrisy as their protective shield. But many of them, the best people, the ones who would like to unfold, will not be able to cope. These are the social "losers," the ones who refuse to succeed as long as things are the way they are. The ones who refuse to be socially well-adjusted.

A lot of children today are on the verge of death or some other kind of destruction in hospitals all around us. They are merely the nuclear family's waste products—or so we can call them to keep from having to mention blood, which sounds so sad.

If society is to function—and a society must always function, that goes without saying—then in my opinion we might just as well stop having kids. Since the Western world has no use for children, it seems to me that we ought to be consistent and abolish them completely once and for all. In the long run, too, it would save us a lot of money.

11 Ah, Knitwear...

It is several years now since pornography came and closed our mouths and ran away with our bodies in the name of liberation.

But never mind. Time will show whether our own wings are not stronger than the plastic ones pornography excels in. I hope and believe that everything will come out all right in the end, despite the inevitable male trump card in any discussion of women's lib, namely, "What's to become of fucking after the revolution?"

And yet the question is a good one, and deserves an answer. Although no one knows what is going to happen, we can still guess, and my guess is that nothing will happen. Because no revolution will ever succeed, and there will be no change in our erotic behavior nor in the relations between the sexes, unless there is first a change in our sexual fantasies.

It is possible, of course, that some revolutionaries have very attractive, generous, humane, and affectionate erotic fantasies. But I do not. I don't rule out the possibility that there are people who can use *Das Kapital* as a masturbatory stimulus and who can have orgasms at the thought of all humanity marching hand in hand beneath red banners to the strains of the "Internationale." But I cannot. What's worse, the fantasies I do have are very unhealthy, and I can't figure out what I'm going to do with them when the revolution comes. For my fantasies are not one whit revolutionary—on the contrary.

To be precise, what we are dealing with in my case is one single erotic fantasy. It has been with me for a long time, and it is always the same without variation—except for one time when I had an orgasm thinking about making love to a splendid imaginary son. Perhaps in real life he would turn down the opportunity, but since he doesn't exist, I can hardly be said to have done anyone any harm. I was very pleased with myself at having increased my repertoire with this new fantasy—but it never amounted to more than the one single episode.

Otherwise, my masturbatory images are eternally the same. And although God knows I don't find them the least bit dull, I would like to know how I'm supposed to adapt to a freer and more sensual society when all I can muster is one single fantasy—and that of the very worst sort.

Well, all right. It goes like this. . . . I sort of turn into a man. There, I've said it. But I don't lose my woman's body, or else nothing doing. It's all in my mind—I identify, as they say. It works like this: Men (preferably not college educated) expose themselves to me, and masturbate, and I cannot escape the sight (thank heaven). It usually happens on the street or in an alley, in doorways and stairwells, or on a bus or down by the waterfront. A man sits down beside me on the bus, say, and whispers something obscene and starts to masturbate, and I always ride two or three stops too far in pure fascination. Don't ask me how the other passengers react, because that has nothing to do with it. And don't ask me how I manage to accompany all those men into all those doorways and stairwells, because the fact is I always just happen to be on the spot when the man exposes himself. He never touches me, partly because he's the type who wouldn't dare, and partly because it would only delay the orgasm—this is a purely voyeuristic relationship. I'm always incredibly elegantly dressed in this fantasy, and he always insinuates something to the effect that I'm a little slut, and what's worse, that I *like* being a little slut. I never contradict him, because to tell the truth I never say anything in my fantasy —I'm always as silent as a post. But I identify with the man to the extent that I myself cease to exist and little by little I become him . . . and in fact his orgasm becomes my own. It is always a particular type of man, a type I'll never actually meet, partly because there is something called class differences, but even more because I don't find them sexually exciting in the usual sense of the word. They're good only in fantasies. It could, for example, be the crabby owner of an ice-cream stand. Or a bankrupt sales manager wearing a windbreaker. They are usually fifty to sixty years old, balding, a little seedy and decrepit. Life has not been easy on them. Maybe my fantasy *will* get through the revolution uncensured, since after all I do identify with somewhat *downtrodden* men. I swear they're never rich and *never* powerful—scout's honor! My fantasy is directed at anxious men who never dare touch me, men who have always been stepped on by their bosses, and that sort of thing. Although I have to admit I can also use an ill-mannered junior executive with glasses and a white nylon shirt and a three-piece suit. To say nothing of a sweaty, traveling, knitwear salesman with an expense account and a light blue Anglia. The important thing is that they're all rather stupid-looking—not terribly bright. My masturbatory images exclude any kind of sympathy, and so of course my fantasy has to be classified among the unhealthy ones. It involves an undeniable misuse of other human beings; there is no trace of a "human" relationship; I don't care about them one bit, in fact they frighten me a little. My relations to them are built on a mixture of contempt, fear, and fascination. This constellation is well-known from male attitudes toward women, nor would I rule out the possibility—in fact I'm sure of it—that my fantasy is the heritage of a six-thousand-year-old masculine society. But all the same it is delicious, my fantasy—even if it isn't anything to brag about.

Now some people may say that fantasies and dreams don't matter, since all you can do with them anyway is to keep them to yourself—so that no one will discover what you're really like at heart. Which may be very smart. Although not in the long run, for mischief will always out somewhere. Even in the new society. Sooner or later, all the pillars of the revolution who don't have their dreams in order will come to grief. Sooner or later, someone will come up and say, "What did you dream about last night?" or "What were you thinking about last time you got your rocks off?" And in the final analysis, it is here that power must stand or fall, according to whether these dreams serve oppression, mediocrity, cruelty, or whether they have the capacity to save us from them. . . . The revolutionary king whose fantasies include a white derriere in a black corset tied to a lamppost—his head will inevitably roll. And then we can start all over again . . . on another revolution.

I know nothing about the erotic fantasies of either Stalin or Hitler, but my guess is that most of us would nod in recognition. However lacking they may have been in charm, those fantasies, they were probably not especially startling, since they can't have been out of keeping with their other ideals.

But now take women. Take, for example, the women

who, by present-day standards, have to be regarded as "liberated." What do they dream about, aside from equal pay for equal work? Maybe some of them don't dream at all. Others, perhaps, dream about things they have no wish to dream about, because they conflict with their social convictions and egalitarian philosophy. These latter women are in trouble.

But the former, the ones who don't dream and are not burdened with sexual fantasies of any kind, are in even worse trouble. Masters and Johnson, among others, have discovered that female frigidity is not entirely due to "technically" inadequate partners, but also to the fact that women in our society suffer from a lack of erotic "pictures"—sexual focus. There is nothing very remarkable about this, since the erotic pictures in this society are painted by men, and women have had to find a place in these pictures as best they could. There is no female parallel to the stimuli used to arouse masculine drives. Women have unconsciously had to adapt their fantasies to fit male fantasies in order to attract a reasonable amount of fornication. Imagine a woman with nettles in her hair leaping about in the trees shrieking in heat. Such a woman has no decent chance today of being mounted. She is more likely to be considered somewhat overwrought, which frightens most men and makes them impotent. Of course no one has ever actually forbidden women to define their own fantasies, but for some mysterious reason they have been slow to do so. Or maybe for a very good reason: fear of being burned at the stake. The kindling for a nice witch-burning has never been far out of reach. Virginia Woolf writes, "The first—killing the angel in the house—I think I solved. She died. But the second, telling the truth about my experiences as a body, I do not think I solved. I doubt that any woman has solved it as yet." And Alfred C. Kinsey states that among the vast numbers of unpublished amateur documents he has seen in the course of his work, he was able to find only three manuscripts written by women that contained erotic elements of the kind commonly found in documents written by men.

The women who suffer from this lack of erotic images do not need to suffer at all, and they are not necessarily cold; they can be terribly affectionate deep down. But they can't get free of themselves, for very few people can experience orgasm in a vacuum—a pictureless room—merely by stroking someone's hair. I don't say that all women with erotic fixations invariably lie there thinking about giant orangutans in raincoats and rubber boots as they embrace their lovers. But they do have to think about something or other every now and then, especially when they're alone, and it is usually something recurrent.

The problem is that we can't (yet) produce a sexual fantasy the same way we can produce a good idea. Very few people can muster an orgasm at the thought of columbine or the teachings of Buddha, however much they might like to. (The fact that we can't, I think, merely shows that we're not entirely sane.) But we cannot choose our erotic images in accordance with our ideals—nor can we pull them out of thin air. A fixation, an erotic fantasy, is always linked to the past, and even if a person has had the healthiest and happiest childhood imaginable, he or she can still grow up with the most revolting fantasies. For they are inherited from and frozen deeply into our culture, which, however magnificent we may consider it, is undeniably cruel and unloving, that is to say—in the broadest sense of the word—*unerotic*. And we cannot free ourselves from that culture completely—no more than we can free ourselves from our parents, even when they are insufferable.

And so a lot of good women lie in bed dreaming about things that are very bad. As liberated a woman as Nora, for example (whom I was just reading about in a magazine), doesn't dare talk about her fantasy in detail. She told a psychiatrist once—he was the only person in her life who knew anything about it—and was very relieved when one day she saw his death announcement in the paper. It made her "free" again. However she does reveal this much, that at the conclusion of her fantasy she is dominated by some men who rip the clothes from her body. They stare at her in their faceless way and grow wild with desire and tear off all her clothes. It is marvelous, apparently. In her erotic fantasies, no one ever loves her for her mind or her good ideas. She swears that in reality there is nothing she wants less than to be dominated. And I believe her. But her fantasy is hardly an uncommon one, neither among women, nor, in its mirror image, among men. The problem is, how shall all those of us who are stuck with the standard clichés—feminine/masculine, subordinate/dominant, masochistic/sadistic—ever adapt to a less prurient but more desirable and ideal and egalitarian world? How are we ever going to break loose from the rubbish we grew up with, which, at the same time, we associate with feelings of the most intense pleasure? How will we ever get our fantasies to live up to what we actually want from life?

Of course we could be consistent, like some people I know who have abolished their unhealthy fantasies for the sake of the future. My hat is off to them. But when I asked them what they had instead, and they answered, "Nothing," I thought to myself, No, then I guess I'd really rather have a sick fantasy than no fantasy at all.

But frankly I did go so far as to consider whether it might not be possible to push the ice-cream vendor, the ex-sales manager, the knitwear salesman, and all the other apparitions into the background a little—by living out my fantasy in real life. I hoped that it might give rise to some new and less unhealthy fantasies—after all, variety is the spice of life.

Now I realize perfectly well that not everyone has the privilege of living out his or her fantasies in concrete terms. But since my propensities fortunately tended neither toward arson nor murder, all I had to do was send for one of the gentlemen in question, which I decided to do. By advertisement, very businesslike and *comme il faut,* as is the custom these days.

I received nearly fifty applications in response to my carefully formulated advertisement but had to eliminate over forty of them out of hand as being from more or less congenial people who were looking for what we call sex. This was very friendly and human of them, and therefore utterly uninteresting. It was not a well-meaning deposit of white semen in the womb that I sought but rather an anonymous slather of dark seed in the face. For everything is so unreal when all you know is the bodies of your own social class. Still, I didn't intend to get to know the unknown on intimate terms but just to *see* the apparition in real life for once. I guess I also showed a certain puerile disregard for the law that says we may never look God in the face.

I chose a wrinkled old man; that is to say, I couldn't see his face in the photo—it faded out in the darkness, which suited me perfectly. But his erection and the chintz covers in the background indicated that I was on the right track. He gave a kiosk on Vesterbro as his return address.

The day he was scheduled to come I was so scared I was ready to go out and buy a ticket to Rome with a rubber check. But that would have been shabby of me. No, I simply had to go through with it. I sat on the bus about four o'clock that afternoon, looking at the men on their way home from work. Some of them were carrying those plastic cases they made twenty years ago when they still didn't know how to imitate leather. I wondered if maybe he might have a plastic case like that, or maybe plastic shoes with pointed toes. Maybe he was sitting there on that very bus, without my knowing it. It felt strange, but not wrong, to be prepared for anyone at all. I suddenly remembered my cat and it scared me, for what if it started to meow when he went for his fly, or if it clawed at his trouser leg and hissed . . . that would spoil everything. . . . And what was I going to *say* to him? I never talk in my fantasy. . . . Well, maybe the time had come to learn to keep my mouth shut—for an hour.

I got home a couple of hours before he was supposed to come and I started to vacuum. I was playing Tchaikovsky on the tape deck. No, I thought, not *Eugene Onegin*, that's not right. . . . But what would be right? What kind of music is appropriate when a stranger comes to jack off? In the end I turned off the tape deck and most of the lights so his face wouldn't hurt my eyes, and I put on my friend Jean's long, green velvet queen's costume that she wore in a Gombrowicz play. Perfect. It might frighten him a little, but that would only make us even, at least at the start. At the last moment I wound a turban around my head, because I didn't want him to see my hair.

There was a short ring on the bell and when I opened the door, there stood a withered, balding little man with glasses, wearing an ordinary sport coat, a tie, and a white shirt—the kind of man who would otherwise be a Jehovah's Witness or an encyclopedia salesman—the kind of man you would normally slam the door in the face of. He stuck out his hand and introduced himself as Benny Nissen. He was perfect, and I wished I could fall dead on the spot. It is almost more than you can bear to shake hands with your own private apparition.

I asked him if he would like a whiskey, and since he

looked confused I hurried to apologize for not having any beer, but "whiskey would be quite all right"—he seemed overwhelmed at being offered anything at all.

He sat on the edge of his chair, holding his glass in one hand and petting the cat with the other. Well, so he was a decent person—but that was exactly what he mustn't be. . . . The cat liked him, which was not a good sign. . . .

"You have a lot of unusual things," he glanced around.

"Yes . . . well . . . I like them. . . ."

"I had a couple of old carriage lamps one time, you know, but I sold them. Only got a hundred crowns. It was dumb of me. They came from my father's farm and I could have got a lot more for them today. . . ."

"Yes, you have to hold onto things. I mean prices go up all the time. . . ."

"Yes."

"But of course you can hold onto too much junk . . ."

"Yes. . . . But still I shouldn't have sold them so cheap. Same thing with three old iron telephones I had, antiques, with wood dials, you know. . . ."

"You sold those too?"

"Yes."

"Oh."

He put down his glass and picked up an elephant-hair bracelet that was lying on the table and asked me if I knew that elephants were plant-eating animals. I'd never thought about it, but he had once had the job of feeding bamboo to some elephants on a freighter from Africa. Now he was a subway checker—one of those men who come and stick you with a 25-crown fine if you've forgotten to stamp your ticket. He couldn't be better. If only he'd go. I didn't want him to have anything to do with my fantasies. I just wanted to get him to leave, any way I could—except by asking him. . . .

He asked me where the toilet was, and I pointed with one hand, refilling my whiskey glass with the other. So he was planning to stay. Oh, no!

I sat there on the sofa, trembling, and watched him walk back into the room with his prick out of his pants. How dare he, in *my* living room. . . . He walked across the room and stopped right in front of me. I don't know what he was thinking, for I didn't dare look at his face, but the thing rose higher and higher and grew more and more rigid and got big and fat and quivering right in front of my eyes. The foreskin was still down around the tip, so only a little round circle of red meat peeked out with a drop of moisture on the point. He waved it up and down in front of my face. I sat very still with a cigarette in one hand and gripping the back of the sofa with the other so I wouldn't pass out. He just kept on standing there, forever and ever, like a giant red exclamation point.

"It's very pretty," I whispered.

"I'm glad you like it."

I scratched it very gently with the nails of the hand in which I was holding my cigarette. He wasn't the least bit afraid I would burn him, and he had no cause to be, because it was gorgeous and I was so happy sitting there looking at it and thinking about all the ugly old men on the street whom you don't know, and how beautiful they are, and how you never get to know them, and how crazy it all is, and he asked me if he could take his clothes off and I said the pants, and he pushed me back on the bed and the whole thing was all wrong because I wasn't going to get close to him, and he knelt down in front of my face and sometimes it hit my cheeks and sometimes it slid into my wet mouth and he pushed it all over my head and up in my hair and down my throat and started pulling at my nipples and boring his fingers up in my pussy and poked at my womb while his prick swept my face and in and out of my mouth, and then he started whacking it off and my whole body throbbed at the thought that pretty soon it would erupt—"Now you're going to get it," he whispered—and it flooded out over my face in several pumping spurts. I put my hands in the warm seed and rubbed it wildly into my skin until my hair was wet at the temples and it burned my eyes.

"Was that good?" he asked.

"Yes, that was lovely. You'll have to excuse me if I seem a little distant; it's only because I can't see you—my eyes are stinging."

"That's quite all right."

Then he stepped out to wash up, and I had survived. When he came back and sat down to finish his drink, he was once again a wizened old ticket checker from the Danish State Railways.

"Well, I hope you found that as satisfying as I did."

"Yes, thank you, I did indeed."

He said it was a good thing to know what you liked. I envied him his simplicity.

And it was a simple old man who gave me his hand in farewell. "I'm always at your service, anytime."

And that, dear reader, was the end of that. I did say hello to my apparition, I acted out my fantasy and had my dream brought to life—although the whole thing suffered from too much cordiality and intimacy and, what's worse, the man had a face. Faces and eyes are simply not compatible with your hard, metallic, misanthropic, alienated fantasy. Faces are one of the most upsetting things in the world. It could never be the same as it had been in my imagination.

Mais je ne regrette rien. A lot of good came out of it. For example, my relations to the State Railways were much improved—I mean, my relationship to the people sitting on the trains. I no longer find them quite so frightening; in fact I'm not afraid to look them right in the eye. But as far as the fantasy itself is concerned, I still have it. Exactly the same as always. In fact, as I now know, it's at its very best when it remains a fantasy, without a face—as I'm sure any psychologist could have told me beforehand. But of course they always know everything beforehand. The rest of us mortals have to pick our way along by trial and error, and I now realize better than all the experts put together that my fantasy will pursue me to the funeral chapel. And I say God bless it, and me, poor sinner that I am.

For even though I'm not very proud of mine, I don't believe people can ever free themselves of their fantasies. Because even if we repress them in keeping with our finest convictions, we can hardly free ourselves from the thinking and the thousand-year-old expectations that created them, that is, from everything that lies behind the images.

In all probability, our dreams and fantasies would be different in a different sort of society, but how can people with fantasies like ours ever really change society? To put it bluntly, we have to change our dreams in order to change our feelings. But even if clever heads decide on brainwashing or seven years of psychoanalysis in an attempt to anticipate the new order and prepare themselves for a fresh start, what will become of the apparitions of the past? Will a different social structure be able to force our ghosts into haunting us only in the cafeteria at lunchtime? In another, more fruitful society where women have equal rights, where their identities and status are independent of men's, where the masculine/feminine syndrome ceases to dictate a checkmate between the two sexes, much of this absurd business of keeping life at arm's length will be abolished. But not all of it. For there will still be a library around the corner, and in it all of *literature.*

Feminist Ti Grace Atkinson was once asked what would happen to literature after the revolution, and her answer was, "What difference does it make?"

But it does make a difference. For even though a lot of people will undoubtedly write very instructive books about princesses who refuse to have chambermaids out of a moral aversion for the exploitation of the working class, nevertheless, little girls of the future will probably go right on reading about Cinderella and all the others who achieve final happiness in the form of a prince. Sleeping Beauty will lie there on her back for hundreds of years—with one eye open and occasionally scratching her butt—waiting patiently for the juicy prince with the big sword—the ultimate salvation.

So unless we go in for massive, systematic book burning, there just aren't going to be any great revolutionary changes in the pattern of sexual roles. Women will continue to be split into an intellectual desire for equality and an emotional need for the opposite, and men will continue as best they can in the same ambivalence and silly dualism, with the same notion of a sharp distinction between nature and culture, instinct and morality, body and soul, devil and god, love and work. Of course it isn't really very funny. But then it isn't boring either, as long as you take the whole thing with a grain of salt.

In one way I'm resigned to letting pleasure get the better of principle. For I would rather live on my back than die on my feet, as it were. And although in many ways I am an advocate of freedom—free opportunity and free choice and free association and free lunch—in erotic terms I tend to let things slide. I admit that this is not a very revolutionary point of view, but if I haven't compromised myself too badly with my reactionary fantasies, and if there should be someone, somewhere who could use me to paste up posters or join in a song, I am free of charge and completely at his or her disposal. As the old man said, "I'm always at your service, anytime."

12 Prohibition

One day in October, 1972, I read in a French weekly about two events that seemed to throw new light on the relationship between mankind and the natural world—culture versus nature. The fact is that they no longer seem to be antagonistic. About forty scientists from various disciplines gathered at a conference at Royaumount, organized by the sociologist Edgar Morin under the auspices of the CEBIAF (Centre International d'Etudes Bioanthropologiques et d'Anthropologie Fondamentale), and by the end of their meeting mankind had, as it were, been incorporated into nature. Among other things, they established that the vast majority of living creatures—not just human beings—have built social organizations and live in societies, and that the pre-ecological notion that places humanity as an unchanging factor at the "center" of the cosmos, separated from nature by the thought process or brain, is no longer valid. Biologists, anthropologists, sociologists, and psychologists were all agreed that even the human brain and "thought" were integrated parts of the ecosystem, and that nature is a historical culture that includes humanity as one of its determining factors. Thus "Man against Nature" or "Culture vs. Nature" are ideologically loaded expressions of mankind's need to assert its individuality or dissimilarity in order to make it easier to dominate and subdue everything not strictly categorized as human.

The second event, anthropologist Serge Moscovici's book *La Société contre Nature* (the title is ironic), also seems to support the supposition that human societies have a predisposition for hierarchical thinking, which, of course, always places what is nonhuman at the bottom of the hierarchy. It is not so very long, for example, since anthropologists tried to prove that blacks were closer to apes, that is, closer to nature, than whites, and there is still a widespread notion that women are more "earthbound" and more "natural" then men. There have even been attempts to measure women's brains to see if they weren't smaller. "Natural," in other words, has been used to designate those things males have striven, with varying results, to dominate.

But for me, the most crucial part of Moscovici's book was his theory of the incest taboo as the original discriminatory mechanism in sexual relations, and as the basic prerequisite for both social inequality and male domination of women—the incest prohibition as the pillar of patriarchy.

The essence of the incest-prohibiting mechanism is *to make distinctions.* To distinguish, for example, between those you may marry and those you may not. The instant you grasp the distinction between two phenomena, you begin to treat them differently. According to Moscovici, every social order reflects a sexual hierarchy, and our masculine society was created and upheld by the incest prohibition, especially as it applies to the mother/son relationship, the only universal incest taboo. This prohibition is the prerequisite for male dominance, because otherwise sons would remain with their mothers and form a different group, a feminine hierarchy, and male power would disintegrate.

Suddenly I saw the whole problem of sexual roles in the light of the incest prohibition. In *The Dialectic of Sex,* Shulamith Firestone writes, "I submit that the only way that the Oedipus Complex can make full sense is in terms of power." Since the essence of the incest taboo is sexual discrimination, and since its implication is a power struggle between the sexes, why not simply abolish the prohibition?

Why are we always talking about the tip of the iceberg, the cutting edge, the symptoms of social inequality and female oppression? Why not strike at the root of the evil, the PROHIBITION itself, instead of merely picking peevishly at the enervating consequences of this lopsided distribution of power?

We worship the dream of a just and egalitarian society. Some of our cleverer intellectuals—the ones who have taken the flesh and made it back into words—have begun to realize that such a world is an impossibility, because the very *language* prevents us from envisioning it. But I suspect that on the day parents began to love their children, mothers their sons, and fathers their daughters, we would find the words. . . . A language would arise.

At present, we talk about equality but are disgusted at the thought of incest. Incest isn't even expressly forbidden. That's not necessary, for the ban is transmitted osmotically through our pores. In every family with brothers and sisters, the first person to show up on puberty's horizon is an individual you must love but not make love to. Everyone knows this, without its having to be explained. What this means to a grown man is that the person he is most closely bound to all his life, namely his mother, is the very person who, in physical terms, inspires the greatest degree of disgust and loathing. The very thought of a sexual relationship with his mother is enough to give almost any man the creeps, even if he loves her. We are aware of the fact that most men marry women who represent the mothers with whom they never achieved a complete relationship, in order that they themselves can become children again. It is not all that uncommon for men to call their wives "mother" or "my old lady." The incest ban in mother/son relationships means that boys never really grow up to be independent male beings, but are arrested in their development, castrated, turned into patchworks of desire and contempt for women. All their lives they pursue a mother's embrace—the total closeness to woman which seduced them from the very beginning, when the bonds of love were absolute, but which was simultaneously denied them by the incest prohibition. Such men are the lifelong victims of an infantile desire to return to the womb—a desire that stands in the way of any kind of give-and-take between the sexes, because one of them, the female sex, is predestined to be the object of a "metaphysical" male yearning. Masculine society's soothing lullaby and sedative—pornography—reflects the howling of the male infant for the teat.

The incest taboo is probably the most fundamental cause of our society's genital fixation, in that the bodily parts excluded from the context of daily life become the objects of worship and obsession. Sexual organs, distinct from the universe, become criteria in themselves. Men become strangers to women because of the incest prohibition, and this gives rise to the alienated female roles that are assigned to women according to the state of their wombs (mother or nonmother) or the degree of their availability (mother/wife or whore)—the ones men may go to bed with and the ones they may not. Of course no child dreams actively of sexual intercourse with its mother, but the exclusion of all genital contact means that conscious awareness of communication and contact eventually comes to focus upon the sexual organs.

It was Freud who asked the famous question, "What do women want?" The answer is that, in all probability, men would know what women wanted if they had not been cut off all along from woman as a totality—and thus from the female within themselves. Shulamith Firestone writes, "As a result of their battle to reject the female in themselves (the Oedipus Complex as we have explained it) they are unable to take love seriously as a cultural matter . . ." (*The Dialectic of Sex*) The standing phrase "*merely* sexual" (used mostly by men but to some extent adopted by women) is a discriminatory designation for those relationships that involve sexuality, as opposed to the relationship with the mother, in which one may not respond sexually and which therefore ranks higher on the emotional scale.

The mother is the first person the child gets to know and the person from whom it learns that the emotional bond is absolute while the sexual bond is taboo. The child discovers that in order to earn its mother's love it must repress its sexuality and distinguish sexual feelings from all others. Thus love is divided right from the beginning into a polarity between sexual love and that love which is "higher" and "indefinable," between Eros and Agape, between flesh and spirit. This nonsense forms the basis for one additional misery in the human condition—the fact that we can never be one with ourselves, or with anyone else either, that is, the fact of our much sung and incurable loneliness.

It is an open question whether elimination of the incest ban—or rather, whether the creation of alternative lifestyles not determined by that ban the way the nuclear family is—would automatically result in a culture of galloping incest. . . . By the same token, it is an open question whether incestuous relationships between mothers and sons would result in more or less mother fixation than most men suffer from already. Experience indicates, however, that "unrequited" love is the most traumatic, that we are fettered more by love relationships that were never consummated than by those that were. It stands to reason, of course, that as long as children are conceived in and born from the wombs of women, that it will also be woman's task to see to the child's independence and make it capable of growing away from her and out into the world. But everything indicates that the incest prohibition simply does not have the liberating character necessary to free the child. On the contrary. And the proof is that our language contains a phrase called "mother fixation," which in practice involves everything from the fear to the hatred of women. Mother fixation is not the result of incestuous relationships, but of the incest ban, that is, of relationships that are traumatic and unfulfilled.

This traditional, almost universal prohibition has taught us to accept as natural a state of affairs where our human psychophysical possibilities are never realized. The dream of a larger community will not enable us to abolish the core of society, the family, overnight, but within the four walls of our own homes we can all abolish the sexual taboo necessary for the perpetuation of the patriarchal family. Since the incest taboo reflects the essence of the sexual hierarchy and social order that masculine society insists upon, and since many people agree that the Western world suffers from an overdose of masculine initiative (in that dynamic growth has become a value in itself), and since both sexes suffer from isolation and long for communication, one is tempted to picture abolition of the incest ban as the absolute condition for the creation of a new life-style. The question is whether an elimination of the basic prohibition would automatically give rise to a completely different social order than the patriarchal—a world of equality, perhaps, or a matriarchy.

I went to Paris to ask Serge Moscovici.

Interview with Serge Moscovici

What is the origin of the incest prohibition? What purpose does it serve?

"First, to divide the world into two kinds of activities, two universes, a feminine and a masculine, and second, to establish a masculine hierarchy over women. There is no biological explanation for the incest prohibition, nor is there any reason to think it's a cultural phenomenon—in the sense that it is something that distinguishes mankind from the animals, because we don't necessarily find promiscuity in the animal world. The incest ban is the original discriminatory mechanism between the sexes and applies not only to sexual union but to every type of intercourse—or rather the lack of intercourse—between these two universes."

Why was the world divided into two universes, a masculine and a feminine?

"That's a very hard question to answer. But we can say this much—that it was this division that made possible the transition from the animal world to the human world. Archaic societies all over the world have been arranged around two axes, the 'discriminatory axis' that separates people into two groups, the ones you may marry and the ones you may not, that is, your allies and your parents, and secondly, the axis that determines the sexual distinctions between men and women, distinctions that pervade every aspect of life—work, space, residence, objects, food, events, language. . . . These distinctions are what characterize humanity, as opposed to animals."

So they were a step forward, these distinctions?

"Forward or backward, we simply don't know. All we can say is that every society preserves certain inequalities and dogmas from the past because they work to its advantage. And the incest taboo has been preserved in order to uphold the power of the males over the females—a situation we find also in the animal world, at least among the primates, who also have the incest taboo, although power and hierarchy are not necessarily exercised in the same manner by all species in all ages. For example, I have an intuitive feeling—in direct contrast to what we usually believe—that women in the so-called primitive societies, where the sexes have very clearly defined places in the social mechanism and live in distinctly different worlds with their own separate activities and spheres of concern—I have the feeling that in such societies women as a group have *more* power than women in our society, where their status is more diffuse, disjointed, and unclear. . . ."

But what does sexual segregation have to do with the incest ban?

"Sexual segregation is primarily a result of the fact that man became a hunter. Hunting is a more collective activity than gathering, and consequently the young males and the adult males developed a special relationship that hadn't existed before. In the animal world, there is no family, even though practically everyone—from ethologists to biologists—says 'family' whenever they see a young animal with two adults of different sexes. But in the animal world there *is* no family. It was not until the first hunting activity, some three to four million years ago, that the particular relationship developed between young and adult males that we would call paternity, or fatherhood, which is the basis of the family as we know it. The children belong to the female group, but since the men must use their sons in the hunt, it becomes crucial for them to figure out some way of appropriating the young men. The males have two ways of securing their power in society. One is by means of secret male societies, which correspond to political groups, and the other is by means of initiation. The males acquire their masculine offspring through ceremonies that symbolize the transition from the feminine world to the masculine. Initiation is a form of rebirth. The adult male 'gives birth' to his son ceremonially, so that he becomes 'his,' or his 'kind.' In my opinion—as in that of anthropologist Robert Jaulin, who was himself initiated in a tribe in Chad—if initiation did not exist, the social universe would be a feminine universe. It is by means of this ceremony, where sons are wrenched from their mothers, that society comes to be male dominated. The ceremonies are secret, as are the surrounding myths and legends and the very terrain, which is known only to the men. Initiation would lose its efficacy if it were not secret, if women were allowed to witness it, for of course they would perceive that it is not possible for a man to give birth to a child, and then the men would lose their power. The whole amorous sexual relationship between men and women is dominated by two things—first, this wrenching away of the sons, and second, the secrecy of the male world."

Wouldn't it be possible to have initiation without having the incest taboo along with it?

"Oh, no, for then mothers could marry their sons, and if the sons stayed with their mothers that would threaten the supremacy of the men. The mothers and sons would then comprise a group of their own—a feminine hierarchy. If the sons didn't move over to the male group—by way of initiation and the incest taboo—the power of the male group would fade away.

"Anthropologists have always given us the impression that the incest ban was universal, and that it applied to all relationships whether mother to son, father to daughter, or brother to sister. But I've tried to show in my book that there is only one real incest prohibition, namely that between mother and son. The other incest relationships are less serious. The relationship between father and daughter is not as strictly forbidden nor as severely punished. This inequality before the law reflects a basic asymmetry in the relations between men and women—*quod licet jovi non licet bovi.* Secondly, I've tried to show that the incest prohibition is not universal but reflects a particular social hierarchy and power struggle. There were places where incest was obligatory—in Cambodia and Persia, for example, where the attainment of power was connected with incest. So on the one hand we have a prohibition against incest which applies to the lower classes and to women, and on the other hand we have a tolerance for it, even an obligation, which applies to the relation of father to daughter and, in certain societies, to the ruling elite as a whole. Which is to say that incest has generally been permitted to those in power. The incest prohibition is the fundamental discriminatory mechanism that lies behind all of the other inequalities society has since added.

"I have also tried to explain the fear and loathing that incest inspires in us. It is not—as many believe—the fear of promiscuity, or the fear that our instincts from an earlier animal stage will break loose and invade our present culture. This kind of fear has no basis in reality, since this kind of promiscuity has never existed. Sexual relations in the animal world are characterized by great regularity as to rhythm and choice of partners. No, this fear is only a reflection of a more basic fear that we have about equality and the division of property—the fear of a world dominated by women. As I was writing *La Société contre Nature* and trying to reinterpret the Oedipus and Antigone myths, I realized that man's authority over woman lay at the very core of the problem. And I didn't know as much then as I know now. Since then the historian Vidal-Naquet has supplied me with comprehensive information about the fear of a gynecocracy in ancient Greece, that is, the fear of female dominance. On both the conscious and unconscious planes, it has been a problem in most of the world, but the fear of women's power assumed grave proportions in Greece, where it came to the surface, and not only in the plays of Aristophanes. The Dionysian festivals, where incest was permitted, were festivals of the people, of the masses. But little by little, through a process of gradual social change, the Dionysian festivals came to be simply the festivals of women. We have a whole list of things to indicate that the fear of incest was the fear that the masculine hierarchy—the social order—would be undermined."

Can people really be that terrified of a different social order?

"Yes, of course. Don't you think the upper class is terrified of the lower class, and that that fear carries with it a whole series of obsessions and bad dreams? You find them all through literature, in religion, everywhere, in parents' feelings toward their children. . . . Everywhere. I believe that every hierarchically constructed universe, every social order, involves this kind of fear, and the fear of women is presumably the oldest. In my book I quote an article by Robert LeVine where he documents the way men feel sexually unresponsive in any situation that is not one of dominance. This is a phenomenon that's also been noticed in conjunction with the women's lib movement in the United States, and I think everyone's sexuality will eventually be affected by these strivings for equality. LeVine also mentions a Nigerian society where women have a dominant position, which again causes sexual problems among the men. The sexual disorders of the Yoruba males are expressed in impotence and in secret rituals where the men dress up as women and "give birth" to children. I also believe that female frigidity reflects a passive resistance to the dominance of the male sex. A woman's most readily available means of proclaiming her freedom is by *not* accepting, *not* taking part."

But today, when men are no longer hunters, what function does the incest taboo have now?

"First of all, we have to realize that the incest prohibition, the world's oldest prohibition, serves as a model for all the other prohibitions society has established down through the ages. The question is, how has it been possible for the first example of the domination of one group over another to serve as the model for all the other types of subjugation and social exploitation that have come into existence since? But it is a fact that all societies profit from and perpetuate the inequalities of earlier societies—because they are convenient. I maintain that the course of history has seen not the elimination of old inequities, but rather the addition of new ones. In actual fact, our social hierarchy is more complex than the one that preceded it, and this is probably what young people are protesting. There used to be only one type of hierarchy, the generational and sexual hierarchy. To that we have added a political hierarchy, a class hierarchy, and now an educational hierarchy—for the technocracy and the bureaucracy are both educational hierarchies that have been added to the others. As for the incest prohibition, it wasn't limited to sexual relations, it represented a world order, a fundamental principle, like the difference between matter and spirit. It dominated the world of work, the concrete world, as well as the world of the imagination. Today, the prohibition and its implications are limited to a single sector: private life, that is, the family, which has been isolated from social life."

What's the purpose of the prohibition in the family?

"To keep family members away from each other."

What would happen to the family if there weren't any incest taboo?

"I don't think there would be any family."

That is to say—the moment the members of a family began loving one another, there would be no more family?

"Yes, something like that. . . ."

I've read that marriage, in anthropological terms, is an exchange or division of women. . . .

"Levi-Strauss says that. But the question is, why do we exchange and share women? It's not a natural phenomenon, but the result of social conditioning, in the sense that one group needs a certain amount of power in order to divide up the members of another. I've tried to show that the apportionment of women has a specific function, namely to strengthen and preserve the masculine hierarchy. When we talk about fatherhood, we're talking about power. But in order to eliminate the power we have to eliminate the weapon, that is to say, marriage and the family. I believe it's possible for society to discover new life-styles and develop new forms for the relationships between men and women, new ways of raising children other than in the family, whose very existence depends on the incest prohibition. A lot of people are frightened and think we're going to see incest everywhere the moment it's no longer forbidden. But considering social mobility and the structure of our society, the chances that incestuous relationships will become dominant seem relatively slight. For example, we have no prohibition against cannibalism, but that doesn't mean we eat each other. The important thing is that the relations between women and men and children have always been and continue to be determined by the incest prohibition, and the psychological price we pay for this is, as everyone knows, enormous."

But what about the children of incestuous relationships, genetically?

"The question with regard to genetic degeneration—and I'll just ignore all the degeneration caused by radioactivity and atomic fallout—is whether the psychological price we pay for the incest prohibition is greater or smaller than the price of having, say, three million genetically damaged individuals. If it is true that the incest prohibition lies at the core of the hierarchy separating the sexes and the generations, and if it is the incest prohibition that forces the individual to fit into a masculine society from which women are excluded, then the primary condition for any attempt to replace the family with other living arrangements must be abandonment of this prohibition. The challenge facing us is whether we can create a world where sex and generation are not locked into place by the incest prohibition, a world that is built not on inequality but on reciprocity, for only in such a world will love be possible. As long as inequalities exist, the question is not simply to love or not to love, but how to love. How to love. As you know, love is a relatively new phenomenon, I mean love as a criterion, a criterion for social behavior. . . . Attraction between the sexes—sexuality—that has always existed, of course, but love as a criterion for behavior is a Western phenomenon, one or two hundred years old. I don't believe marriage for love occurred at all before the nineteenth century."

Can't love be found in the nuclear family?

"I don't think so."

Why not?

"The family wasn't designed for it."

But for the last hundred years it has been built on love. . . .

"We try to make it work, but the family is not built on love. It is love that has forced its way into the family, at a time when the family was already weakened. But the family is not built on the love of parents for their children, nor on their love for each other. In the family, the children are the objects of a power struggle and conflict between the parents."

If "Down with the Incest Taboo" became a slogan of the redstockings, would that be the germ of a new social order?

"That's not where the problem lies. There is too widespread a tendency to believe that something positive will automatically occur as soon as you abolish or break down something negative. The problem is to create something entirely new, to develop something altogether different. . . . A lot of institutions have drained themselves of significance. They no longer have anything to say to people, they've lost their vitality. But they continue to exist, because they still have a certain archaic grip on people. To insist on trying to destroy or abolish these institutions, or 'seize their power,' is like destroying or seizing power from things that are dead. Take the university. In many countries, all over the world almost, the university is a dead institution. It's been devitalized, no one really believes in it anymore, it no longer has any grip on its students. As far as the students are concerned, it's not a question of doing away with the university or of seizing power—students have done that in a lot of places without giving the university any new lease on life. No, it's a question of creating a whole new form for the institution, or for life, so that it can fill our need for knowledge, among other things.

"There is a widespread notion that people can change social structures 'from within.' What they mean by this is that nature is constant, whereas culture can easily be altered. That is a complete misunderstanding. It is very, very difficult to alter social structures. Can you change the language when you want to? Can you change the family? No. You can't reform anything from within. What you have to do is be capable of living a whole new life.

"We have gone through an epoch these last few years where all political and cultural movements have manifested themselves in negative terms: abolish, destroy, down with this or that. Now we ought to start making ourselves felt in affirmative terms, building something new, creating something different. The ideology surrounding the *anti-* and *underground* culture is always defining one thing as being *lesser* in relation to another thing that is *greater*. But in reality, it is always the marginal that is central. It isn't an anticulture or a counterculture, but a DIFFERENT culture. . . ."

But how are all these victims of the incest prohibition, all these oppressed women and castrated men, how are they going to create a different culture?

"I've thought about the castration complex. Freud's theory was that when the boy sees the girl and discovers that she lacks what he has, he is frightened and develops this castration anxiety. But I'm not so sure. As I see it, his anxiety is based on the fact that he sees her as *different*. What upsets him is not that she has no penis, but that she has something *else*. It's the fear of difference, not the fear of becoming like her, that lies behind it. Our entire cultural heritage leads us to think on a hierarchical scale where we place 'ourselves' at the top and define 'others' as being 'without penis,' 'without education,' 'without culture,' 'without class,' and so forth, in order to assure ourselves that we have more than 'they' have. What really frightens us is that these 'others' exist in their own right as different, whether it's a question of women or of some other culture. And therefore I think that the tendency in women's lib to formulate problems in masculine terms—

both in language and in style—is very reassuring to men. It makes the whole thing less frightening, for fear builds on *dissimilarity*. I would even say that the castrating tendencies of the women's movement are reassuring, because men are familiar with castration anxiety and so the feminist movement merely confirms an archaic fear. Women are very powerful, because they represent our oldest anxiety. And so if they want to assert themselves, they should formulate their wishes in places where it is not expected of them. When they demand equal pay or equal representation in parliament, they are only doing what they have a right to do, for the bourgeoisie permits women and workers and blacks to assert their rights in the right places. But why don't women try to rehabilitate femininity? Science, for example, is 'feminine' and 'infantile,' and male artists are said to possess feminine qualities. Appearance is supposed to be important to a woman—why don't women insist that a man's appearance is also very important? Love is supposed to be a thing that mainly concerns women, while men are more hesitant because love is not 'virile'—why don't women insist that love is essential? Of course I don't think that women should limit their activity to the kitchen—but why not insist that the kitchen is the most fantastic place on earth, the center of the universe? Why not insist that the activities that can't be measured in results but that have continuity and involve no distinction between working time and leisure-time, that these activities have tremendous value? All I mean to say is that women should not necessarily prize only the traditional masculine activities, for that merely strengthens the masculine value system. It is more important to alter our whole arrangement of values. I don't think Americans were really scared until the day Negroes declared 'Black Is Beautiful.'. . ."

But as long as we still have the incest prohibition, we're all given stereotyped female roles that force us to be either mothers or whores. . . .

"Yes, but the mother is a whore!"

Right, and the most expensive one of all, because men have to pay with their sexuality in order to make themselves worthy of her "love." . . .

"If a whore is a woman you buy, then all women are whores. Of course we have always made a sharp distinction between the married woman and the slut, and we have set up prostitution as the opposite of the family in order to strengthen monogamy. But institutionalized monogamy and institutionalized prostitution are the same thing. They are only different ways of distributing women, rather as if you put some of them in factories and others in small workshops. It is only recently that there are no great expenses associated with marrying a woman. Once upon a time she cost what a slave cost—at least. In the Arab countries you can buy a wife for two camels. A whore down at the Madeleine costs the same amount. What's the difference?"

But to get back to the incest prohibition—are you saying that it's already a dead institution, that it's not worth the trouble of abolishing?

"The incest prohibition will disappear by itself as soon as group relationships other than the family develop. The problem is one of sexual oppression in general. I think it was Napoleon who said, 'One destroys only what one can replace.' As for the emotional sphere, I don't think it's enough to say 'Down with the family!' or 'Abolish the ban on incest!' We have to find alternative life-styles. And it seems to me that that is precisely what people are busily trying to do, although their attempts come out as explosions and negations. The Gordian knot is the family. Real give-and-take in the relations between men and women will not result from women getting equal pay or an equal number of representatives in parliament. Changes in the relationship of the sexes can only occur with reference to the family. The elimination of that knot will alter all other social relationships, and every society that retains that knot will retain its fundamental inequalities. I don't say that people shouldn't carry on political and social struggles, but those are merely the trimmings—the problem is in the family. It is in the family that the knot is tightened and loosened."

But if mothers and fathers abolished the incest prohibition at home, why that would have wider social implications. . . .

"Today, mothers could go to bed with their sons as much as they wanted and it wouldn't necessarily change society, because private life is separate from social life. The only thing that could change the social structure would be for whole *groups* of women to begin living differently and developing different relationships with their men and children than the ones dictated by marriage and the incest prohibition. For if that happened, the present authoritarian social mechanisms would no longer be able to function, and the mechanisms of oppression would break down. Of course people say it's Utopian to try to find new life-styles that will attend to reproductive functions as well as provide new opportunities for the sexes and the generations to live together in harmony, but I'm not at all convinced that it is Utopian. In the first place, mankind existed for over a million years without the family, and in the second place, human beings have invented a great many institutions and created a wide variety of group structures in the course of history, and in the third place, people are at this very moment in the process of accomplishing this selfsame Utopian feat. . . .

"The most important part of what's happening right

now is not what is succeeding but what is failing. The important thing is not what people are saying, but what they are still incapable of saying. . . . The important aspect of the student demonstrations in Paris is *not* that they are protesting against military service or against some governmental decree—that's not what's at stake. There is something else they want to say, but they don't yet know how to say it. By the same token, I have the feeling that when we talk about sexual relationships, sexual liberation and feminism, that through these things we are talking about something else . . . something we don't yet know how to formulate."

And what is that?

"I don't know. But it's possible . . . that we are using all these things to try to realize this new phenomenon called love. We still haven't had *groups* of people that were in love. Love has been an individual thing, one single individual to another, one certain person to another. But we've never had loving groups, that is, groups of human beings where people could share one another and choose one another, using love as a criterion. All our institutions prevent that. Take the university. If I told you that what students really want is to love and be loved, it would sound ridiculous. But I have been struck in all the student strikes by the feeling that what they're really saying is that the university won't let them have loving relationships—not just in the sexual sense—with their instructors. And the same thing is true of the family. If you analyze the relationships in the family, you will see that the one thing that's difficult to achieve is just that—love.

"Equality and freedom are just words—we don't really know what they involve. . . . Our various attempts at sexual liberation and equal rights are only fumbling approaches and small steps forward in a world where the one real problem is whether or not there can be any love."

13 Bonnie in Prison

In search of what is known to be evil, I have, for the sake of love, thrown myself into adventures that have led me to prison.

—Jean Genet

Bonnie is a friend of mine and a member of a theatrical company. They perform mostly at schools and institutions. Among other places, they have played at several prisons, and one day Bonnie got a letter from an inmate who wrote that their performance had made such an impression on him that he would very much like to talk to her further and discuss some special problems. He had also written a play that he would like to show her, and asked if she would come out and visit him one day.

November 1

Bonnie calls.

"Should I go out? What do you think?"

"Sure, why not?"

"Yes, but why did he write to *me*?"

"You must have made an impression on him, how do I know . . . ? Does it make any difference which one of you goes out to see him? You happen to be the one he wrote to."

"Yes. I have the feeling, too, that the things you do are sort of meaningless if you don't have the guts to follow through on them. . . . On the other hand, there's got to be a limit somewhere—I mean, I'm just afraid I'll come to play some role for him, or take on some meaning that I simply can't live up to. I mean, lonely people . . . scare me enormously. I'm afraid of getting trapped . . . like if I give him my little finger and he takes my whole hand . . . something like that."

"Well, to start with you can start by going out there—and if it turns out you don't have anything to talk about, you can just say 'Thanks anyway,' and that'll be that, right?"

November 9

I call Bonnie.

"How did it go?"

"I don't know if I can tell you, I'm so confused. I'm COMPLETELY . . ."

"So start at the beginning. You took the train . . ."

"Yes, way out to hell and gone—wait a second, I want to light a cigarette. There was something in the letter about how it was right near the station, but the distances out there in the country, I think I must have walked for an hour. . . . Then I rang the doorbell at this house to get directions and they said, 'Oh, PSYCHOPATHIC . . . that's right over there.' So I go trundling off through the garden gate to 'Psychopathic'—what did she mean, 'Psychopathic'?—but anyway, there was a WALL around it. And now I could sort of see the whole thing better in the daylight, and there were a lot of gates and guards you had to pass. And I noticed they sort of wanted it to look like the doors *weren't* locked, because they'd release the lock mechanism *just* before you grabbed the handle, like they wanted to give you the feeling you were just going into a hotel. . . ."

"But what was he like? A psychopath?"

"No, now you've got to listen to the whole thing or you won't understand any of it. First I had to sign a bunch of papers—name, address, telephone number, diaphragm number, the whole scene—and they wanted my identity card, too, but I didn't have it. And then they wanted to know about the *nature* of the relationship, but I wouldn't say—what could I have put down for that?"

"You should have put 'incestuous.' . . ."

"No, just listen, it was a lot worse than that—or better. I sat there in the waiting room and shivered while they sent for number so-and-so, in other words Ebbe Eigild Tarm Pedersen, yes, that's his name. When I've smoked a couple of quick cigarettes, they call me into the visiting room, which they've fixed up so it's supposed to be NICE—a table with four chairs around it, regular white curtains, and some sort of an abstract amusement on the wall, you know, red and black triangles on top of each other and three green spheres. . . . And then he came in, Ebbe, with a tray."

"Right, now tell me EVERYTHING that was on the TRAY."

"Yes, well I'm going to. Two paper mugs in light blue plastic holders, a thermos, and a paper plate with sweet rolls on it. . . ."

"What kind of sweet rolls?"

"Do you want to hear the story or don't you?"

"I'm all ears. . . ."

"Well, then I sat down on one of the chairs, whichever

one was handy, but I wasn't supposed to sit there, he said, I was supposed to sit on this other one. I didn't get it at all. . . . And you know how he acted—it's an awful thing to say, it gives me the cold chills—but he acted like a PSYCHOPATH!"

"What do you mean?"

"You know perfectly well what I mean, it's just so hard to describe. It's one of the most attractive and repulsive things in the world, both at the same time. It's a very special—sort of sinister—charm, a radiance, a sixth sense. . . ."

"Like in cats?"

"I don't know. . . . If you saw him, you'd run out in the street screaming. No, maybe you wouldn't, but . . . Not a hair on his head, a big lump of a head, and one of those big broad faces with huge jaws, you know, and a potato nose and cauliflower ears, a giant mouth and bright green eyes that are a little slanted, slightly Mongolian."

"Sounds interesting genetically. A cross between an orangutan and a poppy. Nice."

"Yes, but that's the awful part . . ."

"And I'll bet that out of the goodness of your heart and your sense of social concern you've promised to visit him every Sunday, right?"

"Almost. . . . No, I haven't promised anything definite, I haven't decided. I think he's the one making the decisions. I'm nervous. . . ."

"Now, very specifically, what did he say? What did you talk about?"

"At the beginning it was mostly about whether I did or didn't want sugar in my coffee—until we got down to brass tacks. It seems that play he wrote—I couldn't help smiling to myself—is in twenty-eight acts, a thousand pages long. He was rather proud of that. He was an artist, he said; he'd been in show business. God knows if he really HAS written it. In a way I don't believe it. But for him it would be like declaring bankruptcy to mention a play in only four acts. No, his has twenty-eight, because you see it's a very important play. He wants to show it to me next time. . . ."

"Next time?"

"Right. Next time. . . ."

"What's he in for?"

"Yes, I asked him that too. But it's pretty much anything you can name—larceny, minors, a little of everything—because those things, all those names for crimes, they're all superfluous and misleading, because no matter what he does, somehow he's always going to do something that's going to be designated criminal, even though I maintain that he ISN'T, he ISN'T a criminal. But if he goes out into society the way it is now, he won't be able to move a muscle without getting whisked right back in again."

"But they get 'resocialized,' as they say."

"Yes, that's what they say, but that man is so completely bughouse. . . . You should have seen the way his whole body shivered when I came in—he even called my attention to it. 'Look how I'm shaking,' he said, as if to say, 'Look what prison has done to me.' 'I'm a broken man,' yes, he said that. . . ."

"But that means he has a sense of the theatrical. That's good!"

"No, he WAS a broken man, believe me. He said he was a faggot and liked little boys best. And so then I asked him—sort of to keep it from descending into pathos right there in the visiting cell—if he absolutely had to snatch them right out of the cradle. But apparently this last one—the one they put him away for—was twelve years old, although he looked seventeen. Well. The rest of us don't always ask about ages either, do we? But his parents, that is, the 'victim's' parents, caught them in the act, so they sent him back to prison again. He's been in several times."

"Well anyway it isn't you he's got the hots for. . . ."

"You're going to be amazed, because it was a great relief for me too, at first. I thought, well, at least I'm out of the picture as far as that's concerned. . . ."

"And you mean you weren't?"

"Yes and no."

"Do you absolutely have to talk in riddles?"

"I'm just trying to figure out what happened. Somehow I can't make head or tail of it, and at the same time I'm still so angry. . . . He asked me in all seriousness if I thought it was wrong of him to be a faggot. 'What do you mean?' I said, '*Wrong?*' So when he realized that it wasn't something I attached much importance to, he went on to say that in everyday life, when he was on the outside, he dressed as a woman. But not even that got him the condemnation or the disapproval he somehow sat there demanding from me. . . ."

"Don't you think he was just happy to be able to talk to someone who didn't load him down with all the current moral value judgments?"

"Yes, that's what he SAID, too, but deep down . . . that man, he loathes himself, I could tell. He sat there with tears in his eyes almost and told me I would never know how much it meant to him to talk to me, and I was so touched I could hardly stand it. We sat there practically crying on each other's shoulders we were so moved—and he took my hand. So I said—sort of to get my mind back—that I couldn't imagine him as a woman, and God knows I can't, either. With that orangutan body he'd make a lousy transvestite. But he just went on and on about how he never had anyone to talk to—no one who understood him."

"They must have psychiatrists and doctors."

"Yes, they're *supposed* to be getting psychiatric treatment. But what good is a psychiatrist going to do him? The minute Ebbe gets out he'll be right back where he started. . . ."

"Don't they have indeterminate sentences?"

"Yes, but they let them out now and then. They give them some air, right? So society can brag about its humane prison policy. I mean they get out into the very air that makes them go back in again. If the psychiatrists wanted to help him, they'd help him get hold of little boys, that's the only honest approach. . . . Can't you see it's hypocrisy to get a homosexual inmate to 'accept himself' when all you're going to do is send him back out where they punish him for it?"

"Yes, but society's got to protect its little boys—the downtrodden bosses of the future."

"Yes, and little boys are a bunch of little lechers, we know that. . . ."

"But we don't want to hear about it. . . . It's really sort of funny when you get right down to it, because the idea of protecting minors is ALSO hypocritical. We claim we want the little tykes to develop their sex lives on their 'own' terms, which really means they're all supposed to go out and establish nuclear families. We want them sucked into the politics of sexual oppression, and so we punish anyone who might keep the system from continuing unnoticed, right?"

"Yes. But to get back to the psychiatrist, Ebbe says too that the treatment is just a pure formality to give the place the appearance of being a rehabilitation center. Because in fact they never see hide nor hair of a doctor or anyone else. If you want to talk to a doctor, you have to apply, and maybe three months later you get a consultation—maybe. . . . And by that time you've forgotten what you wanted to say, and so the doctor puts down that you're crazy in the head. Well, but anyway, what made me mad . . . He told me more and more about himself, because he could see he wasn't running into any walls with me, even though I sort of sensed that he was going further and further in order to find some. . . ."

"Walls?"

"Yes . . . I don't know. He was sort of pathetic the way he seemed to want me to condemn him, and AT THE SAME TIME he was glad he could talk freely. He really is crazy, because he said he was doing time for that homosexual relationship but he told me he denied everything in court. . . ."

"Didn't you just say they caught him in the act?"

"Right. But he goes on denying it, and so he said he didn't dare get involved with any of the men while he was inside, because he's afraid it would hurt him when his case comes up for parole."

"Impossible!"

"Isn't it? But he sat there telling me how awful it was being surrounded by all those men and not being able to touch them. There's one named Gustav that he's in love with, but he just makes coffee for him all the time, he doesn't dare do anything. . . ."

"But they can't punish him more for practicing a sex life he's already doing time for!"

"I don't know. Like I said, he's a little confused, or rather worried sick. But he sits there serving me coffee and apologizing because it's only instant and telling me how dreadful his life is and yet how he's afraid of giving himself away to me. So I said I didn't understand that expression, 'giving yourself away.' "

"The only fun we have with each other is giving ourselves away."

"Yes, but I could see in his face he was scared to death.

So then I asked him what he did every day, how he passed the time, and then he said he was just glad he was in a good section, where they let you wear your jacket."

"What's so great about wearing a jacket?"

"Yes, that's what I wanted to know, and he said, 'Don't you even understand that?' "

"What?"

"Yes, and then I realized he was sitting there with his hand in his pocket. . . . And suddenly I couldn't figure out if he was shivering from fear or lechery. . . ."

"Both maybe."

"Yes, because he kept on asking me if it was wrong of him to give himself away to a stranger. He was wearing those blue prison clothes, sitting there with his hand in his pocket and tears in his green eyes and sweat on his face. And then, stifled with sobs, he told me how much he wanted to have an orgasm—he never got the chance. And so I told him all he had to do was masturbate. But he couldn't do that, he said, not all alone. So we sat there on opposite sides of the table, and I didn't know what to do. I didn't have the least desire to put my arm around him or anything, and of course it didn't occur to me that he might want me. I was simply glued to my chair. There was something touching about him, and I couldn't just leave, could I? And then he asked me if he could do it there, and I said of course he could. And then he asked me, I swear to God, if he could take it out—a somewhat unnecessary question. 'You can't mean it,' he kept saying. 'You can't mean it.' I was completely at a loss, because I couldn't see how he could find me exciting, sitting there in my raincoat and rubber boots."

"Aha! Don't underestimate raincoats and rubber boots!"

"If I'd been dressed up like Marlene Dietrich, then maybe I could understand it. . . ."

"Don't you imagine it's just accumulated energy? He's

probably so desperate that anything on two legs would turn him on, that is, excuse me, I didn't mean . . ."

"And then he said how much he'd like to be a girl like me, and he asked me to wet my lips. I felt really crazy. . . ."

"But you did it?"

"Yes, I did everything he asked me to, and that's what scares me all of a sudden. He said I should spread my legs, and I did, until I was in a panic because I was scared the guards would come and look through the window, and Christ, I was scared I'd wind up in jail! But he said he'd keep an eye out . . . and that's when I realized why he'd insisted on sitting where he had, where he could see everything. . . ."

"He just simply asked you to come and visit so he could jack off for you. He planned the whole thing in advance. . . ."

"I'm beginning to think so too. But why ME?"

"Because when you people went out there and performed, you radiated something that told him you wouldn't deny him so humble a pleasure—his sixth sense, like you said, his cat faculty—cats always know where there's food, right?"

"Well, in any case I suddenly stood up from my chair, because I was scared, but he followed me over to the door and very earnestly begged me to hold his balls for a second. And you know what he said then? 'That's very kind of you.' And then a few seconds later he came. He whimpered. 'Oh,' he said, he was almost crying, but then he got hold of himself and he was sniffling and he said, 'I mustn't say "Oh . . ."' "

"Why mustn't he say 'Oh'?"

"Well you can see what he's like. . . . And it made me feel so funny—appearing to do so much for him without actually doing anything. . . ."

"That was very sweet. . . ."

"Yes, but I'm sick about it, because when the guard stuck his head in and announced that the time was almost up, Ebbe wanted to help me on with my raincoat, and you know what he said? That I should notice he was only touching my coat with one hand—in other words, the hand he hadn't had his semen in. . . ."

"The other hand was unclean, right?"

"I FELT AWFUL! But the trouble is he keeps asking me, well by the end he was simply telling me, that I'm his FRIEND. And I don't know that I'm up to it. You can't just decide to be someone's friend, can you, on the spur of the moment?"

"Can't you just take things as they come?"

"Yes, and I will too, but I can tell already that he's a lot stronger than I am. And it's an awful thing to say, but the worst part of all is that he's counting on being let out soon—they're considering his case right now. . . ."

"In other words you'd like to have him safely behind lock and key, you bitch. . . ."

"Well, I keep having this awful thought: What if they let him out, and what if . . . what if it's ME who turns him in to the police next time?"

November 11

Bonnie calls.

"Everything's going according to plan, just the way I was afraid it would. Now there's a letter from him."

"What does it say?"

"Do you want to hear it?"

"Yes. Wait a second while I turn down the record player. . . . Okay, go ahead."

"Listen, it was written on the *same* day I was out there. . . ."

"Well, he's got plenty of time. . . ."

"Anyway, here's the letter:

Dear Bonnie,

Allow me to express my sincere gratitude for your visit today. Don't misunderstand me, there is a limit to how much two people can discuss in one hour, but I hope you are fully aware that you have given me more peace and self-confidence than at any time during these last four to five years.

New paragraph:

In saying this I am thinking not only of what you did for me, but on the contrary of the understanding I encountered from someone who is otherwise a stranger to me, which is what you are after all. Let me emphasize again that I am *very happy.*

Underlined.

As everyone knows, it is very wonderful to meet people one can *talk* to and be oneself with, and in your visit today you have given me more than words can describe, more than you can ever imagine. Any person who has been deprived of his (or her) freedom will always be happy and grateful for an outstretched hand. Indeed it needn't have anything to do with loss of one's freedom, for it is always good to feel that one can be whoever one may be and still be accepted. You will probably not understand completely what I have just written, Bonnie, but the truth is this, that on my own I have never dared to be myself, mostly out of consideration for my parents and friends, and as a result I have lived a lie, which gave me problems even when I was free and which brought about my present plight."

"He certainly can express himself, can't he?"
"I think it's very touching. Now listen:

In any case I feel that I have suffered a significant social debasement. It always costs something to be away from society, whatever the reason may be, and so I think you should realize that just because a person has been locked up by the society that condemned him does not necessarily mean that he will become "a better person" for that reason.

Your visit today also made me rather proud, because I know that a girl like you, in the theatrical world, has so many interests and friends and consequently very little time. Of course I could talk more to the Institutional Authorities here, as I told you, but this is a *system* they go by and there can *never* be anywhere near the same communication as, for example, between two people. You are probably reading this letter, Bonnie . . .

"Why so you are!"

. . . but don't feel obliged to answer it. You are a good person, Bonnie, and I would sincerely like to be friends with you and talk about all the things, other than the sexual, that make people unhappy and materialistic individuals.

Finally, I would like to ask you in confidence to help me, partly just to be myself, so hopefully I can give something to other people, which I have really wished for. I hope you got at least something out of coming. I can imagine that it isn't always easy to find time for a prison visit, which isn't exactly cheerful, but I hope it will make you happy to hear that you have done me a great deal of *good today.* I have now, and forever, *thrown away my jacket* . . .

"Oh, yes, the jacket . . ."

. . . which there is no longer any reason to wear except for the cold. It was an experience in so very many ways to talk to you. Please do write to me and say you don't regret it.

"Didn't he just say you *shouldn't* write?"

Friday next week I will probably get a furlough from the Institution when my half-sister has her copper wedding anniversary, so if you can, try to make room for it, Bonnie.

"You're going to be one of the family."

Please accept my warmest regards. You know you can come here to visit whenever you want on Saturday/Sunday. You could come both days, and you must *not* bring anything with you. I set more store by trust than mere materialism.

Dear Bonnie, please let me go on believing in your outstretched hand and so be your friend. I cannot be anything to you in purely sexual terms, even though you are so pretty—but I feel in recompense that I can be of use and joy in other areas over the long run. But anyway thank you for accepting me and understanding me.

Have a nice week and write soon,
With loving affection,
Ebbe

P.S. My letters are not censored—they only do that with letters from outside but only now and then.

"You've got yourself a friend, Bonnie!"

"Yes. What shall I do?"

"Not a thing. . . . Just take it very easy, visit him when you've got the time and the inclination, and otherwise—not a thing. . . . He sounds very sensible. . . ."

"Yes, don't you think there's something sort of wonderful about him? Now listen to the next letter, which came today:

Dear Bonnie,

Just a brief greeting to tell you how unbelievably nice it is that you understand me so that we can communicate.

My parents were here and even they noticed a certain change in me, and believe me, everything is going much better.

I just hope you mean it, Bonnie, and you're not making fun of me. I don't think you are, but it sounds so wonderful I can't really believe it. I am now putting the finishing touches on my play, with a couple of new additions, and I so hope that you will actually put it on, and the fact that aside from this I have found a friend in you makes me very happy, and if I didn't mention it in my previous letter, I would very much like to invite you along with my personal friend . . .

"Does he have a friend?"

"I'm sure he doesn't.

. . . to a really good dinner at, for example, Søllerød Inn, which is a nice place.

I've been given a furlough now for the 26th and 27th

of November, so if you can spare the time I want to urge you to come out here and see me this coming weekend. I hope everything is fine with you and thanks again for your visit, and sincere thanks for listening to what I've wanted to say to someone for a long time.

Best wishes,
Ebbe

" 'Søllerød Inn, which is a nice place . . .' "

"I know. But anyway I can't drop him now, can I?"

"No, because then you WILL be making fun of him, in a way. And what's more, you like him, don't you?"

"When I was there he told me he wouldn't have any financial worries when he got out, because some uncle left him eighty thousand crowns. . . ."

"Oh?"

"But I'm not going to Søllerød Inn with him. He also told me to take a taxi out to the institution and he'd pay for it, but I can't do that."

"So you have decided to go out there again."

"I guess I have—in a month or so, but of course not as a regular thing. He's not going to get dependent on me. But I really would like to read that thousand-page play. He's got the material, and I'm sure we could get a lot out of him—authentic stuff, too! But listen, I'll just write him a little card and tell him I'm going to be out of town, because I don't want to go to the copper wedding anniversary or to Søllerød Inn, but that I'll come and see him again sometime, right?"

"Yes, don't insist on making problems. He's got enough people like that already. And he obviously understands that you've got a full schedule, so you can give him just as much time as you want to."

"Still, it scares me a little. . . ."

"But why?"

"What if he gets the feeling I've let him down—even the tiniest bit—imagine his revenge. How do I know what he'd do? . . ."

November 17

Bonnie calls.

"I'm afraid they're going to let him out."

"You really are too much. Either you *are* on his side, or you're *not*. . . ."

"That's easy for you to say, but what if I'm the only one he has? He'd pester me to death. My whole life would be changed, wouldn't it? Just listen to this:

Dear Bonnie,

Many thanks for your card. Let me say how nice it was to hear from you, partly because it's good to hear things are going well and that you are not turning down my desire for friendship on account of my imprisonment and its cause. Please believe me, Bonnie, it's terribly important to have someone to talk to, and having trust gives me a great deal of joy, and more than anything else it gives me *faith* in the things I am doing on my own. It is simply annoying that you're not going to be in Copenhagen during my coming furlough, but you'll be coming out to visit as soon as you can. I have a lot of news about my case to tell you, for example, that they've started the appeal to get me released, so I can expect to be home by Christmas. My guardian and my lawyer have brought the matter before the court, and they're just waiting for an opinion from out here, and as I told you they don't have any objections. Thanks again for your little card. I don't have that gift of expressing myself briefly, plus it seems to me there are so many happy things to tell about, and since I don't get much chance to talk or give much to others at the moment, you will naturally understand what fun it is to speak through a letter.

Try to come out and see me this coming weekend, Bonnie, and you shall have the play, which I'll soon be finished with. And finally, I've been working for a long time crocheting a dress, which I would like to give you when it gets done along toward Christmas. You really must come out in a cab and I'll pay whatever it costs. As you can see from this letter, your visit made me very happy—or is it wrong to be honest?

Your friend,
Ebbe

"It's sweet of him to crochet you a dress, don't you think?"

"He meant it for himself. But you know what, I think I'll go out and visit him again, and then I can get that play. . . ."

"He's a remarkable mixture of unselfish friendship and at the same time he's so . . ."

"Yes, so devouring, because can't you just see it? They'll let him out and he'll just hang on me. . . ."

"What do your colleagues think?"

"They're crazy for me to go out there—they want to get their hands on that play."

"You know what? Why don't you let him be in it? You said he'd been in show business, didn't you? And he must have something—he seduced you, didn't he? So why couldn't he seduce an audience?"

"Sure, and those antennae of his! God knows he has the power to move in on people—if it suits him."

"He simply IS an actor, a born actor!"

"All right, but what if I just don't want to play along?

Because you can see for yourself that more and more it's HE who's defining MY role. . . ."

"Yes, but, Bonnie, you're playing along already, for all you're worth. In any case, you can't beg off NOW. You're right in the middle of the play, so to speak."

"I get the feeling you could use the story. In your book, right?"

"Yes! Maybe . . ."

"What'll you give me to finish the story for you?"

"You'll get the experience."

"Okay. I'm going out there on Sunday, but I'm not going to tell you what happens next. Ha!"

December 4

Bonnie calls.

"I've spoiled everything. I've *really* made a fool of myself. The shithouse is really on fire this time, I can tell you, and I'll never get out of it alive. . . ."

"What happened?"

"In a nutshell: They've moved him to a sort of hotel where they put the ones they're going to let out. That's where I went to visit him."

"Did he have the play?"

"No. There's one more thing he's going to add. We sat in his room, which he shares with a roommate—and then all of a sudden I didn't have any clothes on. . . ."

"What do you mean 'all of a sudden'?"

"Yes, but that's what scares me. I don't understand how it happens—he's actually disgusting. . . ."

"Now you're sounding like a little child, forgive my saying so. . . ."

"Okay, I'll tell you how I *think* it . . . it has something to do with—no, he's fantastic, I don't understand any of it.

It doesn't feel like it was me who was out there at all, but my ghost or something, some sort of demon inside me, because otherwise how could I do something so . . . completely against . . ."

"You mustn't get so upset. Do you want me to come over?"

"No, no, I'm going to bed now. But you know, we were just sitting there with coffee and pastry in this room with all of this teak furniture, and he took out some old yellow photographs, with thumbtack holes in them, out of this box—they were pictures of the Skubbidubbidoo Group. 'God,' he said, 'don't you even know the Skubbidubbidoo Group? I thought you were in show biz!' He was angry. They were pictures of men in tuxedos and ducktail hairdos and women in taffeta dresses and Brigitte Bardot curls and black lines in the corners of their eyes—and down in one yellowed corner of the picture was George Ulmer. 'You must know *him!*' he said, and I nodded. 'He's my friend,' he said and he put his musty pictures back in their box. He was also putting me down because I didn't know Dirch Passer's dresser—who was also his friend. But then he put an Elvis record on a little rubber phonograph and we danced like crazy in our stocking feet—he could dance like Fred Astaire. . . ."

"I can just see you—Ebbe and his fiancée."

"And then he started telling me how unhappy he was about what happened the first time."

"I never got that impression. . . ."

"Neither did I—but suddenly he was sitting there telling me a long, pathetic story about how he wanted to have himself castrated. About how shockingly he had behaved toward me, and what a pig he was, and how ashamed he was, and how that was no way to treat a woman, as nice a woman as I was, and how he'd taken advantage of my friendship, and on and on."

"Sweet Jesus."

"Yes, and then I got all worked up myself and told him how wrong he was, that there was no reason to be ashamed, and then I said the worst thing I could have said . . . it just popped out of my mouth . . . I said . . . that I had enjoyed it too."

"Was that the worst thing you could have said?"

"Yes, and for your information, this is the turning point of the story, because from that moment on he changed completely. . . . It seemed to interest him enormously. He cross-examined me and dragged confessions out of me, which he sat there sort of filing away in his big fat brain. I should have left, but you know I didn't feel like it was me myself sitting there anyway. . . . He changed completely, opened his pants, and pulled my dress off, no, not violently, almost quietly and calmly, and that's practically the worst part, because how did it happen? There was nothing in the world I wanted *less* than to be naked there with him."

"You wanted to please him, didn't you?"

"Yes, maybe. I was so disgusted by his shame, I sort of had to show him there *wasn't* anything swinish about him, you know? And I had the feeling that if I resisted when he took my dress off, then I'd only be confirming the low opinion he had of himself—'She doesn't even want to be naked for me'—and I was supposed to be giving him self-confidence, wasn't I?"

"But there must have been some other way, because you didn't want to be naked, did you?"

"No."

"Was he rough with you?"

"No. He didn't rape me. He's not a criminal, after all. We didn't go to bed together or anything, but he was changed. He ordered me to do all sorts of things, like a marionette. . . . It was as if my saying I'd enjoyed it—

which wasn't completely a lie—had made me like him. As if we were equals. And somehow he couldn't take that, because he got very foul in the mouth and called me a little whore—not contemptuously, but merely as if he were getting even because there was no longer anything to look up to."

"Your social consciousness brought you down off your pedestal with a crash."

"Flat on my face."

"In your altruistic zeal . . ."

"Why don't you call it 'common kindness'? Because I know perfectly well what I should have done to maintain the distance between us—I should have left him in the lurch there with his insecurity, his guilt, and self-loathing. But instead, like an idiot, I talked about equality. I know very well I should have agreed with him when he called himself a pig. He would have accepted that, he would have understood it. But he didn't understand the other stuff."

"So you parted on bad terms, or what?"

"Are you crazy, do you think I'd get on bad terms with *him?* He kept saying we ought to go to the Royal Ballet together and that our relationship shouldn't only be sexual, since he really wasn't 'that kind.' He kept telling me he wasn't from Istedgade, almost like a threat. . . . 'Okay,' I'd say, 'but what's so bad about Istedgade?' And he'd say, 'I'm just telling you I'm not from Istedgade.' You don't understand who he is at all—he's not the violent criminal you think he is. . . ."

"That isn't what I think."

"But there are things that are worse . . . like the way he can make me into . . . a sort of ghost. And I can tell you I have no intention of precipitating some kind of drama.

I'm just going to play it his way and then get out of it sort of quietly without letting him know what I'm doing. I'm going to steal away on little cat feet. . . ."

"How are you going to bring that off? He'll just steal after you, and now that they're going to let him out . . ."

"Yes, but now the whole thing has become so unpleasant I don't intend to see hide nor hair of him again."

"But what are you going to do if he comes and bothers you?"

"I'll call the po . . ."

"No, now you *won't* do that!"

"No, of course not, and what's more I won't have to. The man isn't dumb after all, and when you've been locked up for five years, I guess you're pretty careful about making false steps, don't you think? Because all he has to do is steal so much as a nickel, right?"

December 6

I was over at Bonnie's this evening for dinner—roast pork. About eleven o'clock, the telephone rang. She hesitated a moment before answering it, because she was afraid it might be him. He was allowed to leave the "hotel" and had already called once before that same day, "just to hear her voice." She was about to lose her mind. Obviously it WAS he, for she said she didn't have time to talk, that she had guests, and that he shouldn't call her so often.

And then all of a sudden she put her hand in her hair and her eyes flickered wildly and she said "Well . . ." several times, sometimes harshly and sometimes softly. Finally she said, a little bewilderedly, "You'd better go out there right away," and then in a more neutral tone, "I'm sorry I can't help you."

When she had put down the receiver, she stood up and spoke almost to herself. "He said he wanted to come over. I said he couldn't. Then he said his parents had just been killed in an auto accident an hour ago. They were on their way out to the prison to visit him. They were killed on the road, he said. He was just about to go out to identify the bodies."

"It's a lie."

"Yes. Isn't it?"

"Of course it is. From now on, he'll use any trick to get in touch with you. With those long antennae of his, he's noticed you're about to back out."

"But it's just too awful . . . his parents being killed . . . and what if it IS true? He has the right to common sympathy at least, and in HIS situation . . ."

"And that's what he's counting on. From here on in it's psychological warfare, and you'll have to harden yourself. Even if they ARE dead, you still can't do anything."

"But that's hideous, when you can't even be a decent friend for fear of being eaten up. . . . And don't forget, formally we're not enemies at all. . . . For the time being, things are still the way they were—I'm his best friend. So when he tells me his parents were just killed, I can't just say, 'Up yours,' can I?"

"You might have to."

I offered to stay overnight just to be on the safe side. You never knew but what he might show up, desperate. But Bonnie declined. And we agreed it was best not to let it affect her, but just to go to bed the way she always did. Preparing to be terrified is somehow asking for it. We kissed each other good-bye with forced laughter and, in our thoughts, sent the psychopath out to his damned bodies.

* * *

The telephone rings in the middle of the night, and I tumble out of bed. It's Bonnie, I can tell; I can hear her whispering hysterically far away.

"He's here!"

"Where?"

"Outside. I won't open the door. He's been standing there ringing the bell for half an hour and calling in through the letter slot, 'Bonnie, Bonnie, you have to help me, I know you're in there, Bonnie, open the door,' but I won't open. He can't break in can he? I'm so scared. . . ."

"Why don't you just go out and tell him to go away?"

"Don't you understand? I don't dare go out in the hall in case he's standing out there and might hear me. I have to pee, but I don't dare go out to the bathroom. I don't dare light a cigarette in case he might hear the match. For a long time I didn't dare call you in case he'd hear me dialing, but I couldn't help it, I'm so scared, and what if he's sleeping out there on the mat?"

"So let him sleep on the mat. And if he rings the bell in the morning, then open the door on the chain and tell him you can't see him anymore if he's going to be so inconsiderate as to wake you up at four o'clock in the morning. Period. Bonnie, you mustn't overdramatize, and you don't have to whisper in your own apartment, it's ridiculous. . . ."

"Do you really think I might go out and pee, as long as I don't flush the toilet?"

"I don't know what's gotten into you, but you simply have to get rid of him—and the sooner the better."

"Yes, but what'll become of HIM?"

"That'll have to be HIS headache. You're not responsible for him. My God, Bonnie . . . You can't worry about how HE's going to react; you've got to pull yourself together and go out and pee."

"Yes, I've got to stop caring . . . but just think, it's all turned out just the way I was afraid it would . . . EXACTLY. . . ."

The next morning, 9:30

Bonnie calls. She bursts into tears.

"You've got to come over right away. He raped me. Bring some bread."

When I ring the doorbell at Bonnie's a little while later (with the bread under one arm), I see her staring out through the peephole for a long time. I put on a big smile, but she doesn't open up right away, and when she finally does, the door is on its chain.

"Can I come in? I brought you some breakfast."

She looks awful, disheveled and red-eyed. She's still wearing the clothes she had on the night before, an angora sweater, and her kimono is torn up one side.

"You HAVE been raped."

Her mouth becomes an unrecognizable square as she sobs, and the snot runs down her chin. "I'm so hungry, I haven't even had breakfast," she sobs, reaching out for the bread.

"You haven't even undressed from yesterday."

"I didn't dare. I didn't dare move or anything," she gasps, wiping her face with a paper towel and putting on some water to boil. "Do you know why I'm so miserable? Because a person can't be herself. Everything is misunderstood."

"So he came back this morning?"

"Yes, he rang the bell at eight o'clock. I was already up, because I never closed my eyes. The instant I heard the bell, I knew it had to be him, and I knew I would open the door, just a crack, in order to tell him I never wanted to see him again and get it over and done with once and for all. And there he stood on the mat like a little dog in his cotton coat, mumbling something about his parents and how he only wanted to talk to me for five minutes. Five minutes, he said, and promised to go away again. So I let him come in, and I emphasized that it was the last time, that I never wanted to see him again if he was going to behave like this.

" 'Yes,' he said, 'this is the last time you'll see me, Bonnie. Because last night my parents were killed, you know. And they were my parents, you know. So now there's nothing to live for. I'm going to kill myself.'

" 'Yes, that's a good idea,' I said. And I meant it. Deep down I felt the man ought to die, because he doesn't have a chance."

Bonnie cut herself five pieces of bread and asked me how many I wanted.

"Considering I haven't been raped, I'll make do with two, in honor of the occasion."

"As you can imagine, he played the part beautifully. I mean, the only reason we got to talking was that I was so relieved that he wanted to kill himself that I started to like him again. And he sat there explaining how he wanted to use the morning to go around to his 'friends' and tell them he was going to Sweden. 'But to you, Bonnie, I'll tell the truth. And tomorrow you can read about my death in the papers.' "

"And you believed him?"

"Yes, of course. Because I wanted so badly to be rid of him once and for all. And suddenly he seemed so appealing in his self-recognition, the same way he was the first time I met him. And so we went on talking. . . . He sat there with his sorrowful Mongol eyes and his thick meat-hunk of a tongue swabbing around in his face—'I'm so dry in the mouth, Bonnie. I haven't slept all night.' I gave him some tea. Because of course I was sorry for him, and when a person's going to die, you might just as well talk things out, right?"

"Lord, Bonnie, you're so sweet."

"Well, thanks, but never again. Because of course what it came down to was that he wanted to have one more orgasm before he died. And I said well then he was welcome to it—just so long as it wasn't with me, and I went out and opened the front door and said good-bye and OUT.

"But he just stood there like a little puppy and said he didn't want to touch me, all I had to do was watch, and I couldn't refuse a dying man his last orgasm. I got more and more angry and I said, 'No, I'm not refusing you anything, just go away. . . .' I stood in the door and pointed down the steps and tried to push him out. And standing there just inside my doorway, he opened his pants. And I closed the door. Can you figure that?"

"The mere fact that you closed the door is enough to keep them from ever considering you a rape victim. . . ."

"Yes, but can't you understand why I did it? It was partly fear. You don't want a masturbating man coming out your door and down the stairs; you know, you're scared of the neighbors. Or maybe he'll make a scene and stand out there bellowing. I don't know . . . I just panicked. And then too it seemed better to deal with it myself. I didn't want other people to find out."

"You want to keep your private life to yourself."

"I can't even tell you the rest of it, it's so confused. He wanted me to hit him and tell him he was repulsive. I got desperate and sobbed, 'I *can't* hit you.' Yes, I was practically apologizing because I couldn't hit him, but I added that he really WAS repulsive when he took advantage of my friendship that way. Then he turned absolutely raving and said I should say he was beautiful and had the most beautiful prick in the world, and then a minute later I was supposed to say it was hideous and disgusting. I was about to lose my mind, and I couldn't say all the things I was supposed to say, because all I could think about was when is this nightmare going to end. And I was either the prettiest, loveliest woman in the world or the worst, filthiest whore."

"Dear God!"

"Yes, and I was completely worn out, and he couldn't come, and I was supposed to say he was beautiful and he was disgusting, and he was. 'I'm repulsive, aren't I? I'm repulsive,' he kept saying, and I was absolutely desperate and kept saying yes and no in the wrong places. And when he finally did start to come, he threw himself on top of me and got a stranglehold and pushed into me. . . ."

"I thought he was gay. . . ."

"He's insane. You should have seen his eyes, and the way he was frothing at the mouth. . . . And he didn't take his hands off my throat and I realized he was going to strangle me, yes, I swear he was, and you know what I did? I ran my hand gently over the crown of his head—he's bald, you know—and I whispered 'Sweet little Ebbe' over and over again until he let go. But, my God, I can easily see how some people get killed—because in that situation insanity is rampant—it's all a question of chance. . . ."

I went over and put my arms around her. "God, I'm glad you didn't get strangled."

"Yes, believe me, I am too! But you know what? When he was finally about to leave, he started fantasizing about all the things he was going to do, all about his 'personal friend' and how they were going to South America together. And then I said, 'Yes, but you're going to die!'

" 'No,' he said. 'I've changed my mind!' "

"God, how he took you for a ride, Lord in heaven!"

"He's a genius! He ought to be president of an insurance company or something. Oh, yes, and right after he raped me, he put on this terribly serious expression and told me to call the police. He picked up the receiver himself and asked me to dial the number and report him."

"Well, there has to be some order in the world. He can't stand it unless he gets punished, right?"

"He's absolutely crazy. Afraid of himself. But I told him if I ever saw so much as a hair of his head, I *would* call the police. Because I don't intend to go around being scared for the rest of my life."

December 8

I call Bonnie.

"Listen, Bonnie, I've been thinking I could use your story in my book, because I'm writing some stuff about rape, and it fits in so well. . . . You know, I've been sitting here figuring out why you got raped. . . ."

"Thanks a lot!"

"No, really!"

"I just can't see what could be so interesting about it. I mean after all . . . If the lady invites a psychopath in to tea and then gets raped, why she must be daft, right? I mean that's a very particular and perverse case, and she was asking for it, wasn't she? People will just say that if she's so naïve she thinks she can be friends with a psychopath like he was some ordinary person, why then it's her own fault. If you write about it, it'll just make me look silly. Because any woman who goes out and visits some psychopath in prison and then figures on being treated decently, I mean, not murdered and not raped, why, she must be crazy, right? I'M the one who's going to look ridiculous, because HE only did what you'd expect a psychopath to do. It's MY fault I was raped—I'm the one who tempted the poor man. . . ."

"Oh, sure. It's perfectly normal when a man can't control his sexual drives, because nature has given him so wonderfully many of them that of course someone HAS to suffer for it. *C'est la vie* . . . Well you better believe I can make better sense than that out of your story, because the man isn't such a psychopath but what all his prejudices and values reflect society's standards right down to a T. The only difference between him and the men they don't lock up is that he HAS A HARDER TIME LIVING WITH THEM. His value system is actually so classical, and the whole story is so trite, that they could print it in the family newspaper, that is, if it weren't for your behavior, which they'd have to censor. You might say it's a story about a man who is crushed by the things and the standards he himself believes in, like some member of the Home Guard who's protecting his 'freedom' and who cleans his rifle every Wednesday with the risk that he might accidentally shoot himself. But it's mostly a story about you. You overstepped the standards, and that's what I want to write about—because do you want me to tell you why you got raped?"

"Okay. Wait a minute while I get my cigarettes. . . ."

"I'll just run through it schematically—what you did 'wrong,' I mean, where you broke the sexual rules, okay?"

"Do you absolutely have to get raped, just because you break the sexual pattern?"

"I don't know, but I'm gradually coming to the conclusion that you do. . . . Anyway, in the first place, you should NEVER have gone out there ALONE to visit him. You should have sent him a marble cake and a couple of magazines. 'Best wishes, Bonnie.'

"Point two.

"It was 'wrong' of you to repudiate society's sexual rules by accepting his 'perversities.' You revealed yourself to him as an outsider, and an outsider has no right to the respect due to people who conform to the rules. And that man is an authoritarian if anyone is. He knows from experience that people get punished for breaking the rules. He believes in the rules more than anyone, because he has bodily experience of what it costs to be a lawbreaker. And you have to be punished too.

"Point three.

"You broke the sexual regulations by talking cheerfully about sex with a completely strange man. He didn't know what to make of that. 'What's she after? Is she available? Is she that kind of woman?' You pretended to be liberated, which at the moment is synonymous with the man's liberty to do whatever he pleases, without consideration. By revealing your liberatedness—pardon the stupid word—you surrendered your right to be protected, that is to say, your right not to be raped. I don't think he *consciously* wanted to punish you with rape. He just couldn't handle the freedom you displayed—and there are very few men who can. All of a sudden he didn't know how to behave.

"Point four.

"He probably dreamed about and even planned on using you as a witness to his masturbation, but it never occurred to him you'd go along with it. It's one thing that you're not scandalized by his relations with minors, his homosexuality—whatever it involves—or by his being a transvestite, which he also dishes up as if to test you—it's crude enough that you don't puke at the thought of him. But when you let him masturbate right in front of your nose, that's the last straw. Which is why he kept saying, 'You can't mean it. . . .' In a way it would have made him much happier—and you were on to this yourself—if you had spit in his face and called him a pig and run away. At least he would have understood it, because he thinks he's a pig himself. He doesn't dare touch your coat with his 'unclean' hand, while all the time you're thinking, where are the unclean hands that have made this man what he is?

"Point five.

"It's not enough that you let him masturbate, you little whore. One day you tell him, on top of that, that he *shouldn't* have himself castrated, that he's *not* a pig, that you enjoy him. You sneer at his self-contempt by telling him he's beautiful. Now there's nothing left for him to do but rape you, because if you like *him*, then that's all you deserve, you bitch.

"You've turned into a pig—just like him. You no longer deserve respect—the same way he knows that he doesn't deserve it himself.

"Point six.

"You might possibly have avoided your fate—for that matter, who says that male society is our fate?—if you'd refused to touch him with a ten-foot pole but just let him masturbate while you stared off into space with a superior, all-forgiving, goddesslike expression—like some higher being looking down on an animal. You shouldn't have begrudged him his shame. But instead you crawled down from your pedestal. And that he couldn't forgive. So he started ordering you around. Because you'd shattered his image of the universe, you witch."

"That sounds very good, all of that, but in his case don't you think an ordinary conventional woman would be in danger of getting raped?"

"That would depend on a lot of things, but a conventional woman wouldn't put herself in your situation. She wouldn't tempt 'fate,' as they call it. . . ."

"Yes, but couldn't what happened have been completely irrational? I mean, when he began to realize that he was about to lose me . . ."

"Of course it was irrational. But irrationality is a better reflection of our culture than almost anything else, isn't it? We're marked much more by what escapes us and what we repress than by what occupies our rational faculties.

Because there's no rational connection whatsoever between rape and the fear of losing someone, the fear of being left alone. What about all the women who are afraid of losing their men? They don't run around raping them, do they? And that's no accident, is it? On the contrary, in women the fear goes inward. We creep around our men, whispering and waiting on them. We make ourselves as invisible as we possibly can so our men won't get sick at the sight of us and leave us. Once a woman has reached the point of screaming and hitting, she's dug her own unwomanly grave, because no one would blame a man for leaving a hysterical shrew like that. No, most women keep their mouths shut, because that's what pays.

"And it isn't even very painful, because you forget very quickly what it was you wanted to say."

After talking to Bonnie, I wrote:

December 8, 1972

There are still only goddesses, whores, and then the majority of wives and mothers who follow the sexual rules. These women will never even know what the rules imply, for they are in our blood and in the air we breathe—and are revealed only when we overstep them, which in the most extreme cases means going against human nature.

Oscar Wilde once published a polemical article in favor of better living conditions for the working class in which he wrote, "It will, of course, be said that such a scheme as it is set forth here is quite unpractical, and goes against human nature. This is why it is worth carrying out, and that is why one proposes it." I might say the same about the sexual rules—these codes that hold the sexes in checkmate, these denials of our very being, which we can only expiate by doing away with ourselves once and for all. The only decent grounds for breaking down those rules is that doing so goes utterly against human nature.

14 To Begin With

abolish mankind!
And so we'll meet, some day . . .

—JØRGEN GUSTAVA BRANDT

There is a section of Mysore where irrigation has recently been introduced, with it has come a sudden prevalence of witches.

—ELIZABETH JANEWAY

The people who think about women and what's to become of them are divided, at the moment, into two groups—one that's concerned with whether we should say "girls" or "women," "Mrs." or "Ms.," and another that thinks that all of us—and they mean every last one of us without exception (including you over there in the corner trying to sneak out)—should be HUMAN BEINGS. The first group, the ones who quibble about words, point out that much of what we say is old-fashioned and needs to be updated in order to reflect reality. For these people, the whole question is primarily one of language, which keeps them from having to talk about the way things are. By the same token, a proper understanding of racial tensions has long been dependent on whether a person said "Negro" or "colored" or "black," and it was discriminatory to use the wrong word in the wrong decade. . . . There will always be debates of this kind, and we won't go into them here.

On the other hand, HUMAN BEING doesn't make the whole thing any easier, although clearly it was meant to. I can't avoid the feeling of being pigeonholed—as a human being—whenever group number two, including the vast majority of feminists, insists that we are all human beings and no one gets off scot-free. I feel no immediate attraction to the purely human. I am more interested in biochemistry and miracles, because HUMANITY is always invoked when someone wants to point out that there is nothing new under the sun, and that there is no way out, and so we might just as well drink down the bitter draft, since we can't have our cake and eat it too, and anyway you can't go around giving people the idea that they're going to get away with anything. This is by and large considered to be the human condition, and it is obviously HUMAN BEINGS the feminists want to be when they talk about equality. "Women are people too," has become a well-known slogan.

I can imagine a lot of different things a person might strive to be equated with. . . . To be like blades of grass, for example, would not drive us apart. But to go along voluntarily with the idea of being a human being! To put equality with men on your program, when you stop to consider that men as we know them are about to die out! That I don't understand. These women who want the same opportunities as men, they are looking for hand-me-down answers in outdated books. The women who seek acceptance as human beings are digging their own graves. HUMANITY is a concept hauled out at the convenience of various interest groups in order to camouflage the basic tensions between body and sex, between reality principle and dream. Everything basic is overshadowed by HUMANITY. So I can't understand why creatures as lovely as ladies and tramps, ma'ams and madams, mistresses and ms.'s, housewives and harridans, have all willingly agreed to be people. It can't possibly lead to improvement, but only to more oppression.

We will reach a point someday (and the day has come) when we will have to ask ourselves whether the condition of women or the condition of the earth is more important—if the earth is even to have a condition, if there is to be anything at all upon it. It seems to me it might be fun to have as many different sorts of things as possible. But I don't believe there will be so very many when I see the way women strive for integration into the human thanatocracy, and when I see the way they plead for equal pay for work that ought to be abolished in the first place, because most of the jobs that do exist are boring and to that extent completely worthless.

I believe that all men and women are basically in agreement with the feminists in all the areas that haven't yet been talked about. The strength of the feminists was that people expected everything of them. And so for many people it was something of a disappointment to be fobbed off with the news that we were all simply to be human beings, when they'd been hoping for a little fun and games. There was never any explanation of why in the world we ought to be human beings. Being human didn't mean anything, or rather, it could perfectly well mean we were going to wipe each other out with little green poison pills or napalm bombs. For when you've said "human," you haven't said a thing—though Villy Sørensen nevertheless says this:

> If we didn't all know humanity from ourselves, we would probably be more willing to learn about what was human, the same way we learn about what is characteristic of the other animals. . . . As it is, we assume that we know—even though the language itself suggests conflicting feelings toward humanity. It is definitely good to be human, but if we say that something is "only" human, we mean that it is not especially good, and to say that something shows human interference is the same as saying that it has great faults. For some people it is especially humane to be indulgent toward what is only human. For others, this form of humanity, this humanism, is an old habit that bears part of the responsibility for all sorts of inhumanity. (Villy Sørensen. *Uden Mål og med,* Copenhagen: Gyldendal, 1973)

For Erich Fromm, there is literally no such thing as humanity or human nature.

> . . . man, in contrast to the animal, shows an almost infinite malleability; just as he can eat almost anything, live under practically any climate and adjust himself to it, there is hardly any psychic condition which he cannot endure, and under which he cannot carry on. He can live free, and as a slave. Rich and in luxury, and under conditions of half-starvation. He can live as a warrior, and peaceably; as an exploiter and robber, and as a member of a co-operating and loving fellowship . . . there is no such thing as a nature common to all men, and that would mean in fact that there is no such thing as a species "man," except in a physiological and anatomical sense. (*The Sane Society*)

Mankind is a unique species because its development depends on its having abandoned nature while at the same time remaining a part of it. Mankind has lost its original home by stepping out of nature, and to this extent man is a historical and utterly unnatural reality. What is natural does not necessarily have any human value. And we cannot go on referring to what is natural in order to get an idea of what is human—as various fanatic rat-psychologists are in the habit of doing. If Nixon (he is a human being) declared publicly that he was partial to possessing his daughters from behind, he would lose his job, for he is human, after all, and not some animal. If, on the other hand, he manages to lay waste the land and burn up the people in some part of the world, that can be officially excused by pointing out that he is only human. We can say this much of human culture, that tenderness is an absolute miracle.

> Tenderness does not emerge out of the necessities of social living, for it is beyond society. In tenderness, *Man* is beyond *Homo sapiens;* in being tender, man is more than a mere social animal. It is possible to have a society without tenderness, but *Homo sapiens* has never been able to survive without cruelty. Hence I say "the miracle of tenderness." (Jules Henry, *Pathways to Madness*)

Instead of devoting their time to miracles, the feminists have identified with the male sex in their effort to become human beings and in the belief that equality lies in the obliteration of differences. "Discrimination" has become the root of all evil. In reality it was male society that dictated the manner in which the women's movement was to manifest itself, that is, angrily and aggressively. Militant feminist protest came to express an identification with the oppressor, which led the movement to build on the ideals of the male society and to operate on its conditions. And this was its limitation, for the male society is a thanatocracy and a phenomenon of perdition. But the efforts of the female sex to achieve equal rights have been inescapable. Women seem to strive for the unattainable in an attempt to define what is possible. But is what is possible enough?

The equal rights movement has come to involve skepticism and suspicion toward all differences. I don't want to glorify the erotic promise of the masculine/feminine sexual polarity, for I would like to see lots of different sexes, and I don't believe that the basic power of sexual attraction is threatened by multi- or ambisexuality, but solely and exclusively by uniformity. I find cause for concern in the possibility that we will be left with only one sex, which is where the equal rights movement seems to be taking us. The demand for equality has been stripped of all its revolutionary force today because society itself sets up equality as an ideal. It has discovered that it has a need for human automatons, all of whom resemble one another and work together happily and smoothly, all of whom follow the same drummer although convinced of their individual eccentricities. Our longing for equality, in the sense of a fellowship of dissimilar individuals, turns out, in practice, to lead to standardization.

Since most people are agreed that the world should be different—either because it is out of order, or else because it has not yet really begun—and since quite a few people believe that we suffer from an overdose of masculine initiative and that we ought to encourage a different world view from the one expressed by the present thanatocracy, I would like in passing to propose a miniexperiment. This is not meant to be a solution, of course, but only a tentative step in the right direction: Close the educational sector to men before it is too late.

There are several reasons for thinking this to be a good

idea. For one thing, it would free men from the burdens of power, which they so often bewail. Lord Acton's observation fits the situation perfectly:

> Power tends to corrupt and part of the corruption the powerful suffer from in bad times is a paranoic dislike of their own power, a petulant envy of the weak, and a sudden taste for frivolity. No one, in the end, profits by too clear-cut a division into rulers and ruled. (Lord Acton [John Emerich Dalberg]. In a letter to Bishop Mandell Creighton, 1887)

Obviously the point is not simply to let women take over men's power, for nothing would be gained by that, and it is wishful thinking to ascribe to women the perpetual function of guardian angels. But I do think men need to escape their responsibilities and gather wild flowers or ride horses or play with boats or whittle chess sets or whatever else they never get the time for otherwise—interesting thoughts that have nothing to do with the system, imagination and useless ideas—since in the final analysis it is always the superfluous things that prove to be the most essential. They wouldn't be bored. I really think they would rejoice, for they would not be pushed out into the cold. On the contrary, they would be utilized in a way that would satisfy everyone. (Naturally they would keep the right to vote, for there is no question of taking anything away from them but only of giving them *other* possibilities.) Excluding men from higher education will simultaneously give us a chance to ward off the very real and present risk that women will turn into men. I don't claim that this is a very grand experiment, or that it will solve any fundamental problems. But the educational sector has been virtually closed to women for over five hundred years, so it might be inspiring to change things around and see what that could lead to. At the moment we can say only that never have so many women studied so much with so little social effect. This is because women have had to integrate themselves into a masculine society in order to acquire social benefits and positions of importance, which has not fostered new values nor shaken the male military, industrial, and scientific complex. Maybe it's already too late, but women ought to be given a chance before we reach the point where the only sexual difference left between men and women is in their reproductive organs. Death and collective annihilation are statistically probable, while all of the creative events in history have been statistically unlikely. At the moment I think it might pay to invest a little more heavily in the unlikely.

But women are hardly going to acquire any real influence in the world by tomorrow, and so it's a good idea to remember—if we're to be realists for the sake of the unlikely—that a woman's greatest privilege at the moment is the *right to make a fool of herself*. This is not a right to be sneezed at. A woman has an almost unlimited opportunity to undermine the norms in almost any field she enters, because as a rule she has neither prestige nor position to defend. She can move about freely as a partisan. Her subversive strength lies in the fact that no one has really bargained on her. On top of that she has the advantage of being regarded with a good deal of tolerance because she is weak—"only" a woman—without either responsibility or power. The guerrilla can afford to have ideas, because she has everything to win, while the general's mistakes are always fateful, by reason of the prestige and position it is his function to defend regardless of the cost. Consequently, generals never undertake the unlikely, because there is always a price to be paid for failing to follow the rules of the game. Generals never dare take chances, and therefore men are by definition limited in their capacity for imaginative action. A man who cannot live up to his responsibilities vis-à-vis the status quo is a finished man, while a woman can do what she wants, because the fact that no one takes her seriously anyway gives her greater psychological maneuverability.

And so the greatest weakness of women at the moment is precisely their desire to be taken seriously. Here witches come to our aid. Apparently they have always come when they were needed, which is not to say that they have always come when they were called. Witches have boiled their brews and cast their spells and inspired both fear and respect, but, by God, they have never demanded acceptance or integration or understanding or state support—or asked to be taken seriously. And that's the serious part.

Witches have always popped up as a symptom of social upheaval and the disintegration of traditional power structures, roles, and value systems—whether in Elizabethan England, or in a Europe torn by religious wars, or in modern India and China, or in revolutionary France, where they appeared by the scaffold with their knitting. In India today, social changes seem to be producing an overabundance of witches.

We cannot live without roles. Without roles, we don't know who we are, nor who anyone else is either. But since roles are an expression of predetermined relationships, a society in upheaval has a tendency to negate the established roles. The most well-known negative role is that of the witch. She is the antithesis of the loving mother. Both a mother's and a witch's power are feared (there is no knowing which is feared the most), but the power of the witch is magical. Portnoy's mother is almost a little witch-like—her role becomes negative in the sense of being obsolete, for there is no longer any use for such a woman.

From the moment he comes out of his mother's womb,

a man knows that it costs something to associate with women. Women cost him his freedom. Most men are afraid of women—they represent unconditional love, and at the same time they divide love up into various types and doses which a man must earn and pay for. Women appear to have become more generous recently. They've equipped their sex with a zipper. They wriggle their fannies and at the same time they maintain that they really don't want to be sexual objects. They want to be for sale but they don't want to be bought. They want to have their cake and eat it too, and there wouldn't be anything wrong with that if it weren't for the fact that it's always the women themselves who get both had and eaten. What this reveals is an inaccurate analysis. There is nothing so awful about being a sexual object (unless you suffer from some sexual disorder), for if people were not objects for each other, then who would they be objects for? No, what's upsetting is a woman's price, and that is set by the person who owns the wares. The price women set brings them a short-lived power—and leads eventually to their own long-lived oppression. It is only women themselves who have the power to put an end to these marketing mechanisms by starting to ask no price and set no conditions—and stop trying to please and smile unless there is something to smile for. The witch, woman's negation, is not pleasing in the least, but she asks no price at all, because she is free and has her center of gravity within herself. She laughs only when there is something to laugh about—and she can also hiss with a will. To this extent, the witch's role is an attractive one. But for those women who would like to be accepted by men (on an equal footing), the witch's role is hardly tempting. This is partly because men don't care for witches and women who cost nothing. They have learned that the more expensive something is, the more desirable and worthwhile it becomes. Nor can a witch hope to be supported, since very few men indeed can imagine marrying one. As things now stand, most women prefer to place their centers of gravity outside themselves and to make their homes and husbands the centers of their lives. For most women, the decision to marry is the most important decision they will ever make, in spite of the fact that the world stands open to them and there are no longer any legal or formal impediments to their becoming astronomers or polar explorers. Since most women decide sooner or later that their place is in the home, does that mean that the home is the most satisfying place for them to be? The consumption of tranquilizers and alcohol among housewives does not appear to support such a conclusion.

Technically, everyone is free to refuse to live up to expectations and to repudiate a role. But the fact that women's behavior corresponds so closely to the behavior people expect of them, and the fact that they have such a hard time identifying with more imaginative ideals than that of the housewife (the dream of becoming Mrs. Beethoven), is the result of a mythic conception of woman's place. And since no one is completely free from this mythology, it is probably wisest to take it seriously, regardless of how little it may correspond to real conditions. For a myth is a lie only to the extent that it fails to express some deep desire. It is a waste of time to prove that a myth is untenable, that its content is stuff and nonsense. You can refute it until you are blue in the face and it will still survive, because it is "true" as long as it reflects real feelings.

Countless authors over the last ten years have taken the trouble to demystify the traditional woman's role and to demonstrate how unreasonable is the assumption that anatomy is destiny. One eminent woman after another has thoroughly analyzed the myth of woman's "place," to the point where we might reasonably ask why her place is still there in the home instead of up in the trees or someplace out in the world. . . . But myths are eliminated only to the extent that new knowledge can alter people's feelings. Changing feelings is quite a different thing from invalidating attitudes, and to confuse the two is a kind of mythic thinking of its own. A person can write thousands of well-argued paragraphs about how unreasonable it is for women to limit their activity to a kitchen and a nursery, but it has no effect on the fact that most people—men and women—*feel* that this is essentially where women do belong.

In her book *The Poets' Ladies,* Lise Sørensen writes of being

> at home in the imperturbable center of values. And maybe this is what really lies behind this whole curious cult around the housewife—not that people really believe that the home would be so very different if she left it for a few hours, but that her leaving would be an admission that this imperturbable center, untouched by the alarms and cries of the world, no longer *existed.* But it is also very clear that the more things whirl around in accordance with the desperate law of centrifugal force, the more both men and women need to *believe* in a center which they alone control. A peaceful temple, with unchanging original woman as its priestess. (Lise Sørensen. *Digternes Damer,* Copenhagen: Gyldendal, 1974)

In the United States, two-fifths of all women are employed outside the home (and half of these are married and have children). So the myth that "woman's place is in the home" simply doesn't square with reality. And it doesn't help to go back in history, because until very recently whenever women actually WERE at home, their men were there too, since that was where both sexes worked.

"Woman's place is in the home" probably expresses a less well-defined longing to return to the womb and a golden age when there was no difference between you and me, yours and mine—the desire for a paradise filled with shady trees and succulent fruits that always hang within reach. We can repeat a thousand times that women no longer have any function in that little envelope, the home, but the myth that she belongs there is more powerful than anything we can say, because it expresses basic drives and longings. Logic can invalidate the myth, but not eliminate it. For it is precisely by being illogical or prelogical, detached from reality, that the myth achieves a force of its own as self-fulfilling prophecy. Mythic thinking is a form of wishful thinking, and therefore action in service of the myth can never succeed in altering the conditions that gave birth to the myth. If the Nazi myths had had any scientific validity, the superhuman Aryans would not have been obliged to exterminate the subhuman Jews. Nor did the murder of the Jews lead to that robust Third Reich that they had imagined would last a thousand years. Neuroses and myths have this in common, that they cannot disentangle whatever crisis the society or the individual suffers from at that given moment in history. There is good reason to suppose that the myth and the neurosis are one and the same thing, the one collective, or public, the other private.

It is characteristic of our cultural crisis that "myth" has become synonymous with "lie." When we say "that's a myth," we mean, "that's a lie." The misfortune is that our deepest longings display themselves today as lies, because we no longer have any central values to hold us together. But the original—and more dynamic—function of myths is to present "images" that will give us the chance to identify with one another in our fear, joy, sorrow, and hope. Thus one leading mythologist, Joseph Campbell, defines myths as "public dreams"—the communicative power between the conscious and the unconscious in the collective sense. The problem, Campbell writes, is that this communication has broken down in the Western world. The old myths don't work anymore. "The latest incarnation of Oedipus, the continued romance of Beauty and the Beast stands this afternoon on the corner of 42nd Street and Fifth Avenue, waiting for the traffic light to change." And we have not yet developed any effective new myths to take their place. The result, according to Campbell, is that the Western world is currently undergoing a painful reorientation that can only be compared with the period around 4000 B.C., when the Sumerians conceived the idea of a mathematically ordered cosmos and thereby made a fundamental change in mankind's experience of the universe. And we can't simply pick a new mythology out of the blue, for, as Campbell notes, "To be effective, a mythology must be up-to-date scientifically, based on a concept of the universe that is current, accepted and convincing." So today we find ourselves mythless, because our myths are no longer the images of a unified vision of the world. But we cannot exist without our "public dreams," and therefore the need to spread myths is as great as it ever was. "A world bereft of radical significance is not long tolerated; it leaves men radically unstable, so that they will seize at any myth or pseudo-myth that is offered." For example, it is mythic thinking that asserts itself in the hard-nosed demand for "equality" between the sexes, and also in the struggle to establish an ENTIRELY new system, for example, Socialism. But even if we never satisfy the longing for equality, freedom and brotherhood that these mythic systems represent, still the myth itself must be taken seriously, for even by *not* functioning, it leaves its mark upon the world.

Mythic thinking has in common with religious thinking the fact that both spring from desire. The mythic attitude wants satisfaction HERE and NOW, while the religious attitudes goes beyond personal needs. Prisoners, suffering from hunger and privation and dreaming about bread, can only survive by denying the reality of their situation or by finding values that transcend it. The first reaction is mythic, the second, religious. At the moment we talk mostly about bread, and less about the general privation of captivity. Karen Blixen once said, back in the forties, that it was indecent to give people bread when they were pleading for a stone to scratch pictures into. . . .

Mythic thinking, satisfaction HERE and NOW—either by saving and preserving the good old world or by establishing a wholly new one in the form of a Socialist society that will make Danish pastry of the paving stones—has apparently, but only apparently, taken precedence over all other desires. The belief that all of mankind will be free as soon as the workers have taken over the means of production, and that women's potential will automatically be liberated with the establishment of a new society, and that then we will live in eternal love and harmony is, however, an inoperative myth, for otherwise we would have created such a system long ago. After all, the formula has been at our disposal for more than a hundred years. And it is mythic thinking to ascribe our failure to do so to independent economic processes beyond human control, or to believe that the great capitalists do not want paradise and eternal love and harmony—they undoubtedly want those things more than anyone else.

Leszek Kolakowski writes:

> That we shall be capable of raising ourselves with a single leap from the depths of Hell to the height of Heaven—that revolution will never happen. . . . The idea that the existing world is so rotten that it cannot conceivably be improved, and that precisely because of this the world that replaces it will achieve the wholeness of perfection and final liberation is one of the most monstrous aberrations of the human mind.

The struggle for women's liberation and equal rights *used* to be a real struggle. But today it has become mythic, by denying the fact that, legally, women do have equal opportunities but fail to exploit them. There is no longer any specific woman's destiny, and many women find that traumatic. A woman can suddenly do what she wants with her anatomy. This confrontation with a host of untried possibilities is an utterly new situation for women. And since society demands almost nothing of them, many women have come to envy men their more restricted lives. Consequently, the feminist movement, which is represented largely by well-educated women, does not deal with liberation at all, but with the anxiety of hovering freely in empty space—and with the effort of figuring out how to live there.

"When society asks so little of women," writes Betty Friedan in *The Feminine Mystique*, "every woman has to listen to her own inner voice to find her identity in this changing world." But the problem, a woman's real trauma, which she must face by herself, is that she cannot even listen to her own "inner voice" to discover how to channel her drives and aspirations, for at the moment that inner voice will lead her backward in history. That voice is loaded down with a thousand years of mythical baggage, which is of no use to women at all in an entirely new historical situation.

A curious, painful, almost intolerable situation, not to be able to count on your own feelings, because they reflect a world that no longer exists. Not being able to listen to your own voice, not being able to act in accordance with your own conscience, not being able to base anything on your own emotions—this is a new human condition. And this condition is first and foremost woman's. She has no frame of reference; there are no ideals; there is no one to consult. She is emotionally coded to a program that has been played out. And she cannot fall back on history unless she is prepared to pay for it with her reason, because the anachronistic role that history offers would conflict with her temperament and with what she wants from life. If she is to grow, mutate, and find a new identity—without becoming a man—she must venture out into new waters where she may find herself beyond her depth. No one knows. No one has tried.

15 Wash

I feel them speaking through me, these women who have taken longer to speak than man, because what stirred in them were states which are not articulate in the language of man, but perhaps in the language of music, if this music could be frozen in the air to catch the words it forms.

—Anaïs Nin
(*Diary*, Part 3, 1939–1944.)

Can't love anyone in this country. All the almond-shaped burning brown eyes and the perpetually bulging trousers. Men that get no rest. Can't handle any more oppressed people. Can't handle the code, my body gets stiff, and so do my eyes, smiling all day, stiffly. Every evening the same man stands at the hotel desk and plucks a lily from the bouquet there in the lobby and hands it to me passionately, with all the signs of fascination, fear, and contempt. The way you throw nuts to the apes and wait for some reaction. I would really like to scream, but I smile. He thinks he is worshiping me—female worship is a faith

I do not share. Most of all what I would like to do is strike him, but in all decency I can't do that simply because he gives me a flower. I cannot love anyone in this country, although I honestly did try. But I always found myself approaching a mysterious ritual with sacred relics being brought forth from sacred vestments, while I myself stood far off like a witness to a holy act. The moist embrace was so significant, so fraught with meaning, that there was no place for tenderness—nor for me, for that matter. I was lost among thousands of anonymous supplicants and tried to stand on my toes so that I could better follow what was going on so far away. There was no encounter and my toes begin to hurt. And then they say we are all of the same blood. Ha! Merely blood. Blood is nothing, and flowers cannot relieve the misery, and so every evening I get drunk. My body is gone, and my dreams, for the whole time I can feel those burning brown eyes. Maybe it would be better to crawl off across the ground, and make noises, and practice picking flowers with my teeth.

A sticky, clinging embrace from a contemptible hotel manager who drinks nothing but water so he won't make a fool of himself. I drink a bottle of whiskey in distraction and grow more and more fascinated by this incredibly unattractive person, who is very eager to show me several discotheques in town. He snaps his fingers and demands a glass of water from one of his people, takes a single sip, and tastes it for a long time with his thin, snakelike lips, whereupon—without looking at the waiter—he sends it back and orders more, for, as he explains to me with every indication of triumph, the water has an aftertaste, and his people must learn to obey. "They need to feel a strong hand. They must be trained."

"Like animals?" I ask, hoping he'll say yes so I can have my antipathy confirmed.

"Yes, very true," he says appreciatively and puts his

arm around me to express sympathy for my deep insight into human nature.

There is a bourgeois Jewish marriage being celebrated at the hotel. I nibble at a couple of stuffed peppers with a little saffron rice, but I mostly drink whiskey, having made my excuses. There is belly dancing and an immense amount of jabbering conversation that cannot be heard above the popular music being performed at earsplitting volume by stringed instruments and singers with ecstatic expressions. All of the songs are about the woman you cannot have, which is by definition the one you love. I have long since decided to go to bed for a few seconds with this loathsome, water-drinking individual—as a distraction, or because I have no desire to go to bed alone, or because I want to see if this "seducer" on his steed of flattery is for real, or because I want to protest and feel disgusted by all the love songs about women the singer cannot have (the kind that make me want to say, "Okay, you're going to get me, you little creep, you're going to get so much of me it'll make you sick."), . . . or maybe for no special reason at all, because I am drunk and because this abortive evening demands an adequate conclusion in the form of a thundering anticlimax. But of course the seducer doesn't know I've decided to shake up his bones a little, and so he's very anxious about the effect of his strained poetic phrases, which little by little lead to the suggestion of a distant, impossible, hopeless dream of love. I believe that is the word he uses. If I were a kind and well-bred person, I would allow the man to sit there with his dreams intact and dream for another two hundred years or so, but instead I say, "Yes, just say when."

In the beginning was the word, and it never gets to be much more than that. He clings to me tightly in a bizarre ritual that remains at the back of his mind and never becomes real, and I get sore from standing on my toes to see what's going on far, far away and thousands of years ago. Maybe it really would be better if I were a picture. If we judge a people on the basis of the idols they worship, must we not also judge them on the basis of the dreams that worship gives rise to? Everywhere I sense dreams of distance, dreams of separation, dreams of detachment, hopeless dreams that will never become dreams of hope or union—and I sense a fear of losing these dreams, for then the spell would be broken and people would have to eat their own dung. My dreams are far from warm, but the men with the burning eyes worship conflict and estrangement and illusion, and hate women with their hips and their hollows and their hands.

The seducer's adoration is boundless, and equally boundless is his rage a quarter of an hour later when I arise from the altar and get dressed. He doesn't quite know why I came with him in the first place, but he can't begin to figure out why I'm leaving. He is desperate, for he is afraid to sleep alone. I tell him he can order his people to bring him a glass of water.

Early the next morning, heavy at heart, I flee to another town. A local saint has died on the previous Friday. The shops are closed, and there are black flags flying all over the bazaar. I take a taxi down to the eighth imam's brother's holy tomb. The car is done up like the driver's private apartment. Next to the steering wheel there is a pale blue translucent hand holding a pale blue translucent vase filled with pink nylon tulle flowers. The insides of the car doors are papered with pictures of the prophet Ali in the company of other strong men carrying machine guns and cartridge belts. Second place in this glossy exhibit is held by Elvis Presley with his arms protectively around a pair of slender female shoulders in a sea of enchanting pastel flowers.

At the entrance to the tomb I rent a *chaddar*—way too

short, but it obviously covers enough of me, for a toothless old hag asks me if I am Syrian. There is a lot of bustle at the sacred tomb. It must be a real holiday, for the square in front of Shah Sharag is filled with families using the day for a picnic. They have primus stoves and are making tea and grilling small delicacies. The scene breathes both peace and excitement. The women nurse, the men stare.

Inside the sepulcher, everything is mirrors. The floor is marble. They file past the shiny grave in a steady stream—you really *can* see yourself in it—and kiss the imam's brother, millions of lips impressed in the mirrors. Farther off, the old men sit on the floor, rocking back and forth, intoning—barely audibly—the ancient story of Kerbela. Rocking back and forth in the age-old rhythm, the rhythm of the heart, the rhythm of the cradle, of coitus, of union, and of the ancient story—Kerbela, and the murder of Hossein, Hassan, and Mohammed's daughter Fatima. The women weep, huge tears running down their cheeks. They have heard it a hundred times before. Some of them nurse while they weep over Kerbela, and little boys pad around among the old men, chewing gum. The same rhythm. Everything in life deals with Kerbela—Tazieh too, the classical theater. It takes eight days and eight nights to play all of Kerbela, but the nice part about the performance is that you can always tell the difference between the good characters and the evil ones, for ritual requires that the evil ones talk, while the good ones always sing. There's no making a mistake. When the actors are neither speaking nor singing, they talk to people or eat or sleep. It takes eight days and eight nights to get through Kerbela, but there is no other way.

One always leaves the sepulcher backward. An anthropologist tells me—and I can see it for myself—that the sacred tomb is the center of the community. People go to

Shah Sharag to look at girls or to get a whore—to get whatever they might need. Young lovers arrange to meet at Shah Sharag, because here they can be together without arousing suspicion. The holy tomb is well kept up. Here you can find a *sigheh*—a "contract woman," usually a widow. If you're going to make a long journey through the desert, for example, and don't want to travel without a woman, you can procure a *sigheh.* In practice, a contract can run from an hour to ninety-nine years. Lovers who could not have each other because of their families could, in principle, have recourse to a *sigheh* arrangement. But now the system is falling apart, because people have begun to look down on *sighehs* as prostitutes. It it only in the holiest cities, like Xhum and Mashad, that the system continues to function as it did in the old days, in all of its simplicity.

I would actually like to stay at the tomb and maybe write an honest contract. Who knows . . . maybe someone could use a Syrian widow. The very thought of going back to the Intercontinental Hotel, where my invitation forces me to stay—under the most charming and hospitable circumstances—and picking flowers with my teeth—makes me feel old and tired. The fact is that I am simply not very tolerant, and the bourgeoisie makes me physically ill, especially here in the Third World where it lacks that discreet charm often associated with decadence. If the bourgeoisie is dying in the West, here it is only budding, and with every day that passes it shoots up and bursts forth in luxuriant greenery that will turn the still "underdeveloped" portion of the world into a gigantic discotheque and make insensitivity part of the social system.

Along toward evening I flee the receptions and go down to the bazaar—it is not yet quite closing time. A newly hatched engineer pursues me, apologizing that the whole place hasn't yet been plasticized. He tells me what I see has nothing to do with his country. That his country has nothing to do with the people and the streets I see. I can't get rid of him and I feel more and more alone. He looks self-conscious, he is embarrassed on behalf of his people. Since he won't leave me in peace, I tell him to show me the way to the almonds—I want to buy sugar and almonds. He says Persian carpets would be a better investment. He gets lost in the bazaar and can't find the almonds. A man who gets lost in the bazaar! What an insect! He calls me romantic for insisting on the bazaar when there are smart boutiques near the hotel. He says the bazaar has nothing to do with his country, which I would know for myself if I went to the capital instead of hanging around in this crummy little town.

What a romantic insect. There was a time—under Mossadegh—when a significant share of the political power lay in the bazaar, where people talked and did business. At that time the bazaar was a political forum where people exchanged goods and ideas. If the bazaar has become unimportant, if it has lost its function, if, as he says, it no longer has anything to do with his country, then it's because of this insect who pursues me because I'm from the West, and because of all the other insects who are training themselves to turn their country into a discotheque, where, as we all know, no one can hear what anyone else is saying.

"You may as well go now. I'm going to the *hammam!*"

He shakes his head in bewilderment. "Are you crazy? You are our guest and live in a luxury hotel with showers and bathtubs and swimming pools. What are you going to the *hammam* for? The public baths are filthy."

"Are Iranians filthy?"

"At least you must take your own towel and shampoo and soap, because I would not advise you to use the ones the people use. . . ."

"Is there much disease in this town?"

He doesn't answer, just goes on asking why in the world I want to go to the *hammam*. Why, why?

It's because I'm lonely you little insect, I think, but I don't say anything. Why should I argue with a Persian who's forgotten where to buy almonds? But it's true. I'm so lonely I could cry, and they say that if you go and get a woman to wash you, you can't go completely wrong. A woman's hand is a solace. I don't know why that is, but it has always been so.

It is a yellow clay building with blue-green tiles on the walls in traditional Islamic designs. The cleanest place in the world, I say to myself, thinking of the insect—all of the insects I'm trying to get away from. There I am outfitted with a modest piece of soap, a yellow tube of shampoo called Oasis, a round black stone for the soles of my feet, and a piece of white limestone for who knows what.

The man at the desk shows me into the bathing room alone, but that wasn't what I . . . I'm not dirty in that sense of the word. . . . Outside the bathing room sit a couple of women, wrapped up like mummies in their flowered *chaddars*. One of them is peeling a piece of fruit, holding her *chaddar* in her teeth the way women do in the marketplace when their hands are full. I indicate with gestures that I want to be washed. They giggle shyly. They are probably not used to washing people with blonde hair or to exotic visitors as large as I am. Then one of them, the one with the fruit, says I should just take my clothes off and she'll be along. I am pleased. I really would like to get to know these women whom I know only from the streets—covered, dark, unapproachable, and anonymous. It's hard to imagine what they actually look like, even though they seem more real to me than high society's exhibited bikini bodies.

Then she bustles in and all at once she has taken off

her clothes. After the *chaddar* she removes a flowered, spangled, slightly ragged dress—the sort of fancy finery mothers dress their little girls in for a day at the zoo or some other holiday park. We stand opposite each other and smile a little in greeting. She has kept her pants on, black nylon panties that have run so badly her loins are girded mostly by threads. It has never occurred to me that panties like that could run, but that's probably because I have never known anyone to keep a pair of them so many years. She looks about fifty, my woman. She has little pigtails and tattoos on her forehead and silver rings on her arms. She looks like a friendly woman. We stand there grinning for quite a while—partly because I don't know what else to do. I am completely in her hands. For the first time in Iran I am filled with happiness. She may have given birth to ten children, I have no idea. Her body is more used than mine, even though perhaps she's only thirty. I feel a little embarrassed, as if I had cheated fate. I could never show her how happy I am, for she would not be able to comprehend it. For she doesn't understand the way a person can live packaged in cotton and gauze, odor-free and watertight, and therefore she doesn't understand that my eyes can turn shiny from the very fact that she exists. I don't mean anything special—just the fact that she exists, here in the bath, now that I need her, and that she permits me to enjoy her ancient motions simply as a customer, without formalities.

She runs the shower with the air of an expert and finds the right temperature. She puts her hands in the stream of water and lets it run down her arm in order to find a good temperature for me personally, and that strikes me like a declaration of love, and I feel it deep in my body. Of course I'm paying her, but all the same . . . She could just as well let the water run scalding hot and chase me into it, and maybe I wouldn't even protest, for I am entirely devoted to her. No, she couldn't. She could not chase me into scalding hot water. For she is kind, and that's why I'm devoted to her. There IS no mystery when you get right down to it.

When I am wet from the shower, she draws me down to the floor. I am relaxed from the warmth and the water and her movements that could lead me anyplace. I feel no resistance and she can do anything she wants with me. I can see that her eyes are very pretty—slightly slanted and gray-blue—the same color as the tattoos on her forehead. Her stomach is large and slack, her thighs quite slim by comparison, and her breasts just two thin flaps of skin with nipples that have been sucked dry and brown.

When she takes the Oasis shampoo, I am curious to see what she will do. For if she doesn't like me, now is her chance to show it, considering the way commercial hairdressers tear and rip at your hair. If she doesn't like me, she can, for example, pay no attention to whether or not I get soap in my eyes. But her mind works nothing like mine, for she quietly and calmly massages my scalp and pours a plastic bucket of water over me in several vast, gentle waterfalls, and I feel no soap in my eyes, and then it begins from the beginning, over and over again. She washes my hair four times, which is presumably the custom.

My skin is to be scrubbed, or rather removed. She sits facing me with one of my legs across one of her thighs, for we must sit close together so that she can reach my whole body with her arms. First she rubs the limestone into one of my arms, back and forth, along with some scratchy wool to remove the dead skin. Suddenly I'm a little afraid she'll notice that I'm simply not dirty and realize that my motives have not been entirely honest. But so small a concern disappears in her long, regular movements back and forth. I have no desire to talk to her, ask her her name or about her children or how many she has. I simply don't care. Nor does she expect me to. I enjoy being in a place where silence is in order, where closeness is concrete and movements so simple and ancient that a person is allowed not to care. Then too it's because I am paying for the privilege.

The skin is rubbed loose and dissolved by her long, soothing, regular strokes. Now and then I can't help smiling at her or looking her in the eye—just for fun, just to see what she might be thinking, because she is here too, after all. But I can see that it distracts her. She would rather I ignore her, I can tell. I can't change that, nor do I feel any need to. I pay, and she does her work. She is neither my friend nor my lover, and it doesn't matter. She is the woman who softly limes my Persian breasts. She has tucked one of my feet against her body so that my heel rests in her groin. She rubs the shoulder and arm farthest from her, while one of her breasts brushes across my toes like a steady fan, far beneath her face and her bobbing braids, far away from her and me. Whether or not her brown nipples are as ticklish as my toes is beside the point. It doesn't bother her, it doesn't matter. After the limestone comes the soap. The same movements over again on the same body, only now it foams. Everything is softer and more gliding.

She opens the spigot for the shower and helps me to my feet, so now it must be over, now I must be clean. She steps into the shower herself while I brush my hair. We have agreed in silence that I will brush it myself. That will be easier, because it tangles. It would be wrong to say she wishes me any harm.

In less than a minute she has put on her fancy dress and *chaddar* and vanished like dew under sunlight with the eight crowns I have given her. Double the price. I didn't feel I could give her any less. When I step out on the street in the cool evening air and reluctantly—but light of heart—head back toward my concrete hotel, I suddenly feel that I really was dirty, that indeed I was covered with filth.